C0-GEH-234
3 2711 00135 3626

THE FOREIGN-BORN POPULATION OF THE UNITED STATES: 1850 TO 2000

ENTERED AUG 3 0 2007

THE FOREIGN-BORN POPULATION OF THE UNITED STATES: 1850 TO 2000

CAMPBELL GIBSON
AND
KAY JUNG

Novinka Books
New York

Copyright © 2007 by Nova Science Publishers, Inc.

All rights reserved. No part of this book may be reproduced, stored in a retrieval system or transmitted in any form or by any means: electronic, electrostatic, magnetic, tape, mechanical photocopying, recording or otherwise without the written permission of the Publisher.

For permission to use material from this book please contact us:
Telephone 631-231-7269; Fax 631-231-8175
Web Site: http://www.novapublishers.com

NOTICE TO THE READER

The Publisher has taken reasonable care in the preparation of this book, but makes no expressed or implied warranty of any kind and assumes no responsibility for any errors or omissions. No liability is assumed for incidental or consequential damages in connection with or arising out of information contained in this book. The Publisher shall not be liable for any special, consequential, or exemplary damages resulting, in whole or in part, from the readers' use of, or reliance upon, this material.

This publication is designed to provide accurate and authoritative information with regard to the subject matter covered herein. It is sold with the clear understanding that the Publisher is not engaged in rendering legal or any other professional services. If legal or any other expert assistance is required, the services of a competent person should be sought. FROM A DECLARATION OF PARTICIPANTS JOINTLY ADOPTED BY A COMMITTEE OF THE AMERICAN BAR ASSOCIATION AND A COMMITTEE OF PUBLISHERS.

Library of Congress Cataloging-in-Publication Data

Gibson, Campbell.

The foreign-born population of the United States, 1850 to 2000 / Campbell Gibson and Kay Jung.

p. cm.

"Presents selected decennial census data on the foreign-born population ... [and] provides the background knowledge necessary to examine the tables in a detailed and informed manner. The tables provide statistics that reveal all the trends in immigration during the last century of America's history"--Pref.

Includes bibliographical references and index.

ISBN 10: 1-60021-134-8

ISBN 13: 978-1-60021-134-8

1. United States--Population--Statistics. 2. Immigrants--United States--Statistics. 3. United States--Census. I. Jung, Kay. II. Title.

HA181.G53 2006

304.8'73021--dc22 2006009089

Published by Nova Science Publishers, Inc. ✤ New York

CONTENTS

LIST OF TABLES

PREFACE

Immigration has always been a source of debate for the American public. During the early part of the twentieth century Americans had concerns about the effects of European immigrants. Today similar concerns are being raised about Latin American immigrants. This book presents selected decennial census data on the foreign-born population of the United States from 1850 to 2000. This book provides the background knowledge necessary to examine the tables in a detailed and informed manner. The tables provide statistics that reveal all the trends in immigration during the last century of America's history. It is fully indexed.

Chapter 1

INTRODUCTION

This paper presents selected decennial census data on the foreign-born population of the United States from 1850 to 2000.

This paper updates and supersedes Working Paper No. 29, "Historical Census Statistics on the Foreign-Born Population of the United States: 1850 to 1990." The primary change to table content is the addition of data for 2000. The tables in the Internet version of the new working paper are in Excel and PDF whereas the tables in the previous working paper were in HTML only.

Other reports on historical census statistics for the United States. The following six reports present historical census statistics that are more detailed and/or more recent than historical census statistics published in reports from the decennial census of population or in Historical Statistics of the United States: Colonial Times to 1970 (U.S. Bureau of the Census, 1975a).

- Population of States and Counties of the United States: 1790 - 1990, by Richard L. Forstall. U.S. Bureau of the Census. Washington, DC: U.S. Government Printing Office, 1996. Data for the 1900 to 1990 period are available also on the Census Bureau's Internet site at <www.census.gov/population/www/censusdata/hiscen data.html>.
- Population of the 100 Largest Cities and Other Urban Places in the United States: 1790 to 1990, by Campbell Gibson. U.S. Bureau of the Census, Population Division, Working Paper No. 27, 1998. Available also on the Census Bureau's Internet site at <www.census.gov/population/www/censusdata/hiscendata.html>.
- Historical Census Statistics on the Foreign-Born Population of the United States: 1850 to 1990, by Campbell Gibson and Emily Lennon. U.S. Bureau of the Census, Population Division, Working Paper No. 29, 1999. Available also on the Census Bureau's Internet site at <www.census.gov/population/www/censusdata/hiscen data.html>. This report (No. 29) is superseded by the current report.
- Historical Census Statistics on Population Totals by Race, 1790 to 1990, and by Hispanic Origin, 1970 to 1990, for the United States, Regions, Divisions, and States, by Campbell Gibson and Kay Jung. U.S. Census Bureau, Population Division, Working Paper No. 56, 2002. Available also on the Census Bureau's Internet site at <www.census.gov/population/www/censusdata/hiscendata.html>.

- Demographic Trends in the 20th Century, by Frank Hobbs and Nicole Stoops. U.S. Census Bureau, Census 2000 Special Reports, CENSR-4, 2002. Available also on the Census Bureau's Internet site at <www.census.gov/population/www/censusdata/hiscendata.html>.
- Historical Census Statistics on Population Totals by Race, 1790 to 1990, and by Hispanic Origin, 1970 to 1990, for Large Cities and Other Urban Places in the United States, by Campbell Gibson and Kay Jung. U.S. Census Bureau, Population Division Working Paper No. 76, 2005. Available also on the Census Bureau's Internet site at <www.census.gov/population/www/censusdata/hiscendata.html>.

Chapter 2

NATIONAL TRENDS IN THE FOREIGN-BORN POPULATION

The 1850 decennial census was the first census in which data were collected on the nativity of the population. From 1850 to 1930, the foreign-born population of the United States increased from 2.2 million to 14.2 million, reflecting large-scale immigration from Europe during most of this period.[1] As a percentage of total population, the foreign-born population rose from 9.7 percent in 1850 and fluctuated in the 13 percent to 15 percent range from 1860 to 1920 before dropping to 11.6 percent in 1930. The highest percentages foreign born were 14.4 percent in 1870, 14.8 percent in 1890 and 14.7 percent in 1910.

From 1930 to 1950, the foreign-born population of the United States declined from 14.2 million to 10.3 million, or from 11.6 percent to 6.9 percent of the total population. These declines reflected the extremely low level of immigration during the 1930s and 1940s. The foreign-born population then dropped slowly to 9.6 million in 1970, when it represented a record low 4.7 percent of the total population. Immigration had risen during the 1950s and 1960s, but was still low by historical standards, and mortality was high during this period among the foreign-born population because of its old age structure (reflecting four decades of low immigration).

Since 1970, the foreign-born population of the United States has increased rapidly due to large-scale immigration, primarily from Latin America and Asia. The foreign-born population rose from 9.6 million in 1970 to 14.1 million in 1980, to 19.8 million in 1990, and to 31.1 million in 2000. As a percentage of total population, the foreign-born population increased from 4.7 percent in 1970 to 6.2 percent in 1980, to 7.9 percent in 1990, and to 11.1 percent in 2000, the highest percent foreign born recorded in the decennial census since 11.6 percent in 1930.

Chapter 3

DATA ON THE FOREIGN-BORN POPULATION IN STATISTICAL COMPENDIA

The U.S. Bureau of the Census published historical data on the foreign-born population of the United States in three statistical compendia. The most recent, Historical Statistics of the United States, Colonial Times to 1970, was preceded by Historical Statistics of the United States, 1789-1945 and Historical Statistics of the United States, Colonial Times to 1957 (U.S. Bureau of the Census, 1975, 1949, and 1960, respectively; see references). This working paper, like Working Paper No. 29, is a small reference work that updates and expands data on the foreign-born population presented in the most recent edition of Historical Statistics of the United States.[2]

Chapter 4

ACCURACY OF THE DATA

Since 1940, some data in the decennial census of population have been collected on a sample basis. Sample data are identified in the detailed tables.

The data contained in this paper are partially based on a sample of households or persons that responded to the census long form. As a result, the sample estimates may differ somewhat from the 100 percent figures that would have been obtained if all housing units, people within those housing units, and people living in group quarters had been enumerated using the same questionnaires, instructions, enumerators, and so forth. The sample estimates also differ from the values that would have been obtained from different samples of housing units, and hence of people living in those housing units, and people living in group quarters. The deviation of a sample estimate from the average of all possible samples is called the sampling error.

The sampling variability on data in the detailed tables for 1950 to 2000 is low because the data are for the United States as a whole, for states, and for large metropolitan areas and cities and thus are based on relatively large numbers of sample cases. For more information on sampling variability for each of these censuses, see the sources cited for each detailed table.

In addition to the variability that arises from sampling, both sample data and 100 percent data are subject to nonsampling error. Nonsampling error may be introduced during any of the various complex operations used to collect and process data. Such errors may include: not enumerating every household or every person in the population, failing to obtain all required information from the respondents, obtaining incorrect or inconsistent information, and recording information incorrectly. In addition, errors can occur during the field review of the enumerators'ork, during clerical handling of the census questionnaires, or during the processing of the questionnaires.

Nonsampling error may affect the data in two ways: first, errors that are introduced randomly will increase the variability of the data and, therefore, should be reflected in the standard errors; and second, errors that tend to be consistent in one direction will bias both sample and 100 percent data in that direction. Such biases are not reflected in the standard errors.

The estimates in the tables may vary from actual values due to sampling and nonsampling errors. As a result, the estimates used to summarize statistics for one population group may not be statistically different from estimates for another population group. Further information on the accuracy of the data from the 2000 census is located at <www.census.gov/prod/cen2000/doc.sf3.pdf>.

Chapter 5

SOURCES, DEFINITIONS, AND EXPLANATIONS FOR THE DETAILED TABLES

The format of this section parallels the format in Historical Statistics of the United States. A general discussion of census data on the foreign-born population is followed by descriptions of each table, including sources.

The first decennial census of the U.S. population was taken in 1790, as required by the Constitution, in order to obtain the population counts needed for Congressional apportionment. A question on place of birth, which is the primary source of data on the foreign-born population, was not added until the 1850 census (Bohme et al., 1973).

Prior to 1850, the primary questions on the census were on age, sex, and race, although a few other topics had been included (e.g., the industrial classification of employed persons, with three categories in 1820 and seven categories in 1840). The data were collected not for individuals, but rather as tallies at the household level in predefined categories on the questionnaire (e.g., the number of household members who were White females under 5 years old or who were employed in commerce).

The 1850 census introduced major advances by collecting data for each individual and by permitting write-in responses which could be coded later into a large number of categories. These advances facilitated, most notably, the inclusion of questions on place of birth and on occupation, both of which have been included in every subsequent census. The question on place of birth in the 1850 census required the enumerator to record the state, territory, or foreign country. Individuals who were born in a state or territory of the United States (and the small number of individuals for whom place of birth was not reported) were defined as native, and individuals born in a foreign country were defined as foreign born. The dramatic increase in immigration to the United States during the 1840s may have been a motivation for adding the question on place of birth in the 1850 census.[3]

Data on the total foreign-born population of the United States are generally comparable from 1850 to 2000, although the definition of foreign born has been refined. Since 1890, individuals who were born in a foreign country, but who had at least one parent who was an American citizen, have been defined as native rather than as foreign born.[4]

In the 2000 census, the population was classified by nativity as follows. The native population included all U.S. residents who were born in the United States or an outlying area of the United States (e.g., Puerto Rico), or who were born in a foreign country, but who had at least one parent who was an American citizen. All other residents of the United States were classified as foreign born.

Data in this report are for the United States as defined at each census in census reports. The total population shown in detailed tables for 1890 (62,622,250) is the population in general tabulations in 1890 census reports and excludes the population enumerated in the Indian Territory and on Indian reservations (325,464) for whom information on most topics, including nativity, was not collected. The 1890 census was the first to enumerate the entire American Indian population. Alaska and Hawaii are included in the U.S. population starting in 1960. Data showing the effect of these changes in geographic coverage on total population in 1890 and 1960 are included in Tables 8 and 9, which show data on the U.S. population by race and nativity.

Through 1940, census data on nativity of the population were based on data for the total enumerated population. For 1950 to 2000, data on nativity were based on a sample of the total population ranging from about 1 in 4 in 1960 to about 1 in 6 in 1990 and 2000. In 1970, there were two samples, one 15 percent and one 5 percent. The question on nativity was included on both samples. Data on length of residence in the United States, citizenship status, and on Hispanic origin were based on the 5-percent sample, and thus data on nativity cross-tabulated by these characteristics were based on the 5-percent sample. In the detailed tables, sample data are identified with an asterisk after the year (e.g., 1950*).

General information on census data, including area classifications, definitions of topics, accuracy of the data, and collection and processing procedures, is provided in decennial census publications. The United States census has been taken on a de jure (usual place of residence) basis rather than on a de facto (location at the time of the census) basis. For a general discussion of census coverage and underenumeration, see U.S. Bureau of the Census, 1975, Part 1, Series A 1-371, p. 1. For evaluations of census coverage since 1940, see Fay et al., 1988; Robinson et al., 1993; U.S. Census Bureau, 2001a; and Robinson, 2001. For histories of the census of population, see Wright and Hunt, 1900; Eckler, 1972; and Anderson, 1988.

For a bibliography of all U.S. census publications through 1945, see Dubester, 1950. This catalog was reprinted in the Bureau of the Census Catalog of Publications: 1790-1972 (U.S. Bureau of the Census, 1974). For publications of the 1980 and 1990 censuses, see U.S. Bureau of the Census, 1984 and 1994. Additional information is available in the procedural histories of censuses cited in these catalogs. For publications of the 2000 census, see <http://www.census.gov/prod/cen2000/index.html>. For 2000 census data on the Internet, see <http://www.census.gov/main/www/cen2000.html>.

Sources for each detailed table are included below. All sources are decennial census publications unless otherwise noted. For publications from censuses of 1940 and earlier, sequence numbers are included from the Dubester catalog (Dubester, 1950), which provides Library of Congress call numbers, titles, and descriptions of the contents of each publication.

Table 1. Nativity of the Population and Place of Birth of the Native Population: 1850 to 2000.

Sources: For 1850-1870, 1870 census, Vol. I (Dubester #45), Table XXII, pp. 606-615. For 1880-1960, 1960 census, Vol. II, Subject Reports, Report No. 2A, State of Birth, PC(2)-

2A, Table 1, p. 1. For 1970, 1970 census, Vol. I, Characteristics of the Population, Ch. D, Part 1, PC(1)-D1, Table 191, p. 596. For 1980, 1980 census, Vol. 1, Characteristics of the Population, Ch. D, Part 1, Sect. A, PC80-

D1-A, Table 253, p. 7. For 1990, 1990 census, Social and Economic Characteristics, 1990 CP-2-1, Table 18, p. 18. For 2000, Census 2000, <http://www.census.gov/main/www/cen 2000.html>, Summary File 3, Quick Table QT-P22.

The native population includes all U.S. residents who were born in the United States or an outlying area of the United States (e.g., Puerto Rico), or who were born in a foreign country, but who had at least one parent who was an American citizen. All other residents of the United States are classified as foreign born. As described in the general text, the refinement to define as native those individuals who were born in a foreign country, but who had at least one parent who was an American citizen, was introduced in the 1890 census. It appears, however, that this instruction was not followed consistently by enumerators in 1890 (1890 census, Vol I, Part I, Dubester #177, p. clvii).

The outlying areas are as defined at each census. Thus, for example, individuals born in the Philippines (which was granted independence in 1946) were classified as native in 1940 and as foreign born in 1950. The primary outlying areas in censuses of the United States include Alaska (1880-1950), Hawaii (1900-1950), the Philippines (1900-1940), Puerto Rico (1900-2000), Guam (1900-2000), American Samoa (1900-2000), the Canal Zone (1900-1970), Virgin Islands of the United States (1920-2000), and Trust Territory of the Pacific Islands (1950-1980). See U.S. Bureau of the Census, 1975, Section 1, p. 9. Sources for data in Table 1, footnote 2 for Puerto Rico: For 1900, 1900 census, Supplementary Analysis (Dubester #273), p. 280. For 1910-1950, 1950 census, Vol. IV, Special Reports, Part 3, Ch. D, Puerto Ricans in Continental United States, P-E, No. 3D, Table A, p. 4. For 1960, 1960 census, Vol. II, Subject Reports, Report No. 1D, Puerto Ricans in the United States, PC (2)-2D, Table 1, p. 2. For 1970, 1970 census, Vol. I, Characteristics of the Population, Ch. D, Part 1, PC (1)-D1, Table 191, p. 596. For 1980, 1980 census, Vol. I, Characteristics of the Population, Ch. D, Part 1, PC80-1-D1-A, Table 253, p. 7. For 1990, 1990 census, Social and Economic Characteristics, 1990 CP-2-1, Table 18, p. 18. For 2000, Census 2000, <http://www.census.gov/main/www/cen2000.html>, Summary File 3, Quick Table QT-P22.

With regard to footnote 3 in Table 1, the 1970 census had two samples. In contrast to the 15-percent sample questionnaire, the 5-percent sample questionnaire did not include questions on birthplace of father and mother, but it did include questions on citizenship status and on year of entry for persons born in a foreign country. Sampling variability and differences in the questionnaires and in editing procedures account for the differences between data based on the 15-percent and 5-percent samples. These differences are most pronounced for the categories of "Born in the United States" and of "Born abroad of American parents."

Table 2. World Region of Birth of the Foreign-Born Population: 1850 to 1930 and 1960 to 2000.

Sources: Tables 3 and 4.

Data in Table 2 summarize data from Tables 3 and 4 on region of birth of the foreign-born population (number and percent distribution) in a one-page table. See text for Table 3 regarding definitions of regions and country of birth. See text for Table 4 regarding data for 1940 and 1950.

Table 3. World Region and Country or Area of Birth of the Foreign-Born Population: 1960 to 2000.

Sources: For 1960, 1960 census, Vol. I, Characteristics of the Population, Ch. D, Part 1, PC(1)-D1, Table 162, p. 366. For 1970, 1970 census, Vol. I, Characteristics of the Population, Ch. D, Part 1, PC(1)-D1, Table 192, p. 598. For 1980, 1980 census, Statistical Profile of the Foreign-Born Population: 1980 Census of Population, CB84-179, Table 1, pp. 1-4; Vol. I, Characteristics of the Population, Ch. D, Part 1, Sect. A, PC80-D1-A, Table 254, p. 9; and special tabulations. For 1990, 1990 census, The Foreign-Born Population in the United States: 1990, CPH-L-98, Table 13, pp. 19-21; Social and Economic Characteristics, 1990 CP-2-1, Table 14, p. 14; and special tabulations. For 2000, Census 2000, <http://www.census.gov/main/www/cen2000.html>, Summary File 3, Quick Table QT-P15, and special tabulations.

The countries or areas of birth included in Table 3 are those for which data are available for 2000. Prior to 1960, the earliest year included in this table, census data were published for only a small number of countries outside of Europe, reflecting the small number of non-European countries which were numerically important sources of immigration to the United States. Table 4 shows data for the 1850 to 1930 period and the 1960 to 2000 period for a less detailed list of countries.

The six regions of the world shown in Table 3 are based on the "macro regions" used by the United Nations in its Demographic Yearbook for 2002, <http://unstats.un.org/unsd/demographic/products/dyb/dyb2.htm>. These regions are Europe, Asia, Africa, Oceania, Latin America, and Northern America. In general, the subregions are the "component regions" used in the same publication. The differences are in Oceania and Europe. For Oceania, the component regions of Melanesia, Micronesia, and Polynesia are combined and shown as Pacific Islands as well as being shown separately when data are available. For Europe, the component regions of Northern, Western, Southern, and Eastern Europe are modified to reflect historical groupings and patterns of immigration to the United States: Albania and Yugoslavia (former) are included in Eastern Europe rather than in Southern Europe; and Estonia, Latvia, and Lithuania are included in Eastern Europe rather than in Northern Europe. Table 3 includes various subtotals of historical interest within regions (e.g., within Northern Europe, subtotals are shown for the British Isles and for Scandinavia).

Data on country of birth are based generally on the political boundaries of foreign countries existing at the date of the specified decennial census. Changes in political boundaries are less of a concern for the 1960 to 2000 period covered in Table 3 than for the entire 1850 to 2000 period for which data on country of birth are available and are shown in Table 4. Because of boundary changes, including those made following World War I and World War II, accurate comparisons over time are limited for some countries, such as Austria, Czechoslovakia (reported as Bohemia through 1900), Hungary, and Poland. For a discussion of the effects of these boundary changes, see U.S. Bureau of the Census, 1975, Part 1, text for Series C 228-295, pp. 103-104.

In Tables 3 and 4, the term "country or area of birth" is used (rather than just "country of birth") because the foreign geographic areas of birth for which data are available have not always reflected the United States' diplomatic relations at the date of each census.

Table 4. World Region and Country or Area of Birth of the Foreign-Born Population, With Geographic Detail Shown in Decennial Census Publications of 1930 or Earlier: 1850 to 1930 and 1960 to 2000.

Sources: For 1850, 1850 census, The Seventh Census of the United States: 1850 (Dubester #30), Table XV, p. xxxvii. For 1860, 1860 census, Population of the United States in 1860 (Dubester #37), unnumbered table, pp. 620-623. For 1870, 1870 census, Vol. I (Dubester #45), Table VI, pp. 336-342. For 1880, 1880 census, Vol. I (Dubester #61), Table XIII, pp. 492-495. For 1890, 1890 census, Vol. I, Part I (Dubester #177), Table 32, pp. 606-609. For 1900, 1900 census, Supplementary Analysis (Dubester #273), Table 61, pp. 856-859. For 1910, 1910 census, Vol. I (Dubester #296), Ch. VII, Table 2, p. 784. For 1920, 1920 census, Vol. II, (Dubester #453), Ch. VI, Tables 3-4, pp. 694-695. For 1930, 1930 census, Vol. II (Dubester #653), Ch. 5, Table 4, p. 233. For 1960-2000, see sources for Table 3. In addition, see U.S. Bureau of the Census, 1975, Part 1, Series C 228-295, pp. 117-118.

See text for Table 3 concerning the definitions of regions and countries of birth. Data are not included in Table 4 for 1940 and 1950 because data on the foreign-born population by country of birth in census publications for these years are limited almost entirely to the White population. For data on the foreign-born White population by country of birth for 1910 to 1970, see U.S. Bureau of the Census, 1975, Part 1, Series C 228-295, pp. 117-118.

Table 5. Language Spoken at Home for the Foreign-Born Population 5 Years and Over: 1980 to 2000.

Sources: For 1980, 1980 census, Vol. I, Characteristics of the Population, Ch. D, Part 1, Sect. A, PC80-1-D1-A, Table 256, p. 16, and special tabulations. For 1990, 1990 census, Social and Economic Characteristics, 1990 CP-2-1, Table 13, p. 13; Social and Economic Characteristics of Selected Language Groups for U.S. and States: 1990, CPH-L 159; and special tabulations. For 2000, Census 2000, <http://www.census.gov/main/www/cen2000.html>, Summary File 3, Quick Table QT-P16, and special tabulations.

Data on language spoken at home are based on the question, "Does this person speak a language other than English at home?," and if the answer was yes, also on the question "What is this language?" (If the answer was yes, individuals were asked also "How well does this person speak English - Very well, Well, Not well, Not at all.") If individuals spoke both English and another language at home, they were classified by the non-English language in data shown in Table 5, regardless of how well they spoke English.

The categories used to group data on language spoken at home are both linguistic and geographic and are based generally on Classification and Index of the World's Languages (Voegelin, C.F. and F.M., 1977). The classification used in Table 5 includes three major language groups (Indo-European languages, Asian and Pacific Island languages, and Other languages) and selected language families within each of the three groups (e.g., Romance languages within the Indo-European language group). As a result, these categories do not always correspond to the regions and subregions of the world used to group countries of birth (Tables 3 and 4). For example, unlike most languages spoken in European countries, Finnish and Hungarian are included with Other languages rather than with Indo-European languages.

All individual languages spoken at home with 10,000 or more foreign-born speakers in 1980 or 1990 or 2000 are listed separately in Table 5. Data for language families include languages not listed separately.

Table 6. Mother Tongue of the Foreign-Born Population: 1910 to 1940, 1960, and 1970.

Sources: For 1910-1920, 1920 census, Vol. II (Dubester #453), Ch. X, Table 1, p. 973. For 1930-1940, 1940 census, Nativity and Parentage of the White Population (Dubester #1001), Mother Tongue, Table 1, p. 7. For 1960, 1960 census, Vol. II, Subject Reports, Report 1E, Mother Tongue of the Foreign Born, PC(2)-1E, Tables 1-2, pp. 1-2. For 1970, 1970 census, Vol. II, Subject Reports, Report 1A, National Origin and Language, PC(2)-1A, Table 19, p. 492.

Data on mother tongue are based on a question on language spoken in this person's home when he was a child or, when the question was limited to the foreign-born population, on a question on what language was spoken in this person's home before he came to the United States. Data on mother tongue for 1910 to 1940 were tabulated only for the White population, which represented over 98 percent of the foreign-born population during this period (Table 9). For 1960 and 1970, data are shown for both the White foreign-born population (to compare with data for 1910 to 1940) and for the total foreign-born population. Starting with the 1980 census, a question on language spoken at home replaced the question on mother tongue. Data on language spoken at home for the foreign-born population are shown in Table 5.

To the extent possible, the language groups and families used to group data on mother tongue are the same as used in Table 5 to group data on language spoken at home. However, the concepts of mother tongue and language spoken at home differ considerably, and thus data in Tables 5 and 6 are not comparable.

Table 7. Age and Sex of the Foreign-Born Population: 1870 to 2000.

Sources: For 1870, 1870 census, Vol. II (Dubester #49), Table XXII, pp. 552-553. For 1880, 1880 census, Vol. I (Dubester #61), Table XVII, p. 542, and Table XX, pp. 548-551. For 1890, 1890 census, Vol. I, Part 1 (Dubester #177), Table 20, pp. 486-487, and Vol. I, Part 2, (Dubester #178), Table 1, pp. 3 and 5. For 1900, 1900 census, Vol. II, Part II (Dubester #254), Table XVI, pp. xxxvi-xxxviii. For 1910, 1910 census, Vol. I (Dubester #296), Ch. IV, Table 29, pp. 310-313. For 1920, 1920 census, Vol. II (Dubester #453), Ch. III, Table 9, pp. 162-165. For 1930-1940, 1940 census, Vol. II, Part 1 (Dubester #957), Table 7, p. 22, and Vol. IV, Part 1 (Dubester #971), Table 3, p. 13. For 1910-1940 for total foreign-born population (all races by sex, but not by age), 1940 census, Vol. I, Part 1 (Dubester #957), Table 4, p. 19. For 1950, 1950 census, Vol. II, Characteristics of the Population, Ch. C, Part 1, Bulletin P-C1, Table 96, p. 171, and Table 101, p. 178. For 1960, 1960 census, Vol. I, Characteristics of the Population, Ch. D, Part 1, PC(1)-D1, Table 156, p. 354, and Table 161, p. 364. For 1970, 1970 census, Vol. I, Characteristics of the Population, Ch. D, Part 1, PC(1)-D1, Table 191, p. 596. For 1980, 1980 census, Vol. I, Characteristics of the Population, Ch. D, Part 1,

Sect. 1, PC80-1-D1-A, Table 253, p. 7, and special tabulations. For 1990, 1990 census, Foreign-Born Population in the United States, 1990 CP-3-1, Table 1, pp. 1-2, and special tabulations. For 2000, Census 2000, special tabulations.

In censuses of 1880, 1890, and 1910 to 1940, published census data on the age and sex distribution of the foreign-born population were limited primarily to the foreign-born White population. During this period, the foreign-born population of races other than White, which peaked at 220,744 in 1930, represented between 1 percent and 2 percent of the total foreign-born population (Table 9). Because age data for the total foreign-born population are available for 1870, 1900, and 1950 to 2000, and because the foreign-born population of races other than White represented such a small proportion of the total foreign-born population from 1880 to 1940, the population universe for Table 7 is the total foreign-born population. The foreign-born population of races other than White is included in the category "age data not available" for 1880, 1890, and 1910 to 1940.

Table 8. Race and Hispanic Origin of the Population by Nativity: 1850 to 1990.

Sources: For 1850-1860, 1870 census, Vol. I (Dubester #45), Table XXII, pp. 606-615. For 1870-1890, 1900 census, Vol. II, Part II (Dubester #254), Table I, p. xvii. For 1900-1940, 1940 census, Vol. II, Part I (Dubester #971), Table 4, p. 19. For 1940 for White population with Spanish mother tongue, 1940 census, Nativity and Parentage of the White Population (Dubester #1001), Mother Tongue, Table 1, p. 7. For 1950, 1950 census, Vol. II, Characteristics of the Population, Ch. C, Part 1, Bulletin P-C1, Table 96, p. 171, and Vol. IV, Special Reports, Part 3, Ch. B, Nonwhite Population By Race, Tables 1-7, pp. 15-21. For 1960, 1960 census, Vol. I, Characteristics of the Population, Ch. C, Part 1, PC(1)-C1, Table 66, p. 201, and Part 3, PC(1)-C1, Table 38, p. 50, and Part 13, PC(1)-C1, Table 38, p. 50. For 1960 for nativity of the Black population and the Asian and Pacific Islander population, 1960 census, Vol. II, Subject Reports, Report 1C, Nonwhite Population by Race, PC(2)-1C, Tables 1-8, pp. 1-8. For 1970, 1970 census, Vol. I, Characteristics of the Population, Ch. D, Part 1, PC(1)-D1, Table 189, p. 591, and Table 190, pp. 593-594, and Vol. II, Subject Reports, Report No. 1C, Persons of Spanish Origin, PC(2)-1C, Table 4, p. 32. For 1980, 1980 census, Vol. I, Characteristics of the Population, Ch. C, Part 1, PC80-1-C1, Table 101, p. 70, Table 122, pp. 95-96, Table 132, p. 117, and Table 167, p. 164. For 1990, 1990 census, Social and Economic Characteristics, 1990 CP-2-1, Table 43, p. 43.

The racial and Hispanic origin categories shown in the boxhead of Table 8 reflect the guidelines set forth in Statistical Policy Directive No. 15, "Race and Ethnic Standards for Federal Statistics and Administrative Reporting" (U.S. Office of Management and Budget, 1977).[5] Data by race or color for all censuses since 1850 have been made consistent with Directive No. 15 to the extent possible. Data for the Hispanic origin category are available since 1970, and data for the category of White, not of Hispanic origin are included also since 1970. Individuals of Hispanic origin, the vast majority of whom report themselves by race as White or as "Other race," may be of any race.

There was a dramatic population increase in Other race from 1970 to 1980. This reflected the addition of a question on Hispanic origin to the 100-percent questionnaire, an increased propensity for Hispanics not to identify themselves as White, and a change in editing procedures to accept reports of "Other race" for respondents who wrote in Hispanic entries such as Mexican, Cuban, or Puerto Rican. In 1970, such responses in the Other race category were reclassified and tabulated as White.

The classification of the population by race reflects common or social usage. It does not denote any clear-cut scientific definition of biological stock. Through 1950, the classification of the population by race was usually obtained by the census enumerator's observation. Individuals of mixed White and other parentage were usually classified with the other race. In 1960, census data on race were collected by a combination of self-classification, direct interview, and observation. In the 1970 census, data on race and Hispanic origin were obtained primarily through self-classification. In the 1980 and 1990 censuses, the data were obtained entirely through self-classification.

In the 1850 census, the only racial classifications in census reports were for White and Black. It is not clear how the unknown, but clearly very small, number of enumerated individuals who were not White or Black were classified by race. Chinese and American Indian classifications were added in the 1860 census; however, prior to 1890, the enumeration of American Indians excluded Indian reservations and American Indians living elsewhere in tribal society (not taxed). Japanese was added in 1870, and other Asian "races" were added starting in 1910. In the 1930 census only, Mexican was defined as a race. Tabulations for 1930 were revised to include Mexicans with White and were included in 1940 census reports and are included in this report.

In the 1950 census, an "Other races" category was added in an attempt to identify individuals of mixed White, Black, and Indian ancestry. This attempt was only partially successful; however, the "Other races" category was retained, and with self-identification of race and Hispanic origin, there has been a dramatic increase since 1970 in the "Other races" population. This is due primarily to individuals who are of Hispanic origin and who choose not to report in a specific racial category, such as White or Black.

Data by race for 1950 and for 1960 in Table 8 are based on more than one tabulation of the data and in some cases on more than one sampling rate. As a result, the totals for races other than White differ slightly from the sum of the component races. Data for 1950 on the population by nativity for these component races are highly inconsistent and are not included in Table 8. See sources for Table 8.

For more detailed discussions of data on race and Hispanic origin, see U.S. Bureau of the Census, 1975, Section 1, text for Series A 91-104, pp. 3-4, and the sources listed above for Table 8.

Table 9. Race and Hispanic Origin of the Foreign-Born Population: 1850 to 1990.

Source: Table 8.

Table 9 summarizes data on the foreign-born population by race and Hispanic origin and shows the corresponding percent distribution of the foreign-born population. See text for Table 8 regarding data on race and Hispanic origin.

Table 10. Race and Hispanic Origin of the Population by Nativity and of the Foreign-Born Population: 1990 and 2000.

Sources: For 1990, 1990 census, Social and Economic Characteristics, 1990 CP-2-1, Table 43, p. 43, and Table 107, pp. 109-110. For 2000, Census 2000, <http://www.census.gov/main/www/cen2000.html>, Summary File 4, Detailed Table PCT 43.

Table 10 shows data on the foreign-born population by race and Hispanic origin for 2000, reflecting "Revisions to the Standards for the Classification of Federal Data on Race and Ethnicity" (U.S. Office of Management and Budget, 1997), and data for 1990. The revisions implemented in the 2000 census permitted individuals to report more than one race and divided the Asian and Pacific Islander category into two categories. The division of the Asian and Pacific Islander category into the categories of Asian and of Native Hawaiian and Other Pacific Islander does not present any major issues of comparability since the 1990 data can be divided; however, the option in 2000 to report more than one race means that the data for 1990 and 2000 are not directly comparable. Data for 2000 are shown for race alone and for race alone or in combination with one or more other races, which represent the minimum and maximum definitions, respectively, of the population in a race category (e.g., for Asian). These data provide a minimum-maximum range for change since 1990 when respondents could report only one race. For more information on 2000 data by race, see U.S. Census Bureau, 2001b.

Table 11. Length of Residence in the United States of the Foreign-Born Population: 1900 to 1930 and 1970 to 2000.

Sources: For 1900-1910, 1910 census, Vol. I (Dubester #296), Ch. X, Table 1, p. 1017. For 1920, 1920 census, Vol. II (Dubester #453), Ch. VII, Table 1, p. 779. For 1930, 1930 census, Vol. II (Dubester #653), Ch. 9, Table 4, p. 498. For 1970, 1970 census, Vol. I, Characteristics of the Population, Ch. D, Part 1, PC(1)-D1, Table 195, p. 600, and Vol. II, Subject Reports, Report 1A, National Origin and Language, PC(2)-1A, Table 17, p. 440. For 1980, 1980 census, Vol. I, Characteristics of the Population, Ch. C, Part1, PC80-1-C1, Table 99, p. 68. For 1990, 1990 census, Social and Economic Characteristics, 1990 CP-2-1, Table 13, p. 13, and Social and Economic Characteristics of Selected Language Groups for U.S. and States, CPH-L-159. For 2000, Census 2000, <http://www.census.gov/main/www/cen2000.html>, Summary File 3, Quick Table QT-P14, and special tabulations.

Data on length of residence in the United States of the foreign-born population are available from the censuses of 1900 to 1930 and 1970 to 2000 and are based on a question on the year of immigration (for 1900-1930) or on a question on the year when this person came to the United States to stay (for 1970-1990) or to live (for 2000). For presentation in Table 11, the data have been converted to length of residence in years. This conversion is approximate, reflecting the reference dates of pertinent censuses: June 1 in 1900, April 15 in 1910, Jan. 1 in 1920, and April 1 for 1930 and 1970 to 2000.

Length of residence in (completed) years is based on published data on year of immigration or on year came to stay or to live as follows. For 1900: under 4 (1896-1900), 4-8 (1891-95), 9-13 (1886-90), 14-18 (1881-85), 19+ (before 1881). For 1910: under 4 (1906-10), 4-8 (1901-05), 9-13 (1896-1900), 14-18 (1891-95), 19+ (before 1891). For 1920: under 4 (1916-1920), 4-8 (1911-15), 9-13 (1906-10), 14-18 (1901-05), 19+ (before 1901). For 1930:

under 5 (1925-30), 5-9 (1920-24), 10-14 (1915-19), 15-18 (1911-14), 19-28 (1901-10), 29+ (before 1901). For 1970: under 5 (1965-70), 5-9 (1960-64), 10-14 (1955-59), 15-19 (1950-54), 20-24 (1945-49), 25-34 (1935-44), 35-44 (1925-34), 45-54 (1915-24), 55+ (before 1915). For 1980: under 5 (1975-80), 5-9 (1970-74), 10-14 (1965-69), 15-19 (1960-64), 20-29 (1950-59), 30+ (before 1950). For 1990: under 5 (1985-90), 5-9 (1980-84), 10-14 (1975-79), 15-19 (1970-74), 20-24 (1965-69), 25-29 (1960-64), 30-39 (1950-59), 40+ (before 1950). For 2000: under 5 (1995-2000), 5-9 (1990-94), 10-14 (1985-89), 15-19 (1980-84), 20-24 (1975-79), 25-29 (1970-74), 30-34 (1965-69), 35-39 (1960-1964), 40-44 (1955-1959), 45-49 (1950-1954), 50-54 (1945-1949), 55+ (before 1945).

Table 12. Citizenship Status of the Foreign-Born Population: 1890 to 1950 and 1970 to 2000.

Sources: For 1890-1930, 1930 census, Vol. II (Dubester #653), Ch. 8, Table 4, p. 405. For 1940, 1940 census, Vol. II, Part 1 (Dubester #957), Tables 27-29, pp. 79-81. For 1950, 1950 census, Vol. II, Characteristics of the Population, Ch. C, Part 1, Bulletin P-C1, Table 101, p. 178. For 1970, 1970 census, Vol. I, Characteristics of the Population, Ch. D, Part 1, PC(1)-D1), Table 194, p. 599. For 1980, 1980 census, Vol. I, Characteristics of the Population, Ch D, Part 1, Sect. A, PC80-1-D1-A, Table 253, p. 7, and special tabulations. For 1990, 1990 census, Foreign-Born Population of the United States, 1990 CP-3-1, Table 1, p. 1. For 2000, Census 2000, <http://www.census.gov/main/www/cen2000.html>, Summary File 4, Detailed Table, PCT44, and special tabulations.

In 1960, a question on citizenship status was not included on the general census questionnaire (although it was included on the questionnaire used in New York state). Prior to the 1920 census, published census data on citizenship status were restricted to males 21 years and over. Starting with the 1930 census, data on citizenship status have been published by sex for all ages as well as for the voting age population. For years prior to 1940, when age not reported was not allocated, the data on citizenship status by age assume that all individuals for whom age was not reported were 21 years and over.

Table 13. Nativity and Parentage of the Population: 1890 to 1930, 1960, and 1970.

Sources: For 1890, 1890 census, Vol. I, Part I (Dubester # 177), Table 20, pp. 486-487, and Tables 35-36, pp. 681-683. For 1900-1930, 1930 census, Vol. II (Dubester #653), Ch. 2, Table 6, p. 33. For 1960, 1960 census, Vol. II, Subject Reports, Report 1A, Nativity and Parentage, PC(2)-1A, Table 1, p. 2. For 1970, 1970 census, Vol. II, Subject Reports, Report 1A, National Origin and Language, PC(2)-1A, Table 1, p. 1.

The terms native population and foreign-born population were defined earlier (see text for Table 1). Information on birthplace of parents may be used to classify the native population by parentage: native of native parentage (both parents native), native of foreign parentage (both parents foreign-born) and native of mixed parentage (one parent native and one parent foreign born). The term foreign stock includes the foreign-born population and the native population of foreign or mixed parentage. Just as the native population and foreign-born population comprise the total population, the native population of native parentage and the foreign-stock population also comprise the total population.

A question on birthplace of parents was included in the census from 1870 to 1970; however, data on parentage for the total population are available only since 1890. For data on the parentage of the White population from 1870 to 1970, see U.S. Bureau of the Census, Part 1, 1975, Series A 135-142, p. 19. Starting in the 1980 census, a question on ancestry (based on self-identification) replaced the question on birthplace of parents.

The approach to classifying only the native population by parentage was adopted in census reports for 1910. In census reports for 1890 and 1900, the total population was classified by nativity and parentage, even though a very small proportion of foreign-born individuals were of native parentage. Data published in 1890 for races other than White do not permit adjustment of the data to be consistent with the current approach; however, the adjustment was made in the data presented here based on the assumption that the relatively small foreign-born population of races other than White in 1890 (127,680) was entirely of foreign or mixed parentage. This is a reasonable assumption because a large majority of the foreign-born population of races other than White was Asian (Chinese or Japanese), as shown in Table 9.

Table 14. Nativity of the Population, for Regions, Divisions, and States: 1850 to 2000.

Sources: For 1850-1890, 1890 census, Vol. I, Part 1 (Dubester #177), Table 1, pp. 2-3, and Table 12, p. 399. For 1900-1920, 1920 census, Vol. II (Dubester #453), Ch. 1, Table 10, p. 36. For 1930, 1930 census, Vol. II (Dubester #653), Ch. 2, Table 15, p. 39. For 1940, 1940 census, Vol. II (Dubester #956), Parts 1-7, Table 4 (for the United States and for each state). For 1950, 1950 census, Vol. II, Characteristics of the Population, Ch. C, Part 1, Table 96, p. 171 (for the United States), and Parts 2-50, Table 54 (for each state). For 1960, 1960 census, Vol. I, Characteristics of the Population, Ch. C, Part 1, PC(1)-C1, Table 108, p. 251. For 1970, 1970 census, Vol. I, Characteristics of the Population, Ch. C, Part 1, PC(1)-C1, Table 143, p. 472. For 1980, 1980 census, Vol. I, Characteristics of the Population, Ch. C, Part 1, PC80-1-C1, Table 99, p. 68, Table 183, pp. 181-182, and Table 236, pp. 291-296. For 1990, 1990 census, Social and Economic Characteristics, 1990 CP-2-1, Table 143, pp. 173-179. For 2000, Census 2000, Summary Social, Economic, and Housing Characteristics, PHC-2-1, Part 1, Table 1, p. 1, <http:www.census.gov/prod/cen2000/phc-2-1-pt.1.pdf>.

Data on the population by nativity for regions, divisions, and states are consistent with data in Table 1 for the United States. For information on the boundaries of states and of territories preceding statehood, see Forstall, 1996. The groupings of states into regions and divisions of the United States are those currently used by the Census Bureau. For the history of census regions and divisions and their predecessor areas, see Dahmann, 1992.

Table 15. Foreign-Born Population by Historical Section and Subsection of the United States: 1850 to 2000.

Source: Table 14, and Dahmann, 1992.

The four regions -- Northeast, North Central (subsequently renamed Midwest), South, and West --were introduced in the 1940s and replaced the three sections introduced in the 1910 census: North, South, and West. For the presentation of historical data, including data on the foreign-born population, the three sections are in some ways preferable because they permit direct comparisons of North and South. The North is divided into two subsections

(Northeast and North Central), and the South is divided into two subsections (Southeast and South Central). These subsections recognize the westward expansion of settlement from the Atlantic seaboard and facilitate comparisons of the eastern and central portions of the United States.

Table 16. Nativity of the Population by Type of Residence: 1960 to 2000.

Sources: For 1960, 1960 census, Vol. I, Characteristics of the Population, Ch. C, Part 1, PC(1)-C1, Table 101, p. 238. For 1970, 1970 census, Vol. I, Characteristics of the Population, Ch. C, Part 1, PC(1)-C1, Table 108, p. 414. For 1980, 1980 census, Vol. I, Characteristics of the Population, Ch. C, Part 1, PC80-1-C1, Table 110, p. 81. For 1990 as defined effective June 30, 1990, 1990 census, Social and Economic Characteristics, 1990 CP-2-1, Table 27, p. 27. For 1990 as defined effective June 30, 1993, 1990 census, Supplementary Reports, Metropolitan Areas as Defined by the Office of Management and Budget, June 30, 1993, Section 1, 1990 CPH-S-1-1, Table 5, pp. 262-408. For 2000, Census 2000, <http://www.census.gov/main/www/cen2000.html>, Summary File 3, Detailed Tables, Table P21, and special tabulations.

Under OMB standards prior to December 2000, and in data in general data products through the 2000 census, the United States was divided into two type-of-residence categories: metropolitan and nonmetropolitan, with the latter referring to all territory that did not qualify as metropolitan. The general concept of a metropolitan area (MA) is that of a core area containing a large population nucleus, together with adjacent communities that have a high degree of economic and social integration with that core. Some MAs are defined around two or more cores. The component units of MAs are counties, except in the New England states where the component units are cities and towns. In each MA, the largest place (usually an incorporated city) and, in some cases, additional places are designated as "central cities." With some exceptions, each MA includes at least one central city with 50,000 or more population. For more information about these definitions, see the sources listed for Table 16.

OMB standards issued in December 2000 define metropolitan (metro) statistical areas and micropolitan (micro) statistical areas (collectively labeled as core-based statistical areas), with all other territory being defined as outside core-based statistical areas. Both metro and micro counties are composed of one or more whole counties (or county equivalents, such as independent cities). Metro areas include at least one Census Bureau-defined urbanized area of 50,000 or more population, and micro areas include at least one urban cluster of 10,000 to 49,999 population. For more information, see <http://www.census.gov/population/www/ estimates/html> and the links provided there. For the December 2000 standards, see <http://www.census.gov/population/www/estimates/00-32997.pdf>. Urbanized areas and urbanized clusters are discussed at <http://www.census.gov/geo/www/ua/ua_2k.html>.

Table 17. Nativity of the Population for Metropolitan Statistical Areas With 1,000,000 or More Population and Their Component Metropolitan Divisions: 2000.

Source: Census 2000, special tabulations.

A metropolitan division is a county or group of counties within a core-based statistical area that contains a core with a population of at least 2.5 million. A metropolitan division consists of one or more main/secondary counties that represent an employment center or centers, plus adjacent counties associated with the main county or counties through commuting ties. See <http://www.census.gov/population/www/estimates/00-32997.pdf> for more information.

Table 18. Nativity of the Population for Combined Statistical Areas With 1,000,000 or More Population and Their Component Metropolitan and Micropolitan Statistical Areas: 2000.

Source: Census 2000, special tabulations.

A combined statistical area is a geographic entity consisting of two or more adjacent core-based statistical areas with substantial employment interchange. See <http://www.census.gov/population/www/estimates/00-32997.pdf> for more information.

Table 19. Nativity of the Population for Metropolitan Statistical Areas (MSAs) and Consolidated Metropolitan Statistical Areas (CMSAs) With 1,000,000 or More Population: 2000.

Source: Census 2000, Summary Social, Economic, and Housing Characteristics, PHC-2-1, Part 1, Table 17, pp. 17-36. <http://www.census.gov/prod/cen2000/phc-2-1-pt.1.pdf>.

Table 19 shows 2000 census data using OMB standards in effect at the time of the census (April 2000). See Census 2000, Summary Social, Economic, and Housing Characteristics, PHC-2-A, pp. A-16 and A-17, <http://www.census.gov/prod/cen2000/phc-2-a.pdf>.

For a general description of metropolitan areas (MAs), see text for Table 16. To meet the needs of various data users, the standards for defining MAs permit an MA to be classified either as a metropolitan statistical area (MSA), or as a Consolidated Metropolitan Statistical Area (CMSA) that is divided into primary metropolitan statistical areas (PMSAs). For purposes of ranking MAs by total population in 2000 in Table 19, MSAs and CMSAs are used, and component PMSAs are shown for each CMSA.

Table 20. Nativity of the Population for Metropolitan Areas With 500,000 or More Population: 1960.

Source: For 1960, 1960 census, Vol. I, Characteristics of the Population, Ch. C, Parts 2-52 (for each state), PC(1)-C1 to C52, Table 72.

For a general description of metropolitan areas (MAs), see text for Table 16. MAs for which data were shown in 1960 census reports were standard metropolitan statistical areas (SMSAs). In addition, two standard consolidated areas (SCAs) were included, for New York and Chicago. These correspond generally to standard metropolitan areas (SMAs) for New York and Chicago shown in 1950 census reports. For purposes of ranking MAs by total population in 1960 in Table 20, the two SCAs and the SMSAs outside of the New York and Chicago SCAs are used. On this basis, there are 49 MAs with 500,000 or more population shown in Table 20.

Table 21. Nativity of the Population for Metropolitan Districts With 250,000 or More Population: 1940.

Source: 1940 census, Vol. II (Dubester #956), Parts 1-7, Table 4 (for each state).

Metropolitan districts were defined by the Census Bureau for use in presenting decennial census data from 1910 to 1940; however, data by nativity of the total population for metropolitan districts were published only for 1940. Metropolitan districts, which were replaced starting in 1950 with county-based metropolitan areas, were defined in 1940 in general as cities with 50,000 or more population and all contiguous minor civil divisions or incorporated places with an average population density of 150 or more persons per square mile. For more information, see the source cited for Table 21.

Table 22. Nativity of the Population by Urban-Rural Residence and Size of Place: 1870 to 1940 and 1960 to 2000.

Source: For 1870, 1870 census, Vol. I (Dubester #45), Table III, pp. 77-296, and Table IV, p. 299. For 1880, 1880 census, Vol. I (Dubester #61), Table VII, p. 426, and Table IX, pp. 447-456. For 1890-1900, 1900 census, Supplementary Analysis (Dubester #273), Table XXII, p. 51, Tables 10-11, pp. 620-627. For 1900-1940 for urban and rural, 1940 census, Vol. II, Part 1 (Dubester # 957), Tables 4-5, pp. 19-20. For 1910, 1910 census, Vol. I (Dubester #296), Ch. II, Table 37, p. 178. For 1920, 1920 census, Vol. II (Dubester #453), Ch. I, Table 13, p. 47. For 1930, 1930 census, Vol. II (Dubester #653), Ch. 2, Table 23, pp. 67-73. For 1940, 1940 census, Vol. II, Part 1-7 (Dubester #956), Table 36 (for each state). For 1960, 1960 census, Vol. I, Characteristics of the Population, Ch. C, Part 1, PC(1)-C1, Table 100, p. 233. For 1970, 1970 census, Vol. I, Characteristics of the Population, Ch. C, Part 1, PC(1)-C1, Table 97, p. 403. For 1980, 1980 census, Vol. I, Characteristics of the Population, Ch. C, Part 1, PC80-1-C1, Table 99, p. 68. For 1990, 1990 census, Social and Economic Characteristics, 1990 CP-2-1, Table 13, p. 13. For 2000, Census 2000,

<http://www.census.gov/main/www/cen2000.html>, Summary File 3, Detailed Tables, Table P21.

In 2000, the urban population was defined as the population of urbanized areas (50,000 or more population) and urban clusters (2,500 to 49,999 population) where both urbanized areas and urban clusters encompassed densely settled territory without regard to corporate boundaries. The remainder of the population was defined as rural. The definition of urban in 2000 differs from that of 1990 and earlier, which relied heavily on corporate boundaries. For more information on the 2000 definition of urban, see <http://www.census.gov/prod/cen2000/phc-1-1-pt2.pdf>.

In 1990, the urban population was defined as the population in (1) incorporated places (e.g., cities) of 2,500 or more population, (2) census designated places (CDPs) (i.e., unincorporated places) of 2,500 or more population, and (3) other territory, incorporated or unincorporated, in urbanized areas. The remainder of the population was defined as rural.

In 1990, urbanized areas were defined as one or more "central places" and the adjacent densely settled (with at least 1,000 population per square mile) surrounding territory ("urban fringe") that together had at least 50,000 population.

Changes in the definitions of urban, rural, and urbanized areas were relatively minor from 1950, when urbanized areas were first delineated, to 1990. Prior to 1950, the urban population was defined generally as the population in incorporated places of 2,500 or more population. The population threshold of 2,500 for defining places as urban was adopted in the 1910 census; however, data on the nativity of the population using this population threshold are available for 1890 and 1900 and are included in Table 22.

The rural population is classified as rural nonfarm or rural farm. The farm population consists of individuals in households living in farm residences. In the 2000 census, a one-family house or mobile home was classified as a farm residence if (1) it was located on a property of 1 acre or more and (2) at least $1,000 of agricultural products were sold from the property in 1999. Data on the nativity of the rural farm and rural nonfarm population are available since 1930; however, the definition of farm changed considerably between 1930 and 2000. From 1930 to 1950, the farm population included all individuals living on farms. The definition of a farm depended primarily upon local usage and the respondent's view of what constituted a farm. In 1960, acreage and sales were introduced in the decennial census as criteria for defining farms.

For more detailed discussions of definitions of urban, urban place, urbanized area, rural, rural nonfarm, and rural farm see the sources for Table 22. For more detailed discussions of the changes in definitions of urban and urban place, see also Truesdell, 1949, and Gibson, 1998.

Table 23. Nativity of the Population for the 50 Largest Urban Places: 1870 to 2000.

Sources: For 1870 for all places, 1870 census, Vol. I (Dubester #45), Table III, pp. 77-296. For 1880 for places of 4,000+ population, 1880 census, Vol. I (Dubester # 61), Table IX, pp. 447-456. For

1890 for places of 2,500+ population, 1890 census, Vol. I, Part 1 (Dubester #177), Table 19, pp. 451-485. For 1900 for places of 2,500+ population, 1900 census, Vol. I, Part 1 (Dubester #252), Table 23, pp. 609-646. For 1910 for places of 100,000+ population, 1910 census, Vol. I (Dubester #296), Ch. II, Table 37, p. 178; and for places of 25,000-99,999 population, Ch. VII, Table 38, pp. 860-865. For 1920 for places of 100,000+ population, 1920 census, Vol. I (Dubester # 453), Ch. I, Table 13, p. 47; and for places of 25,000-99,999 population, Ch. VI, Table 17, pp. 760-767. For 1930 for places of 100,000+ population, 1930 census, Vol. II (Dubester #653), Ch. 2, Table 23, pp. 67-73; and for places of 50,000-99,999 population, Ch. 4, Table 35, pp. 199-201. For 1940 for places of 100,000+ population, 1940 census, Vol. II, Parts 1-7 (Dubester # 956), Table 36 (for each state); and for places of 10,000-99,999 population, Table 31 (for each state). For 1950 for places of 100,000+ population, 1950 census, Vol. II, Characteristics of the Population, Ch. C, Parts 2-50 (for states), Bulletin P-C2 to C50, Table 55. For 1960 for places of 10,000+ population, 1960 census, Vol. I, Characteristics of the Population, Ch. C, Parts 2-52 (for states), PC(1)-C2 to C52, Table 72. For 1970 for places of 50,000+ population, 1970 census, Vol. I, Characteristics of the Population, Ch. C, Parts 2-52 (for states), PC(1)-C1 to C52, Table 81; and for places of 10,000-49,999 population, Table 102. For 1980 for places of 50,000+ population, 1980 census, Vol. I, Characteristics of the Population, Ch. C, Parts 2-52 (for states), PC (1)-C2 to C52, Tables 118 and 118a; for places of 10,000-49,999 population, Tables 156 and 156a; and for places of 2,500-9,999 population, Tables 166 and 166a. For 1990 for places of 10,000+ population, 1990 census, Social and Economic Characteristics, 1990 CP-2-2 to 52, Table 167; and for places of 2,500-9,999 population, Table 195. For 2000,

Census 2000, Summary Social, Economic, and Housing Characteristics, PHC-2-1, Part 2, Table 49, pp. 836-839. <http://www.census.gov/prod/cen2000/phc-2-1- pt.2.pdf>.

Table 23 includes data starting with the 1870 census, the first census for which reports showed data on a comprehensive basis on the nativity of the population for places. The lists of the 50 largest urban places at each census through 1990 are from Gibson, 1998. With a few exceptions, the urban places shown in Table 23 are incorporated cities. Honolulu, which is included from 1960 to 2000, is a census designated place (CDP). (See text for Table 22 regarding CDPs.) Three cities included in Table 23 from 1970 to 2000 reflect consolidations of city and county governments: Indianapolis, Jacksonville, and Nashville. The first two are listed as cities in census publications while the last is listed as Nashville-Davidson. See sources for Table 23 for more information on consolidated cities.

Table 24. Nativity of the Population for the 25 Largest Urban Places and for Selected Counties: 1860.

Source: 1860 census, Population of the United States in 1860 (Dubester #37), recapitulation section, pp. 608-615, and state sections, Tables 3-4.

Table 24 presents available data on the population of the 25 largest urban places in 1860, along with data for their parent counties when data are not available for the individual urban places in 1850 or 1860. In the 1870 census, in which data are available for both counties and places, the percent foreign born in the population in these cities was usually higher than in their respective parent counties.

Table 25. Nativity of the Population for the 25 Largest Urban Places and for Selected Counties: 1850.

Source: 1850 census, The Seventh Census of the United States: 1850 (Dubester # 30), Table of Counties, Districts, and Parishes in the United States, 1850, pp. xcv-cii, and Census of 1852 for California, Tables I-II, p. 982; and Statistical View of the United States (Dubester # 33) Appendix, Table III, p. 399.

Table 25 presents available data on the population of the 25 largest urban places in 1850, along with data for their parent counties when data are not available for the individual urban places in 1850 or 1860. In the 1870 census, in which data are available for both counties and places, the percent foreign born in the population in these cities was usually higher than in their respective parent counties.

Table 26. Nativity of the Population for Urban Places Ever Among the 50 Largest Urban Places Since 1870: 1850 to 2000.

Sources: See sources for Table 23.

Each urban place included for any year in Table 23 is included in Table 26. Available data on nativity of the population are included for each year, regardless of whether or not the urban place was among the 50 largest urban places in that year. Ranks in total population for 1950 to 1990 among all urban places in the United States, which are based on sample data, differ in a few cases from those shown in Gibson, 1998, which are based on complete-count data for all censuses in the 1850 to 1990 period.

ACKNOWLEDGMENTS

This working paper was prepared in Population Division. The authors thank Frank Hobbs, Cynthia Davis, Paul Mackun, and Phil Gbur for their review and comments.

Table 1. Nativity of the Population and Place of Birth of the Native Population: 1850 to 2000 (Leading dots indicate subparts)

(See text for sources, definitions, and explanations)

Year [1]	Total population	Native population					Foreign-born population
		Total	Born in the United States	Born abroad			
				Total	In outlying areas[2]	Of American parents	
Number							
2000*	281,421,906	250,314,017	246,786,466	3,527,551	1,606,634	1,920,917	31,107,889
1990*	248,709,873	228,942,557	225,695,826	3,246,731	1,382,446	1,864,285	19,767,316
1980*	226,545,805	212,465,899	210,322,697	2,143,202	1,088,172	1,055,030	14,079,906
1970* [3]	203,210,158	193,590,856	191,329,489	2,261,367	891,266	1,370,101	9,619,302
1960* [1]	179,325,671	169,587,580	168,525,645	1,061,935	660,425	401,510	9,738,091
1950*	150,216,110	139,868,715	139,442,390	426,325	329,970	96,355	10,347,395
1940	131,669,275	120,074,379	119,795,254	279,125	156,956	122,169	11,594,896
1930	122,775,046	108,570,897	108,304,188	266,709	136,032	130,677	14,204,149
1920	105,710,620	91,789,928	91,659,045	130,883	38,020	92,863	13,920,692
1910	91,972,266	78,456,380	78,381,104	75,276	7,365	67,911	13,515,886
1900	75,994,575	65,653,299	65,583,225	70,074	2,923	67,151	10,341,276
1890 [1]	62,622,250	53,372,703	53,362,371	10,332	322	10,010	9,249,547
1880	50,155,783	43,475,840	43,475,498	342	51	291	6,679,943
1870	38,558,371	32,991,142	32,990,922	220	51	169	5,567,229
1860 [4]	31,443,321	27,304,624	27,304,624	-	-	-	4,138,697
1850 [4]	23,191,876	20,947,274	20,947,274	-	-	-	2,244,602
Percent Distribution							
2000*	100.0	88.9	87.7	1.3	0.6	0.7	11.1
1990*	100.0	92.1	90.7	1.3	0.6	0.7	7.9
1980*	100.0	93.8	92.8	0.9	0.5	0.5	6.2
1970* [3]	100.0	95.3	94.2	1.1	0.4	0.7	4.7

Table 1. Continued

Year [1]	Total population	Native population					Foreign-born population
		Total	Born in the United States	Born abroad			
				Total	In outlying areas [2]	Of American parents	
1960* [1]	100.0	94.6	94.0	0.6	0.4	0.2	5.4
1950*	100.0	93.1	92.8	0.3	0.2	0.1	6.9
1940	100.0	91.2	91.0	0.2	0.1	0.1	8.8
1930	100.0	88.4	88.2	0.2	0.1	0.1	11.6
1920	100.0	86.8	86.7	0.1	-	0.1	13.2
1910	100.0	85.3	85.2	0.1	-	0.1	14.7
1900	100.0	86.4	86.3	0.1	-	0.1	13.6
1890 [1]	100.0	85.2	85.2	-	-	-	14.8
1880	100.0	86.7	86.7	-	-	-	13.3
1870	100.0	85.6	85.6	-	-	-	14.4
1860 [4]	100.0	86.8	86.8	-	-	-	13.2
1850 [4]	100.0	90.3	90.3	-	-	-	9.7

* Indicates sample data.

- Represents zero or rounds to zero.

[1] Starting in 1960, includes population of Alaska and Hawaii. For 1890, excludes population enumerated in the Indian Territory and on Indian reservations for whom information on most topics, including nativity, was not collected. See Table 6.

[2] Puerto Rico is the only outlying area for which the number has ever exceeded 100,000. The numbers for Puerto Rico: 1,439,674 in 2000; 1,190,533 in 1990; 1,002,863 in 1980; 810,087 in 1970; 617,056 in 1960; 226,010 in 1950; 69,967 in 1940; 52,774 in 1930; 11,811 in 1920; 1,513 In 1910; and 678 in 1900. See text for Table 1.

[3] The data shown in Table 1 are based on the 15-percent sample. For 1970, data based on the 5-percent sample show total population as 203,193,774, native population as 193,590,856, born in the United States as 191,836,655, born abroad as 1,617,396, in outlying areas as 873,241, of American parents as 744,155, and foreign-born population as 9,739,723. See text for Table 1.

[4] In 1850 and 1860, information on nativity was not collected for slaves. The data in the table assume, as was done in 1870 census reports, that all slaves in 1850 and 1860 were native. Of the total Black population of 4,880,009 in 1870, 9,645, or 0.2 percent, were foreign-born (1870 census, Vol. I, Dubester #45, Table XXII, pp. 606-615).

Internet Release Date: February 2, 2006

Table 2. World Region of Birth of the Foreign-Born Population: 1850 to 1930 and 1960 to 2000
(Leading dots indicate subparts)

(See text for sources, definitions, and explanations)

Year	Total	Region of birth reported [1]							Region of birth not reported [1]
		Total	Europe	Asia	Africa	Oceania	Latin America	Northern America	
Number [2]									
2000*	31,107,889	31,107,573	4,915,557	8,226,254	881,300	168,046	16,086,974	829,442	316
1990*	19,767,316	18,959,158	4,350,403	4,979,037	363,819	104,145	8,407,837	753,917	808,158
1980*	14,079,906	13,192,563	5,149,572	2,539,777	199,723	77,577	4,372,487	853,427	887,343
1970*	9,619,302	9,303,570	5,740,891	824,887	80,143	41,258	1,803,970	812,421	315,732
1960*	9,738,091	9,678,201	7,256,311	490,996	35,355	34,730	908,309	952,500	59,890
1930	14,204,149	14,197,553	11,784,010	275,665	18,326	17,343	791,840	1,310,369	6,596
1920	13,920,692	13,911,767	11,916,048	237,950	16,126	14,626	588,843	1,138,174	8,925
1910	13,515,886	13,506,272	11,810,115	191,484	3,992	11,450	279,514	1,209,717	9,614
1900	10,341,276	10,330,534	8,881,548	120,248	2,538	8,820	137,458	1,179,922	10,742
1890	9,249,547	9,243,535	8,030,347	113,383	2,207	9,353	107,307	980,938	6,012
880	6,679,943	6,675,875	5,751,823	107,630	2,204	6,859	90,073	717,286	4,068
1870	5,567,229	5,563,637	4,941,049	64,565	2,657	4,028	57,871	493,467	3,592
1860	4,138,697	4,134,809	3,807,062	36,796	526	2,140	38,315	249,970	3,888
1850	2,244,602	2,202,625	2,031,867	1,135	551	588	20,773	147,711	41,977
Percent Distribution FOR Region OF Birth Reported									
2000*	(X)	100.0	15.8	26.4	2.8	0.5	51.7	2.7	(X)
1990*	(X)	100.0	22.9	26.3	1.9	0.5	44.3	4.0	(X)
1980*	(X)	100.0	39.0	19.3	1.5	0.6	33.1	6.5	(X)
1970*	(X)	100.0	61.7	8.9	0.9	0.4	19.4	8.7	(X)
1960*	(X)	100.0	75.0	5.1	0.4	0.4	9.4	9.8	(X)

Table 2. Continued

Year	Total	Region of birth reported [1]							Region of birth not reported [1]
		Total	Europe	Asia	Africa	Oceania	Latin America	Northern America	
1930	(X)	100.0	83.0	1.9	0.1	0.1	5.6	9.2	(X)
1920	(X)	100.0	85.7	1.7	0.1	0.1	4.2	8.2	(X)
1910	(X)	100.0	87.4	1.4	-	0.1	2.1	9.0	(X)
1900	(X)	100.0	86.0	1.2	-	0.1	1.3	11.4	(X)
1890	(X)	100.0	86.9	1.2	-	0.1	1.2	10.6	(X)
1880	(X)	100.0	86.2	1.6	-	0.1	1.3	10.7	(X)
1870	(X)	100.0	88.8	1.2	-	0.1	1.0	8.9	(X)
1860	(X)	100.0	92.1	0.9	-	0.1	0.9	6.0	(X)
1850	(X)	100.0	92.2	0.1	-	-	0.9	6.7	(X)

* Indicates sample data.

(X) Not applicable.

\- Rounds to zero.

[1] In 2000, for the first time, includes imputed data on country of birth if country of birth was not reported.

Born at sea included with not reported.

[2] See text for Table 4 regarding data for 1940 and 1950.

Internet Release Date: February 2, 2006

Table 3. World Region and Country or Area of Birth of the Foreign-Born Population: 1960 to 2000
(Leading dots indicate subparts)

(See text for sources, definitions, and explanations)

Region and country or area	2000*	1990*	1980*	1970*	1960*
Total	**31,107,889**	**19,767,316**	**14,079,906**	**9,619,302**	**9,738,091**
Reported by region and/or country [1]	31,107,573	18,959,158	13,192,563	9,303,570	9,678,201
Europe	4,915,557	4,350,403	5,149,572	5,740,891	7,256,311
Northern and Western Europe	.2,070,466	2,058,853	2,384,257	2,629,200	3,334,971
Northern Europe	974,619	968,271	1,083,499	1,271,591	1,694,430
British Isles	834,225	809,972	866,966	937,474	1,171,777
United Kingdom	677,751	640,145	669,149	686,099	833,055
Great Britain (total)	.664,574	623,614	649,318	645,262	764,893
England	423,609	405,588	442,499	458,114	528,205
Scotland	88,445	104,168	142,001	170,134	213,219
Wales	10,948	10,638	13,528	17,014	23,469
Great Britain n.e.c	141,572	103,220	51,290	(NA)	(NA)
Northern Ireland	13,177	16,531	19,831	40,837	68,162
Ireland	156,474	169,827	197,817	251,375	338,722
Scandinavia	140,394	158,299	216,533	334,117	522,653
Denmark	31,422	34,999	42,732	61,410	85,060
Finland	21,408	22,313	29,172	45,499	67,624
Iceland	5,553	5,071	4,156	2,895	2,780
Norway	32,207	42,240	63,316	97,243	152,698
Sweden	49,724	53,676	77,157	127,070	214,491
Western Europe	1,095,847	1,090,582	1,300,758	1,357,609	1,640,541
Low countries	130,615	132,617	142,748	155,513	173,069
Belgium	.33,895	34,366	36,487	41,412	50,294
Luxembourg	2,150	2,053	3,125	3,531	4,360
Netherlands	94,570	96,198	103,136	110,570	118,415

Table 3. Continued

Region and country or area	2000*	1990*	1980*	1970*	1960*
Austria	63,648	87,673	145,607	214,014	304,507
France	151,154	119,233	120,215	105,385	111,582
Germany	706,704	711,929	849,384	832,965	989,815
Switzerland	43,106	39,130	42,804	49,732	61,568
Southern and Eastern Europe	2,840,721	2,285,513	2,748,547	3,090,991	3,907,020
Southern Europe	934,665	1,054,141	1,336,805	1,363,195	1,541,441
Greece	165,750	177,398	210,998	177,275	159,167
Italy	473,338	580,592	831,922	1,008,533	1,256,999
Malta	8,560	9,614	10,182	(NA)	(NA)
Portugal (total) [2]	203,119	210,122	209,968	119,899	80,276
Azores Islands	26,599	29,656	32,531	28,865	22,586
Portugal	175,571	180,466	177,437	91,034	57,690
Spain	82,858	76,415	73,735	57,488	44,999
Eastern Europe	1,906,056	1,231,372	1,411,742	1,727,796	2,365,579
Albania	.38,663	5,627	7,381	9,180	9,618
Bulgaria	35,090	8,579	8,463	8,609	8,223
Czechoslovakia (former)	.83,081	87,020	112,707	160,899	227,618
Estonia	.9,785	9,210	12,169	12,163	13,991
Hungary	92,017	110,337	144,368	183,236	245,252
Latvia	27,232	26,179	34,349	41,707	50,681
Lithuania	28,490	29,745	48,194	76,001	121,475
Poland	466,742	388,328	418,128	548,107	747,750
Romania	135,966	91,106	66,994	70,687	84,575
Soviet Union (former) [3]	*838,809*	333,725	406,022	463,462	690,598
In Europe	710,676	(NA)	(NA)	(NA)	(NA)
Belarus	38,503	(NA)	(NA)	(NA)	(NA)
Moldova	19,507	(NA)	(NA)	(NA)	(NA)

Table 3. Continued

Region and country or area	2000*	1990*	1980*	1970*	1960*
Russia	340,177	(NA)	(NA)	(NA)	(NA)
Ukraine	275,153	(NA)	(NA)	(NA)	(NA)
USSR n.e.c	37,336	(NA)	(NA)	(NA)	(NA)
Yugoslavia (former)	278,314	141,516	152,967	153,745	165,798
Yugoslavia	92,483	(NA)	(NA)	(NA)	(NA)
Bosnia and Herzegovina	98,766	(NA)	(NA)	(NA)	(NA)
Croatia	40,908	(NA)	(NA)	(NA)	(NA)
Macedonia	18,680	(NA)	(NA)	(NA)	(NA)
Slovenia	5,973	(NA)	(NA)	(NA)	(NA)
Serbia	10,284	(NA)	(NA)	(NA)	(NA)
Kosovo	11,220	(NA)	(NA)	(NA)	(NA)
Europe n.e.c	4,370	6,037	16,768	20,700	14,320
Asia	8,226,254	4,979,037	2,539,777	824,887	490,996
Eastern Asia	2,739,510	1,784,702	956,491	(NA)	(NA)
China [4]	988,857	529,837	286,120	172,132	99,735
Hong Kong [4]	203,580	147,131	80,380	(NA)	(NA)
Japan	347,539	290,128	221,794	120,235	109,175
Korea (total)	864,125	568,397	289,885	38,711	11,171
Macau	6,718	5,107	2,959	(NA)	(NA)
Taiwan [4]	326,215	244,102	75,353	(NA)	(NA)
South Central Asia	1,745,201	819,378	373,535	(NA)	(NA)
Afghanistan	45,195	28,444	3,760	(NA)	(NA)
Bangladesh	95,294	21,414	4,989	(NA)	(NA)
India	1,022,552	450,406	206,087	51,000	12,296
Iran	283,226	210,941	121,505	(NA)	(NA)
Nepal	11,715	2,262	844	(NA)	(NA)
Pakistan	223,477	91,889	30,774	6,182	1,708

Table 3. Continued

Region and country or area	2000*	1990*	1980*	1970*	1960*
Soviet Union (former, part)	38,120	(NA)	(NA)	(NA)	(NA)
Kazakhstan	9,154	(NA)	(NA)	(NA)	(NA)
Kyrgyzstan	2,376	(NA)	(NA)	(NA)	(NA)
Tajikistan	2,665	(NA)	(NA)	(NA)	(NA)
Turmenistan	896	(NA)	(NA)	(NA)	(NA)
Uzbekistan	23,029	(NA)	(NA)	(NA)	(NA)
Sri Lanka	25,263	14,022	5,576	(NA)	(NA)
South Eastern Asia	3,044,288	1,968,210	919,646	(NA)	(NA)
Burma	32,588	19,835	11,236	(NA)	(NA)
Cambodia	136,978	118,833	20,175	(NA)	(NA)
Indonesia	72,552	48,387	29,920	(NA)	(NA)
Laos	204,284	171,577	54,881	(NA)	(NA)
Malaysia	49,459	33,834	10,473	(NA)	(NA)
Philippines	1,369,070	912,674	501,440	184,842	104,843
Singapore	20,762	12,889	5,598	(NA)	(NA)
Thailand	169,801	106,919	54,803	(NA)	(NA)
Vietnam	988,174	543,262	231,120	(NA)	(NA)
Western Asia	658,603	400,313	281,426	174,053	132,697
Cyprus	11,087	10,060	8,806	(NA)	(NA)
Iraq	89,892	44,916	32,121	(NA)	(NA)
Israel	109,719	86,048	66,961	35,858	17,724
Jordan	46,794	31,871	21,587	(NA)	(NA)
Kuwait	20,367	8,889	4,337	(NA)	(NA)
Lebanon	105,910	86,369	52,674	22,396	22,217
Palestine [5]	(NA)	21,070	(NA)	(NA)	(NA)
Saudi Arabia	21,083	12,632	17,317	(NA)	(NA)
Soviet Union (former, part)	90,013	(NA)	(NA)	(NA)	(NA)

Table 3. Continued

Region and country or area	2000*	1990*	1980*	1970*	1960*
Armenia	65,280	(NA)	(NA)	(NA)	(NA)
Azerbaijan	14,205	(NA)	(NA)	(NA)	(NA)
Georgia	10,528	(NA)	(NA)	(NA)	(NA)
Syria	54,561	36,782	22,081	14,962	16,717
Turkey	78,378	55,087	51,915	48,085	52,228
United Arab Emirates	6,744	1,656	534	(NA)	(NA)
Yemen	19,210	4,933	3,093	(NA)	(NA)
Middle East n.e.c	(NA)	(NA)	(NA)	52,752	23,811
Asia n.e.c. [5]	38,652	6,434	8,679	77,732	19,371
Africa	881,300	363,819	199,723	80,143	35,355
Eastern Africa	213,299	72,300	26,036	(NA)	(NA)
Eritrea	17,518	(NA)	(NA)	(NA)	(NA)
Ethiopia	69,531	34,805	7,516	(NA)	(NA)
Kenya	40,682	14,371	6,250	(NA)	(NA)
Somalia	35,760	2,437	691	(NA)	(NA)
Tanzania	11,389	6,282	3,246	(NA)	(NA)
Uganda	11,741	6,684	3,804	(NA)	(NA)
Zambia	5,987	2,954	1,346	(NA)	(NA)
Zimbabwe	10,686	4,767	3,183	(NA)	(NA)
Middle Africa	26,900	8,800	3,719	(NA)	(NA)
Angola	4,365	2,252	1,094	(NA)	(NA)
Cameroon	11,765	3,161	1,214	(NA)	(NA)
Zaire (Democratic Republic of Congo)	4,989	3,387	1,411	(NA)	(NA)
Northern Africa	190,491	99,044	69,777	32,396	15,903
Algeria	10,882	4,629	3,853	(NA)	(NA)
Egypt	113,396	66,313	43,424	20,666	8,316

Table 3. Continued

Region and country or area	2000*	1990*	1980*	1970*	1960*
Libya	5,364	4,037	6,427	(NA)	(NA)
Morocco	34,682	15,541	9,896	(NA)	(NA)
Sudan	19,790	4,423	2,711	(NA)	(NA)
Tunisia	6,330	4,101	3,466	(NA)	(NA)
Northern Africa n.e.c	(NA)	(NA)	(NA)	11,730	7,587
Southern Africa	66,496	34,707	16,103	(NA)	(NA)
South Africa	63,558	34,707	16,103	7,667	5,394
Western Africa	326,507	111,566	50,002	(NA)	(NA)
Cape Verde [6]	26,606	14,368	10,457	18,680	8,302
Gambia	5,765	1,485	(NA)	(NA)	(NA)
Ghana	65,572	20,889	7,564	(NA)	(NA)
Guinea	5,062	1,032	(NA)	(NA)	(NA)
Ivory Coast (Cote d'Ivoire)	7,173	1,388	(NA)	(NA)	(NA)
Liberia	39,029	11,455	3,728	(NA)	(NA)
Nigeria	134,940	55,350	25,528	(NA)	(NA)
Senegal	10,534	2,287	762	(NA)	(NA)
Sierra Leone	20,831	7,217	1,963	(NA)	(NA)
Africa n.e.c	57,607	37,402	34,086	21,400	5,756
Oceania	168,046	104,145	77,577	41,258	34,730
Australia and New Zealand	83,837	57,682	47,533	32,388	28,035
Australia	60,965	42,267	36,120	24,271	22,209
New Zealand	22,872	15,415	11,413	8,117	5,826
Pacific Islands	84,209	46,463	30,044	8,870	6,695
Melanesia	32,305	16,759	8,241	(NA)	(NA)
Fiji	30,890	15,935	7,538	(NA)	(NA)
Micronesia	16,469	6,143	1,399	(NA)	(NA)
Marshall Islands	6,318	1,086	(NA)	(NA)	(NA)

Table 3. Continued

Region and country or area	2000*	1990*	1980*	1970*	1960*
Micronesia [7]	7,088	2,741	(NA)	(NA)	(NA)
Polynesia	35,194	23,471	19,578	(NA)	(NA)
Samoa (Western Samoa)	16,438	11,408	12,582	(NA)	(NA)
Tonga	17,269	10,668	5,619	(NA)	(NA)
Oceania n.e.c	241	90	826	(NA)	(NA)
Latin America	16,086,974	8,407,837	4,372,487	1,803,970	908,309
Caribbean	2,953,066	1,938,348	1,258,363	675,108	193,922
Antigua & Barbuda	18,324	12,022	3,920	(NA)	(NA)
Aruba	3,814	3,363	2,597	(NA)	(NA)
Bahamas	28,076	21,633	13,993	(NA)	(NA)
Barbados	52,172	43,015	26,847	(NA)	(NA)
Cuba	872,716	736,971	607,814	439,048	79,150
Dominica	15,639	19,529	3,296	(NA)	(NA)
Dominican Republic	687,677	347,858	169,147	61,228	11,883
Grenada	29,272	17,730	7,101	(NA)	(NA)
Haiti	419,317	225,393	92,395	28,026	4,816
Jamaica	553,827	334,140	196,811	68,576	24,759
Montserrat	3,905	3,493	1,212	(NA)	(NA)
Netherlands Antilles	3,428	3,426	5,123	(NA)	(NA)
St. Kitts-Nevis	11,054	7,447	1,903	(NA)	(NA)
St. Lucia	13,524	6,959	1,901	(NA)	(NA)
St. Vincent & the Grenadines	19,984	12,824	4,044	(NA)	(NA)
Trinidad & Tobago	197,398	115,710	65,907	20,673	(NA)
Other Caribbean	22,939	26,835	54,352	57,557	73,314
West Indies n.e.c	13,546	18,509	(NA)	57,557	73,314
Other	9,393	8,326	54,352	(NA)	(NA)
Central America	11,203,637	5,431,992	2,553,113	873,624	624,851

Table 3. Continued

Region and country or area	2000*	1990*	1980*	1970*	1960*
Mexico	9,177,487	4,298,014	2,199,221	759,711	575,902
Other Central America	2,026,150	1,133,978	353,892	113,913	48,949
Belize	40,151	29,957	14,436	8,860	2,780
Costa Rica	71,870	43,530	29,639	16,691	5,425
El Salvador	817,336	465,433	94,447	15,717	6,310
Guatemala	480,665	225,739	63,073	17,356	5,381
Honduras	282,852	108,923	39,154	19,118	6,503
Nicaragua	220,335	168,659	44,166	16,125	9,474
Panama	105,177	85,737	60,740	20,046	13,076
Central America n.e.c	7,764	6,000	8,237	(NA)	(NA)
South America	1,930,271	1,037,497	561,011	255,238	89,536
Argentina	125,218	92,563	68,887	44,803	16,579
Bolivia	53,278	31,303	14,468	6,872	2,168
Brazil	212,428	82,489	40,919	27,069	13,988
Chile	80,804	55,681	35,127	15,393	6,259
Colombia	509,872	286,124	143,508	63,538	12,582
Ecuador	298,626	143,314	86,128	36,663	7,670
Guyana	211,189	120,698	48,608	(NA)	(NA)
Paraguay	11,980	6,057	2,858	(NA)	595
Peru	278,186	144,199	55,496	21,663	7,102
Suriname	5,579	2,860	1,433	(NA)	(NA)
Uruguay	25,038	20,766	13,278	5,092	1,170
Venezuela	107,031	42,119	33,281	11,348	6,851
South America n.e.c	11,042	9,324	17,020	22,797	14,572
Northern America	829,442	753,917	853,427	812,421	952,500
Canada	820,771	744,830	842,859	812,421	952,500
Other Northern America	8,671	9,087	10,568	(NA)	(NA)

Table 3. Continued

Region and country or area	2000*	1990*	1980*	1970*	1960*
Bermuda	8,379	7,972	8,844	(NA)	(NA)
Northern America n.e.c	292	1,115	1,724	(NA)	(NA)
Region or country not reported [1]	316	808,158	887,343	315,721	59,890

Footnotes:

* Indicates sample data. (NA) Not available. n.e.c. Not elsewhere classified.

[1] In 2000, for the first time, includes imputed data on country of birth if country of birth was not reported.

Born at sea included with not reported.

[2]In 2000, data for Portugal (total) include Madeira Islands.

[3]Data for the former Soviet Union include the part in Asia, as shown in this table under Asia.

[4]In 1960 and 1970, data for China include Taiwan. In source for 2000 census data, a total is shown also for China including Hong Kong and Taiwan (1,518,652).

[5]In 2000, data for Palestine (shown separately in 1990) included in Asia n.e.c.

[6]In 1960 and 1970, data shown for Cape Verde are for Other Atlantic Islands.

[7]Includes Federated States of Micronesia. Internet Release Date: February 2, 2006

Table 4. World Region and Country or Area of Birth of the Foreign-Born Population, With Geographic Detail Shown in Decennial Census Publications of 1930 or Earlier: 1850 to 1930 and 1960 to 2000

(See text for sources, definitions, and explanations)

Line nu	Region and country or area	2000*	1990*	1980*	1970*	1960*	1930	1920	1910	1900	1890	1880	1870	1860	1850	Line num
1	**Total**	**31,107,889**	**19,767,316**	**14,079,906**	**9,619,302**	**9,738,091**	**14,204,149**	**13,920,692**	**13,515,886**	**10,341,276**	**9,249,547**	**6,679,943**	**5,567,229**	**4,138,697**	**2,244,602**	**1**
2	Reported by region and/or country [1]	31,107,573	18,959,158	13,192,563	9,303,570	9,678,201	14,197,553	13,911,767	13,506,272	10,330,534	9,243,535	6,675,875	5,563,637	4,134,809	2,202,625	2
3	Europe	4,915,557	4,350,403	5,149,572	5,740,891	7,256,311	11,784,010	11,916,048	11,810,115	8,881,548	8,030,347	5,751,823	4,941,049	3,807,062	2,031,867	3
4	Northern and Western Europe	2,070,466	2,058,853	2,384,257	2,629,200	3,334,971	5,850,256	6,241,916	7,306,325	7,204,649	7,288,917	5,499,889	4,845,679	3,773,347	2,022,195	4
5	Northern Europ	974,619	968,271	1,083,499	1,271,591	1,694,430	3,415,551	3,501,149	3,953,947	3,917,815	4,056,160	3,212,431	2,867,926	2,271,661	1,358,887	5
6	British Isles	834,225	809,972	865,966	937,474	1,171,777	2,147,733	2,172,723	2,573,534	2,783,082	3,122,911	2,772,169	2,626,241	2,199,079	1,340,812	6
7	United Kingdom	677,751	640,145	669,149	686,099	833,055	1,402,923	(X)	(X)	(X)	(X)	(X)	(X)	(X)	(X)	7
8	Great Britain	664,574	623,614	649,318	645,262	764,893	1,224,091	1,135,489	1,221,283	1,167,623	1,251,402	917,598	770,414	587,775	379,093	8
9	England	423,609	405,588	442,499	458,114	528,205	809,563	813,853	877,719	840,513	908,141	662,676	550,924	431,692	278,675	9
10	Scotland	88,445	104,168	142,001	170,134	213,219	354,323	254,570	261,076	233,524	242,231	170,136	140,835	108,518	70,550	10
11	Wales	10,948	10,638	13,528	17,014	23,469	60,205	67,066	82,488	93,586	100,079	83,302	74,533	45,763	29,868	11
12	Great Britain n.e.c	141,572	103,220	51,290	(NA)	(NA)	(NA)	(NA)	(NA)	(NA)	951	1,484	4,122	1,802	(NA)	12
13	Northern Ireland	13,177	16,531	19,831	40,837	68,162	178,832	(X)	(X)	(X)	(X)	(X)	(X)	(X)	(X)	13
14	Ireland	156,474	169,827	197,817	251,375	338,722	744,810	1,037,234	1,352,251	1,615,459	1,871,509	1,854,571	1,855,827	1,611,304	961,719	14
15	Scandinavia	140,394	158,299	216,533	334,117	522,653	1,267,818	1,328,426	1,380,413	1,134,733	933,249	440,262	241,685	72,582	18,075	15
16	Denmark	31,422	34,999	42,732	61,410	85,060	179,474	189,154	181,649	153,690	132,543	64,196	30,107	9,962	1,838	16
17	Finland	21,408	22,313	29,172	45,499	67,624	142,478	149,824	129,680	62,641	(NA)	(NA)	(NA)	(NA)	(NA)	17
18	Iceland	5,553	5,071	4,[illegible]56	2,895	2,780	2,764	(NA)	(NA)	(NA)	(NA)	(NA)	(NA)	(NA)	(NA)	18
19	Norway	32,207	42,240	63,316	97,243	152,698	347,852	363,863	403,877	336,388	322,665	181,729	114,246	43,995	12,678	19
20	Swede	49,724	53,676	77,157	127,070	214,491	595,250	625,585	665,207	582,014	478,041	194,337	97,332	18,625	3,559	20
21	Other Scandinavia	80	(NA)	(NA)	(NA)	(NA)	(NA)	(NA)	(NA)	(NA)	(NA)	(NA)	(NA)	(NA)	(NA)	21
22	Western Europe	1,095,847	1,090,582	1,300,758	1,357,609	1,640,541	2,434,705	2,740,767	3,352,378	3,286,834	3,232,757	2,287,458	1,977,753	1,501,686	663,308	22
23	Low countries	130,615	132,617	1[illegible]2,748	155,513	173,069	206,375	207,038	172,534	127,719	107,349	86,461	65,157	37,353	11,161	23
24	Belgium	33,895	34,366	36,487	41,412	50,294	64,194	62,687	49,400	29,757	22,639	15,535	12,553	9,072	1,313	24
25	Luxembourg	2,150	2,053	3,125	3,531	4,360	9,048	12,585	3,071	3,031	2,882	12,836	5,802	(NA)	(NA)	25
26	Netherlands	94,570	96,198	103,136	110,570	118,415	133,133	131,766	120,063	94,931	81,828	58,090	46,802	28,281	9,848	26
27	Austria	63,648	87,673	1[illegible]5,607	214,014	304,507	370,914	575,627	626,341	275,907	123,271	38,663	30,508	25,061	946	27
28	France	151,154	119,233	120,215	105,385	111,582	135,592	153,072	117,418	104,197	113,174	106,971	116,402	109,870	54,069	28
29	Germany	706,704	711,929	8[illegible]9,384	832,965	989,815	1,608,814	1,686,108	2,311,237	2,663,418	2,784,894	1,966,742	1,690,533	1,276,075	583,774	29
30	Switzerland	43,106	39,130	4[illegible],804	49,732	61,568	113,010	118,659	124,848	115,593	104,069	88,621	75,153	53,327	13,358	30
31	Other Western Europe	620	(NA)	(NA)	(NA)	(NA)	(NA)	263	(NA)	(NA)	(NA)	(NA)	(NA)	(NA)	(NA)	31

Table 4. Continued

Line nu	Region and country or area	2000*	1990*	1980*	1970*	1960*	1930	1920	1910	1900	1890	1880	1870	1860	1850	Line num
32	Southern and Eastern Europe	2,840,721	2,285,513	2,748,547	3,090,991	3,907,020	5,918,982	5,670,927	4,500,932	1,674,648	728,851	248,620	93,824	32,312	9,672	32
33	Southern Europe	934,665	1,054,141	1,336,805	1,363,195	1,541,441	2,133,092	1,939,600	1,544,149	539,968	216,387	66,249	30,416	21,726	8,152	33
34	Greece	165,750	177,398	210,998	177,275	159,167	174,526	175,976	101,282	8,515	1,887	776	390	328	86	34
35	Italy	473,338	580,592	831,922	1,008,533	1,256,999	1,790,429	1,610,113	1,343,125	484,027	182,580	44,230	17,157	11,677	3,679	35
36	Portugal (total) 2	203,119	210,122	209,968	119,899	80,276	108,775	103,976	77,634	40,376	25,735	15,650	8,973	5,477	1,274	36
37	Azores	26,599	29,656	32,531	28,865	22,586	35,611	33,995	18,274	9,768	9,739	7,512	4,431	1,361	(NA)	37
38	Portugal	175,571	180,466	177,437	91,034	57,690	73,164	69,981	59,360	30,608	15,996	8,138	4,542	4,116	1,274	38
39	Spain	82,858	76,415	73,735	57,488	44,999	59,362	49,535	22,108	7,050	6,185	5,121	3,764	4,244	3,113	39
40	Other Southern Europe	9,600	9,614	10,182	(NA)	(NA)	(NA)	(NA)	(NA)	(NA)	(NA)	472	132	(NA)	(NA)	40
41	Eastern Europe	1,906,056	1,231,372	1,411,742	1,727,796	2,365,579	3,785,890	3,731,327	2,956,783	1,134,680	512,464	182,371	63,408	10,586	1,520	41
42	Albania	38,663	5,627	7,381	9,180	9,618	8,814	5,608	(NA)	(NA)	(NA)	(NA)	(NA)	(NA)	(NA)	42
43	Bulgaria	35,090	8,579	8,463	8,609	8,223	9,399	10,477	11,498	(NA)	(NA)	(NA)	(NA)	(NA)	(NA)	43
44	Czechoslovakia	83,081	87,020	112,707	160,899	227,618	491,638	362,438	219,214	156,891	118,106	85,361	40,289	(NA)	(NA)	44
45	Estonia	9,785	9,210	12,169	12,163	13,991	3,550	(NA)	(NA)	(NA)	(NA)	(NA)	(NA)	(NA)	(NA)	45
46	Hungary	92,017	110,337	144,368	183,236	245,252	274,450	397,283	495,609	145,714	62,435	11,526	3,737	(NA)	(NA)	46
47	Latvia	27,232	26,179	34,349	41,707	50,681	20,673	(NA)	(NA)	(NA)	(NA)	(NA)	(NA)	(NA)	(NA)	47
48	Lithuania	28,490	29,745	48,194	76,001	121,475	193,606	135,068	(NA)	(NA)	(NA)	(NA)	(NA)	(NA)	(NA)	48
49	Poland	466,742	388,328	418,128	548,107	747,750	1,268,583	1,139,979	937,884	383,407	147,440	48,557	14,436	7,298	(NA)	49
50	Romania	135,966	91,106	66,994	70,687	84,575	146,393	102,823	65,923	15,032	(NA)	(NA)	(NA)	(NA)	(NA)	50
51	Soviet Union (former) 3	*838,809*	333,725	406,022	463,462	690,598	1,153,628	1,400,495	1,184,412	423,726	182,644	35,722	4,644	3,160	1,414	51
52	In Europe	710,676	(NA)	(NA)	(NA)	(NA)	(NA)	(NA)	(NA)	(NA)	(NA)	(NA)	(NA)	(NA)	(NA)	52
53	Turkey in Europe	(NA)	(NA)	(NA)	(NA)	(NA)	2,257	5,284	32,230	9,910	1,839	1,205	302	128	106	53
54	Yugoslavia	278,314	141,516	152,967	153,745	165,798	211,416	169,439	(NA)	(NA)	(NA)	(NA)	(NA)	(NA)	(NA)	54
55	Other Eastern Europe	(NA)	(NA)	(NA)	(NA)	(NA)	1,483	2,433	10,013	(NA)	(NA)	(NA)	(NA)	(NA)	(NA)	55
56	Europe n.e.c.	4,370	6,037	16,768	20,700	14,320	14,772	3,205	2,858	2,251	12,579	3,314	1,546	1,403	(NA)	56
57	Asia	8,226,254	4,979,037	2,539,777	824,887	490,996	275,665	237,950	191,484	120,248	113,383	107,630	64,565	36,796	1,135	57
58	Armenia	(X)	(X)	(X)	(X)	(X)	32,166	36,628	(NA)	(NA)	(NA)	(NA)	(NA)	(NA)	(NA)	58
59	China 4	988,857	529,837	286,120	172,132	99,735	46,129	43,560	56,756	81,534	106,688	104,468	63,042	35,565	758	59
60	India	1,022,552	450,406	206,087	51,000	12,296	5,850	4,901	4,664	2,031	2,143	1,707	586	(NA)	(NA)	60
61	Japan	347,539	290,128	221,794	120,235	109,175	70,993	81,502	67,744	24,788	2,292	401	73	(NA)	(NA)	61
62	Palestine 5	(NA)	21,070	(NA)	(NA)	(NA)	6,137	3,203	(NA)	(NA)	(NA)	(NA)	(NA)	(NA)	(NA)	62
63	Syria	54,561	36,782	22,081	14,962	16,717	57,227	51,901	(NA)	(NA)	(NA)	(NA)	(NA)	(NA)	(NA)	63
64	Turkey in Asia	78,378	55,087	51,915	48,085	52,228	46,654	11,019	59,729	(NA)	(NA)	(NA)	(NA)	(NA)	(NA)	64
65	Other Asia	5,734,367	3,595,727	1,751,780	418,473	200,845	10,509	5,236	2,591	11,895	2,260	1,054	864	1,231	377	65
66	Africa	881,300	363,819	199,723	80,143	35,355	18,326	16,126	3,992	2,538	2,207	2,204	2,657	526	551	66

Table 4. Continued

Line nu	Region and country or area	2000*	1990*	1980*	1970*	1960*	1930	1920	1910	1900	1890	1880	1870	1860	1850	Line num
67	Africa excl. Atlantic Islands	854,694	349,451	189,266	61,463	27,053	8,859	5,781	3,992	2,538	2,207	2,204	2,657	526	551	67
68	Atlantic Islands	26,606	14,368	10,457	18,680	8,302	9,467	10,345	(NA)	(NA)	(NA)	(NA)	(NA)	(NA)	(NA)	68
69	Oceania	168,046	104,145	77,377	41,258	34,730	17,343	14,626	11,450	8,820	9,353	6,859	4,028	2,140	588	69

Footnotes:

* Indicates sample data.

(X) Not applicable.

(NA) Not available.

n.e.c. Not elsewhere classified.

[1] In 2000, for the first time, includes imputed data on country of birth if country of birth was not reported. Born at sea included with not reported.

[2] In 2000, data for Portugal (total) include Madeira Islands.

[3] Data for the former Soviet Union include the part in Asia.

[4] Prior to 1980, Taiwan included with China. See Table 3.

[5] In 2000, data for Palestine (shown separately in 1990) included in Asia n.e.c.

Internet delete date:

Table 5. Language Spoken at Home for the Foreign-Born Population 5 Years and Over: 1980 to 2000
(Leading dots indicate subparts)

(See text for sources, definitions, and explanations)

Language	2000*	1990*	1980*
Total	30,709,064	19,506,238	13,859,059
English only	5,212,041	4,075,804	4,129,722
Non-English languages	25,497,023	15,430,434	9,729,337
Language data available	25,496,726	15,428,619	9,639,071
Indo-European languages	18,926,524	11,196,120	7,502,923
English-based pidgin creoles	16,632	13,111	4,398
Jamaican Creole	11,997	12,124	3,237
Germanic languages	642,729	690,339	878,236
German	504,343	529,678	627,998
Yiddish	39,191	72,779	157,252
Dutch	83,545	82,558	87,767
Afrikaans	14,819	4,754	2,586
Scandinavian languages	79,720	80,700	103,615
Swedish	35,146	33,224	42,580
Danish	20,400	20,334	23,113
Norwegian	20,581	23,726	34,903
Romance languages	15,041,799	8,713,899	5,235,425
Italian	394,252	493,439	705,407
French (including creoles)	821,132	534,192	376,060
French (excluding creoles)	472,276	387,915	359,870
Patois	16,055	5,778	1,477
French Creole (Haitian)	332,696	140,433	14,519
Spanish (including creoles)	13,340,264	7,350,512	3,896,505
Spanish (excluding creoles)	13,340,125	7,346,270	3,896,060
Portuguese (including creoles)	390,232	281,635	232,794
Portuguese (excluding creoles)	389,646	281,034	232,467
Romanian	94,671	53,493	24,058

Table 5. Continued

Language	2000*	1990*	1980*
Celtic languages	15,506	17,747	14,260
Irish Gaelic	13,148	15,233	11,661
Greek	164,140	181,965	215,700
Albanian	62,090	13,608	9,671
Slavic languages	1,377,095	663,450	626,668
Russian	619,113	186,514	127,605
Ukranian	93,138	50,725	70,117
Czech	31,051	27,739	35,147
Polish	388,369	286,896	260,341
Slovak	15,301	16,459	24,159
Bulgarian	26,657	4,554	4,363
Macedonian	13,166	4,524	3,595
Serbo-Croatian	183,792	80,222	91,811
Baltic languages	33,864	39,903	57,689
Lithuanian	19,683	20,758	32,535
Lettish	14,181	19,145	25,154
Armenian	156,555	115,017	69,995
Iranian languages	270,726	186,913	97,590
Persian	254,466	178,354	94,395
Indic languages	1,065,668	479,468	189,676
Hindi (including Urdu)	497,544	287,067	115,774
Hindi	278,040	(NA)	(NA)
Urdu	219,504	(NA)	(NA)
Bengali	114,214	33,814	11,516
Panjabi	118,498	43,184	16,820
Marathi	30,934	12,580	5,426
Gujarati	191,570	87,539	32,065
Sinhalese	12,974	7,019	3,057
Asian and Pacific Island languages	5,511,790	3,637,263	1,718,934

Table 5. Continued

Language	2000*	1990*	1980*
Turkic languages	62,116	32,564	22,651
Turkish	59,220	32,024	21,827
Dravidian languages	250,123	82,990	34,458
Telugu	80,433	19,052	8,572
Kannada	22,096	7,602	4,525
Malayalam	68,657	31,143	10,345
Tamil	77,764	24,575	9,691
Chinese	1,627,588	1,088,296	494,855
Thai (including Laotian)	204,249	173,226	73,542
Thai	92,381	(NA)	(NA)
Laotian	111,868	(NA)	(NA)
Burmese	18,386	8,643	3,791
Miao-yao, Mien	11,201	8,144	722
Miao (Hmong)	103,185	62,699	14,638
Japanese	285,771	245,294	171,715
Korean	716,492	530,860	237,516
Mon-Khmer (Cambodian)	131,178	113,910	15,089
Vietnamese	830,428	434,731	182,890
Indonesian languages	51,578	33,009	12,498
Indonesian	41,548	22,102	9,457
Malay	9,071	10,245	2,662
Philippine languages	1,164,424	793,365	428,470
Tagalog	1,074,351	746,443	402,968
Biscayan	13,406	6,349	2,153
Ilocano	63,532	35,098	21,233
Micronesian languages	11,019	3,057	2,384
Polynesian languages	30,266	21,430	18,876
Samoan	15,122	11,309	12,234
Tongan	14,061	8,878	3,920

Table 5. Continued

Language	2000*	1990*	1980*
Melanesian languages	3,229	2,002	1,222
Asian and Pacific Island languages n.e.c	10,557	3,043	3,617
Other languages	1,058,412	595,236	417,214
Uralic languages	97,195	108,289	135,318
Finnish	14,725	14,324	19,437
Hungarian	76,859	87,024	105,298
Caucasian	3,835	710	521
Basque	1,239	1,327	1,783
Semitic languages	641,031	382,997	230,184
Arabic	432,295	251,409	164,953
Hebrew	87,535	74,985	49,044
Syriac	46,932	27,494	5,844
Amharic	74,269	29,109	10,343
Afro-Asiatic languages	42,048	4,373	2,257
Cushite	38,977	3,037	798
Nilo-Saharan languages	5,485	630	478
Niger-Congo languages	229,670	80,676	33,886
Swahili	27,206	7,544	3,881
Bantu	21,125	8,019	4,455
Mande	10,692	2,821	1,057
Fulani	10,956	2,045	450
Kru, Ibo, Yoruba	154,620	58,172	22,454
African languages n.e.c	10,390	5,608	3,323
Native American languages	27,519	10,626	9,464
Language data not available [1]	297	1,815	90,266

Footnotes:

* Indicates sample data. n.e.c. Not elsewhere classified.

[1] For 1980, includes 11,136 cases of "Indian" with no other information provided to classify the language as Indic or Native American. Internet Release Date: February 2, 2006

Table 6. Mother Tongue of the Foreign-Born Population: 1910 to 1940, 1960, and 1970
(Leading dots indicate subparts)

(See text for sources, definitions, and explanations)

	All Races		White					
Language	**1970***	**1960***	**1970***	**1960***	**1940***	**1930**	**1920**	**1910**
Total	9,619,302	9,738,155	8,733,770	9,294,045	11,109,620	13,983,405	13,712,754	13,345,545
Mother tongue data available	9,523,155	9,360,179	8,651,756	8,962,711	10,861,120	13,941,172	13,705,588	13,229,273
Indo-European languages	8,452,466	8,685,423	7,991,298	8,415,894	10,408,000	13,481,337	13,216,190	12,841,870
English and Celtic [1]	1,743,284	1,979,949	1,577,719	1,889,228	2,506,420	3,097,021	3,007,932	3,363,792
English	1,697,825	1,937,184	1,532,260	(NA)	(NA)	(NA)	(NA)	(NA)
Celtic [1]	45,459	42,765	45,459	(NA)	(NA)	(NA)	(NA)	(NA)
Germanic languages	1,788,286	1,996,740	1,757,567	1,961,835	2,648,080	3,586,069	3,541,184	3,962,624
German	1,201,535	1,332,399	1,197,205	1,329,660	1,589,040	2,188,006	2,267,128	2,759,032
Yiddish [2]	438,116	503,605	437,083	503,062	924,440	1,222,658	1,091,820	1,051,767
Dutch	127,834	130,482	123,279	129,113	102,700	133,142	136,540	126,045
Flemish	20,801	30,254	(NA)	(NA)	31,900	42,263	45,696	25,780
Scandinavian languages	283,991	466,515	283,260	463,361	778,200	1,142,645	1,194,933	1,272,150
Swedish	131,408	225,607	131,087	225,421	423,200	615,465	643,203	683,218
Danish	58,218	85,421	58,007	85,338	122,180	178,944	187,162	183,844
Norwegian	94,365	152,687	94,166	152,602	232,820	345,522	362,199	402,587
Romance languages	3,301,184	2,551,982	3,166,837	2,521,725	2,475,880	3,242,033	2,816,296	2,267,009
Italian	1,025,994	1,277,585	1,023,217	1,276,338	1,561,100	1,808,289	1,624,998	1,365,110
French	410,580	330,220	377,752	325,588	359,520	523,297	466,956	528,842
Spanish [3]	1,696,240	813,429	1,602,322	793,134	428,360	743,286	556,111	258,131
Portuguese	140,299	91,592	137,618	88,680	83,780	110,197	105,895	72,649
Romanian	26,055	38,019	25,928	37,985	43,120	56,964	62,336	42,277
Greek	193,745	180,781	192,415	180,458	165,220	189,066	174,658	118,379
Albanian	7,528	7,297	(NA)	(NA)	(NA)	7,586	5,515	2,312
Slavic languages	921,330	1,301,520	918,652	1,300,342	1,671,540	1,992,533	2,255,798	1,690,703
Russian [4]	149,277	276,834	148,644	276,362	356,940	315,721	392,049	57,926
Ukranian	96,635	106,974	96,294	106,864	35,540	68,485	55,672	25,131

Table 6. Continued

Language	All Races 1970*	All Races 1960*	White 1970*	White 1960*	White 1940*	White 1930	White 1920	White 1910
Czech	70,703	91,711	70,564	91,633	159,640	201,138	234,564	228,738
Polish	419,912	581,936	419,006	581,591	801,680	965,899	1,077,392	943,781
Slovak	82,561	125,000	82,429	124,943	171,580	240,196	274,948	166,474
Bulgarian	(NA)	(NA)	(NA)	(NA)	(NA)	12,128	12,853	18,341
Serbo-Croatian [5]	83,064	86,957	82,652	86,860	70,600	109,923	125,844	105,669
Slovene	19,178	32,108	19,063	32,089	75,560	77,671	80,437	123,631
Baltic languages	95,188	99,043	94,848	98,945	122,660	172,643	182,227	140,963
Lithuanian	95,188	99,043	94,848	98,945	122,660	165,053	(NA)	(NA)
Lettish	(NA)	(NA)	(NA)	(NA)	(NA)	7,590	(NA)	(NA)
Armenian	38,323	37,270	(NA)	(NA)	40,000	51,741	37,647	23,938
Iranian languages	17,329	7,503	(NA)	(NA)	(NA)	(NA)	(NA)	(NA)
Persian	15,986	6,936	(NA)	(NA)	(NA)	(NA)	(NA)	(NA)
Indic languages	22,173	3,561	(NA)	(NA)	(NA)	(NA)	(NA)	(NA)
Hindi	22,017	3,493	(NA)	(NA)	(NA)	(NA)	(NA)	(NA)
Indo-European languages n.e.c. [6]	40,105	53,262	(NA)	(NA)	(NA)	(NA)	(NA)	(NA)
Asian and Pacific Island languages	555,445	306,624	8,988	9,107	(NA)	10,457	6,627	4,709
Turkish languages	16,646	14,063	(NA)	(NA)	(NA)	10,457	6,627	4,709
Turkish	16,646	14,063	(NA)	(NA)	(NA)	10,457	6,627	4,709
Dravidian languages	7,535	1,030	(NA)	(NA)	(NA)	(NA)	(NA)	(NA)
Chinese	190,260	89,609	4,734	3,892	(NA)	(NA)	(NA)	(NA)
Thai (Laotian)	11,695	1,666	(NA)	(NA)	(NA)	(NA)	(NA)	(NA)
Japanese	118,090	95,027	4,254	5,215	(NA)	(NA)	(NA)	(NA)
Korean	34,748	8,550	(NA)	(NA)	(NA)	(NA)	(NA)	(NA)
Indonesian languages	6,915	7,273	(NA)	(NA)	(NA)	(NA)	(NA)	(NA)
Philippine languages	152,498	73,500	(NA)	(NA)	(NA)	(NA)	(NA)	(NA)
Tagalog	152,498	73,500	(NA)	(NA)	(NA)	(NA)	(NA)	(NA)

Table 6. Continued

Language	All Races		White					
	1970*	1960*	1970*	1960*	1940*	1930	1920	1910
Polynesian languages	4,956	1,372	(NA)	(NA)	(NA)	(NA)	(NA)	(NA)
Asian and Pacific Island languages n.e.c.	13,102	14,534	(NA)	(NA)	(NA)	(NA)	(NA)	(NA)
Other languages	325,074	360,019	273,500	314,745	389,240	446,026	481,543	382,048
Uralic languages	199,543	266,286	198,749	265,963	338,300	378,196	423,986	349,180
Finnish	38,290	53,168	38,069	53,094	97,080	124,994	132,543	119,948
Hungarian	161,253	213,118	160,680	212,869	241,220	250,393	290,419	229,094
Caucasian	421	192	(NA)	(NA)	(NA)	(NA)	(NA)	(NA)
Basque	2,169	1,580	(NA)	(NA)	(NA)	(NA)	(NA)	(NA)
Semitic languages	110,527	88,516	72,024	48,782	50,940	67,830	57,557	32,868
Arabic	73,657	49,908	72,024	48,782	50,940	67,830	57,557	32,868
Hebrew [2]	36,112	38,346	(NA)	(NA)	(NA)	(NA)	(NA)	(NA)
African languages	6,605	982	(NA)	(NA)	(NA)	(NA)	(NA)	(NA)
Native American languages	5,809	2,463	2,727	(NA)	(NA)	(NA)	(NA)	(NA)
Mother tongue n.e.c	189,170	8,113	377,970	222,965	63,880	3,352	1,228	646
Mother tongue data not available	96,147	377,976	82,014	331,334	248,500	42,233	7,166	116,272

Footnotes:

* Indicates sample data. (NA) Not available.

[1] For 1970, assumes that all individuals with Celtic mother tongue are White

[2] For 1910-1940, Hebrew included with Yiddish

[3] For White in 1960, the published estimate (794,714) includes Basque. The estimate here assumes that all individuals with Basque mother tongue (1,580) are Whit

[4] For 1920, probably includes a "considerable proportion" of individuals of Yiddish mother tongue erroneously reported as of Russian mother tongue. See sources in te

[5] For White in 1960, the published estimate (87,997) includes Dalmatian. The estimate here assumes that all individuals with Dalmatian mother tongue (1,137) are Whit

[6] For 1970, includes 10,031 cases of Breton (which appears to be too high), and 10,208 cases of Other Balto-Slavonic languages. In 1960, the 535 cases of Breton were included with French. For 1960, includes 49,610 cases of Other Balto-Slavonic languages. Internet Release Date: February 2, 2006

Table 7. Age and Sex of the Foreign-Born Population: 1870 to 2000 (Leading dots indicate subparts)

(See text for sources, definitions, and explanations)

		2000*			1990*			1980*	
Subject	Total	Male	Female	Total	Male	Female	Total	Male	Female
AGE									
Total	31,107,889	15,478,793	15,629,096	19,767,316	9,670,861	10,096,455	14,079,906	6,581,094	7,498,812
Age data available [1]	31,107,889	15,478,793	15,629,096	19,767,316	9,670,861	10,096,455	14,079,906	6,581,094	7,498,812
Under 5 years	398,825	200,735	198,090	261,078	134,079	126,999	220,847	111,303	109,544
5 to 9 years	749,137	382,572	366,565	486,854	249,438	237,416	436,890	225,619	211,271
10 to 14 years	1,141,145	587,182	553,963	736,234	380,340	355,894	587,394	299,821	287,573
15 to 19 years	1,731,988	946,509	785,479	1,161,997	628,491	533,506	872,935	458,465	414,470
20 to 24 years	2,720,704	1,494,537	1,226,167	1,797,420	997,074	800,346	1,198,394	627,268	571,126
25 to 29 years	3,403,552	1,797,621	1,605,931	2,238,030	1,197,162	1,040,868	1,306,561	658,419	648,142
30 to 34 years	3,587,974	1,868,985	1,718,989	2,283,636	1,189,686	1,093,950	1,331,858	643,054	688,804
35 to 39 years	3,549,941	1,817,944	1,731,997	2,000,389	1,008,317	992,072	1,101,498	514,454	587,044
40 to 44 years	3,123,440	1,574,371	1,549,069	1,752,918	854,453	898,465	996,737	460,209	536,528
45 to 49 years	2,528,854	1,248,179	1,280,675	1,380,576	653,597	726,979	843,990	383,657	460,333
50 to 54 years	2,056,672	985,160	1,071,512	1,171,783	540,321	631,462	819,282	355,372	463,910
55 to 59 years	1,502,161	687,823	814,338	941,211	421,206	520,005	795,050	354,864	440,186
60 to 64 years	1,281,999	567,865	714,134	859,592	363,634	495,958	588,116	264,191	323,925
65 to 69 years	1,019,781	433,278	586,503	785,589	330,058	455,531	687,701	301,778	385,923
70 to 74 years	869,747	349,346	520,401	522,610	218,183	304,427	720,154	309,328	410,826
75 to 79 years	668,670	265,305	403,365	515,628	204,011	311,617	686,839	280,426	406,413
80 to 84 years	369,687	140,560	229,127	420,902	155,326	265,576	478,722	181,612	297,110
85 years and over	403,612	130,821	272,791	450,869	145,485	305,384	406,938	151,254	255,684
Age data not available [1]	-	-	-	-	-	-	-	-	-
Median age (years)	37.6	36.3	38.9	37.3	35.3	39.3	39.9	37.6	42.2
BROAD AGE GROUPS									
Total	31,107,889	15,478,793	15,629,096	19,767,316	9,670,861	10,096,455	14,079,906	6,581,094	7,498,812
Age data available [1]	31,107,889	15,478,793	15,629,096	19,767,316	9,670,861	10,096,455	14,079,906	6,581,094	7,498,812

Table 7. Continued

		2000*			1990*			1980*	
Subject	Total	Male	Female	Total	Male	Female	Total	Male	Female
Under 15 years	2,289,107	1,170,489	1,118,618	1,484,166	763,857	720,309	1,245,131	636,743	608,388
15 to 64 years	25,487,285	12,988,994	12,498,291	15,587,552	7,853,941	7,733,611	9,854,421	4,719,953	5,134,468
15 to 44 years	18,117,599	9,499,967	8,617,632	11,234,390	5,875,183	5,359,207	6,807,983	3,361,869	3,446,114
15 to 24 years	4,452,692	2,441,046	2,011,646	2,959,417	1,625,565	1,333,852	2,071,329	1,085,733	985,596
25 to 44 years	13,664,907	7,058,921	6,605,986	8,274,973	4,249,618	4,025,355	4,736,654	2,276,136	2,460,518
45 to 64 years	7,369,686	3,489,027	3,880,659	4,353,162	1,978,758	2,374,404	3,046,438	1,358,084	1,688,354
65 years and over	3,331,497	1,319,310	2,012,187	2,695,598	1,053,063	1,642,535	2,980,354	1,224,398	1,755,956
18 years and over [2]	27,901,599	13,818,539	14,083,060	17,674,856	8,584,582	9,090,274	12,360,336	5,698,044	6,662,292
21 years and over [2]	26,597,286	13,088,312	13,508,974	16,791,311	8,095,967	8,695,344	11,733,838	5,363,748	6,370,090
Age data not available [1]	-	-	-	-	-	-	-	-	-
PERCENT DISTRIBUTION									
Age data available [1]	100.0	100.0	100.0	100.0	100.0	100.0	100.0	100.0	100.0
Under 15 years	7.4	7.6	7.2	7.5	7.9	7.1	8.8	9.7	8.1
15 to 64 years	81.9	83.9	80.0	78.9	81.2	76.6	70.0	71.7	68.5
15 to 44 years	58.2	61.4	55.1	56.8	60.8	53.1	48.4	51.1	46.0
15 to 24 years	14.3	15.8	12.9	15.0	16.8	13.2	14.7	16.5	13.1
25 to 44 years	43.9	45.6	42.3	41.9	43.9	39.9	33.6	34.6	32.8
45 to 64 years	23.7	22.5	24.8	22.0	20.5	23.5	21.6	20.6	22.5
65 years and over	10.7	8.5	12.9	13.6	10.9	16.3	21.2	18.6	23.4
18 years and over [2]	89.7	89.3	90.1	89.4	88.8	90.0	87.8	86.6	88.8
21 years and over [2]	85.5	84.6	86.4	84.9	83.7	86.1	83.3	81.5	84.9
MALES PER 100 FEMALES									
Total	99.0	(X)	(X)	95.8	(X)	(X)	87.8	(X)	(X)
Age data available [1]	99.0	(X)	(X)	95.8	(X)	(X)	87.8	(X)	(X)
Under 15 years	104.6	(X)	(X)	106.0	(X)	(X)	104.7	(X)	(X)

Table 7. Continued

Subject	Total	2000* Male	Female	Total	1990* Male	Female	Total	1980* Male	Female
15 to 64 years	103.9	(X)	(X)	101.6	(X)	(X)	91.9	(X)	(X)
15 to 44 years	110.2	(X)	(X)	109.6	(X)	(X)	97.6	(X)	(X)
15 to 24 years	121.3	(X)	(X)	121.9	(X)	(X)	110.2	(X)	(X)
25 to 44 years	106.9	(X)	(X)	105.6	(X)	(X)	92.5	(X)	(X)
45 to 64 years	89.9	(X)	(X)	83.3	(X)	(X)	80.4	(X)	(X)
65 years and over	65.6	(X)	(X)	64.1	(X)	(X)	69.7	(X)	(X)
18 years and over [2]	98.1	(X)	(X)	94.4	(X)	(X)	85.5	(X)	(X)
21 years and over [2]	96.9	(X)	(X)	93.1	(X)	(X)	84.2	(X)	(X)
Age data not available [1]	(X)	(X)	(X)	(X)	(X)	(X)	(X)	(X)	(X)

Subject	Total	1970* Male	Female	Total	1960* Male	Female	Total	1950* Male	Female
AGE									
Total	9,619,302	4,403,687	5,215,615	9,738,091	4,760,432	4,977,659	10,347,395	5,258,255	5,089,140
Age data available [1]	9,619,302	4,403,687	5,215,615	9,738,091	4,760,432	4,977,659	10,347,395	5,258,255	5,089,140
Under 5 years	102,926	52,581	50,345	101,886	51,442	50,444	65,860	32,895	32,965
5 to 9 years	220,477	112,954	107,523	165,858	84,098	81,760	64,440	32,435	32,005
10 to 14 years	283,438	141,941	141,497	237,042	119,935	117,107	68,145	35,890	32,255
15 to 19 years	348,506	173,640	174,866	202,899	98,724	104,175	97,600	50,610	46,990
20 to 24 years	502,529	225,048	277,481	307,365	137,519	169,846	222,335	94,065	128,270
25 to 29 years	597,387	259,025	338,362	387,304	171,310	215,994	370,765	165,695	205,070
30 to 34 years	642,270	285,459	356,811	478,816	204,769	274,047	337,740	156,730	181,010
35 to 39 years	606,534	270,735	335,799	571,485	262,716	308,769	548,950	259,040	289,910
40 to 44 years	640,421	277,423	362,998	457,744	219,307	238,437	815,615	403,305	412,310
45 to 49 years	658,532	297,134	361,398	644,391	315,526	328,865	1,090,530	555,815	534,715
50 to 54 years	508,776	238,495	270,281	846,313	422,367	423,946	1,257,845	647,580	610,265
55 to 59 years	644,203	304,699	339,504	1,063,247	541,383	521,864	1,348,530	717,930	630,600
60 to 64 years	788,146	375,377	412,769	1,095,696	542,483	553,213	1,334,375	728,515	605,860

Table 7. Continued

		2000*			1990*			1980*	
Subject	Total	Male	Female	Total	Male	Female	Total	Male	Female
65 to 69 years	892,110	411,562	480,548	1,118,190	566,414	551,776	1,124,735	591,040	533,695
70 to 74 years	825,283	368,503	456,780	977,166	504,663	472,503	753,645	381,535	372,110
75 to 79 years	658,907	303,070	355,837	614,916	306,872	308,044	453,405	223,175	230,230
80 to 84 years	435,567	196,637	238,930	304,480	141,429	163,051	252,870	120,505	132,365
85 years and over	263,290	109,404	153,886	163,293	69,475	93,818	140,010	61,495	78,515
Age data not available [1]	-	-	-	-	-	-	-	-	-
Median age (years)	52	52.2	51.9	57.2	57.7	56.7	55.9	56.4	55.3
BROAD AGE GROUPS									
Total	9,619,302	4,403,687	5,215,615	9,738,091	4,760,432	4,977,659	10,347,395	5,258,255	5,089,140
Age data available [1]	9,619,302	4,403,687	5,215,615	9,738,091	4,760,432	4,977,659	10,347,395	5,258,255	5,089,140
Under 15 years	606,841	307,476	299,365	504,786	255,475	249,311	198,445	101,220	97,225
15 to 64 years	5,937,304	2,707,035	3,230,269	6,055,260	2,916,104	3,139,156	7,424,285	3,779,285	3,645,000
15 to 44 years	3,337,647	1,491,330	1,846,317	2,405,613	1,094,345	1,311,268	2,393,005	1,129,445	1,263,560
15 to 24 years	851,035	398,688	452,347	510,264	236,243	274,021	319,935	144,675	175,260
25 to 44 years	2,486,612	1,092,642	1,393,970	1,895,349	858,102	1,037,247	2,073,070	984,770	1,088,300
45 to 64 years	2,599,657	1,215,705	1,383,952	3,649,647	1,821,759	1,827,888	5,031,280	2,649,840	2,381,440
65 years and over	3,075,157	1,389,176	1,685,981	3,178,045	1,588,853	1,589,192	2,724,665	1,377,750	1,346,915
18 years and over [2]	(NA)	(NA)	(NA)	9,114,168	4,445,251	4,668,917	10,096,555	5,128,740	4,967,815
21 years and over [2]	(NA)	(NA	(NA)	8,979,524	4,382,844	4,596,680	10,020,450	5,092,230	4,928,220
Age data not available [1]	-	-	-	-	-	-	-	-	-
PERCENT DISTRIBUTION									
Age data available [1]	100.0	100.0	100.0	100.0	100.0	100.0	100.0	100.0	100.0
Under 15 years	6.3	7.0	5.7	5.2	5.4	5.0	1.9	1.9	1.9
15 to 64 years	61.7	61.5	61.9	62.2	61.3	63.1	71.8	71.9	71.6
15 to 44 years	34.7	33.9	35.4	24.7	23.0	26.3	23.1	21.5	24.8

Table 7. Continued

		2000*			1990*			1980*	
Subject	Total	Male	Female	Total	Male	Female	Total	Male	Female
15 to 24 years	8.8	9.1	8.7	5.2	5.0	5.5	3.1	2.8	3.4
25 to 44 years	25.9	24.8	26.7	19.5	18.0	20.8	20.0	18.7	21.4
45 to 64 years	27.0	27.6	26.5	37.5	38.3	36.7	48.6	50.4	46.8
65 years and over	32.0	31.5	32.3	32.6	33.4	31.9	26.3	26.2	26.5
18 years and over [2]	(NA)	(NA)	(NA)	93.6	93.4	93.8	97.6	97.5	97.6
21 years and over [2]	(NA)	(NA)	(NA)	92.2	92.1	92.3	96.8	96.8	96.8
MALES PER 100 FEMALES									
Total	84.4	(X)	(X)	95.6	(X)	(X)	103.3	(X)	(X)
Age data available [1]	84.4	(X)	(X)	95.6	(X)	(X)	103.3	(X)	(X)
Under 15 years	102.7	(X)	(X)	102.5	(X)	(X)	104.1	(X)	(X)
15 to 64 years	83.8	(X)	(X)	92.9	(X)	(X)	103.7	(X)	(X)
15 to 44 years	80.8	(X)	(X)	83.5	(X)	(X)	89.4	(X)	(X)
15 to 24 years	88.1	(X)	(X)	86.2	(X)	(X)	82.5	(X)	(X)
25 to 44 years	78.4	(X)	(X)	82.7	(X)	(X)	90.5	(X)	(X)
45 to 64 years	87.3	(X)	(X)	99.7	(X)	(X)	111.3	(X)	(X)
65 years and over	82.4	(X)	(X)	100.0	(X)	(X)	102.3	(X)	(X)
18 years and over [2]	(NA)	(X)	(X)	95.2	(X)	(X)	103.2	(X)	(X)
21 years and over [2]	(NA)	(X)	(X)	95.3	(X)	(X)	103.3	(X)	(X)
Age data not available [1]	(X)	(X)	(X)	(X)	(X)	(X)	(X)	(X)	(X)
		1940			1930			1920	
Subject AGE	**Total**	**Male**	**Female**	**Total**	**Male**	**Female**	**Total**	**Male**	**Female**
Total	11,594,896	6,121,647	5,473,249	14,204,149	7,647,090	6,557,059	13,920,692	7,675,435	6,245,257
Age data available [1]	11,419,138	6,011,015	5,408,123	13,972,689	7,495,824	6,476,865	13,692,490	7,514,590	6,177,900
Under 5 years	8,321	4,219	4,102	34,009	17,232	16,777	44,984	22,857	22,127
5 to 9 years	21,584	10,937	10,647	142,373	71,872	70,501	169,884	85,774	84,110

Table 7. Continued

		2000*			1990*			1980*	
Subject	Total	Male	Female	Total	Male	Female	Total	Male	Female
10 to 14 years	53,751	27,114	26,637	178,534	90,104	88,430	331,362	167,152	164,210
15 to 19 years	164,785	82,391	82,394	377,106	183,215	193,891	527,942	259,270	268,672
20 to 24 years	209,509	98,917	110,592	747,188	368,631	378,557	926,844	456,988	469,856
25 to 29 years	424,276	193,647	230,629	1,114,932	571,039	543,893	1,454,363	792,088	662,275
30 to 34 years	709,091	342,991	366,100	1,320,810	693,851	626,959	1,651,475	946,818	704,657
35 to 39 years	1,048,395	530,164	518,231	1,702,431	933,999	768,432	1,737,805	1,008,677	729,128
40 to 44 years	1,263,070	656,782	606,288	1,745,900	992,135	753,765	1,428,099	803,195	624,904
45 to 49 years	1,503,905	816,955	686,950	1,610,052	907,537	702,515	1,299,675	744,423	555,252
50 to 54 years	1,565,568	883,342	682,226	1,345,130	737,822	607,308	1,167,377	651,546	515,831
55 to 59 years	1,318,750	735,848	582,902	1,048,476	565,334	483,142	908,722	503,789	404,933
60 to 64 years	1,068,875	573,300	495,575	925,893	491,843	434,050	715,731	392,629	323,102
65 to 69 years	812,528	422,760	389,768	721,899	383,135	338,764	519,226	275,400	243,826
70 to 74 years	602,159	310,106	292,053	466,351	246,334	220,017	381,325	194,732	186,593
75 to 79 years	379,249	193,630	185,619	491,605	241,741	249,864	246,487	124,170	122,317
80 to 84 years	178,892	88,890	90,002	(NA)	(NA)	(NA)	118,935	56,701	62,234
85 years and over	86,430	39,022	47,408	(NA)	(NA)	(NA)	62,254	28,381	33,873
Age data not available [1]	175,758	110,632	65,126	231,460	151,266	80,194	228,202	160,845	67,357
Median age (years)	51	51.4	50.5	43.9	44.1	43.7	40	40.1	39.9
BROAD AGE GROUPS									
Total	11,594,896	6,121,647	5,473,249	14,204,149	7,647,090	6,557,059	13,920,692	7,675,435	6,245,257
Age data available [1]	11,419,138	6,011,015	5,408,123	13,972,689	7,495,824	6,476,865	13,692,490	7,514,590	6,177,900
Under 15 years	83,656	42,270	41,386	354,916	179,208	175,708	546,230	275,783	270,447
15 to 64 years	9,276,224	4,914,337	4,361,887	11,937,918	6,445,406	5,492,512	11,818,033	6,559,423	5,258,610
15 to 44 years	3,819,126	1,904,892	1,914,234	7,008,367	3,742,870	3,265,497	7,726,528	4,267,036	3,459,492
15 to 24 years	374,294	181,308	192,986	1,124,294	551,846	572,448	1,454,786	716,258	738,528
25 to 44 years	3,444,832	1,723,584	1,721,248	5,884,073	3,191,024	2,693,049	6,271,742	3,550,778	2,720,964

Table 7. Continued

Subject	2000* Total	2000* Male	2000* Female	1990* Total	1990* Male	1990* Female	1980* Total	1980* Male	1980* Female
45 to 64 years	5,457,098	3,009,445	2,447,653	4,929,551	2,702,536	2,227,015	4,091,505	2,292,387	1,799,118
65 years and over	2,059,258	1,054,408	1,004,850	1,679,855	871,210	808,645	1,328,227	679,384	648,843
18 years and over [2]	11,260,319	5,930,974	5,329,845	(NA)	(NA)	(NA)	12,859,490	7,097,340	5,762,150
21 years and over [2]	11,123,950	5,863,510	5,260,440	(NA)	(NA)	(NA)	12,478,456	6,914,720	5,563,736
Age data not available [1]	175,758	110,632	65,126	231,460	151,266	80,194	228,202	160,845	67,357
PERCENT DISTRIBUTION									
Age data available [1]	100.0	100.0	100.0	100.0	100.0	100.0	100.0	100.0	100.0
Under 15 years	0.7	0.7	0.8	2.5	2.4	2.7	4.0	3.7	4.4
15 to 64 years	81.2	81.8	80.7	85.4	86.0	84.8	86.3	87.3	85.1
15 to 44 years	33.4	31.7	35.4	50.2	49.9	50.4	56.4	56.8	56.0
15 to 24 years	3.3	3.0	3.6	8.0	7.4	8.8	10.6	9.5	12.0
25 to 44 years	30.2	28.7	31.8	42.1	42.6	41.6	45.8	47.3	44.0
45 to 64 years	47.8	50.1	45.3	35.3	36.1	34.4	29.9	30.5	29.1
65 years and over	18.0	17.5	18.6	12.0	11.6	12.5	9.7	9.0	10.5
18 years and over [2]	98.6	98.7	98.6	(NA)	(NA)	(NA)	93.9	94.4	93.3
21 years and over [2]	97.4	97.5	97.3	(NA)	(NA)	(NA)	91.1	92.0	90.1
MALES PER 100 FEMALES									
Total	111.8	(X)	(X)	116.6	(X)	(X)	122.9	(X)	(X)
Age data available [1]	111.1	(X)	(X)	115.7	(X)	(X)	121.6	(X)	(X)
Under 15 years	102.1	(X)	(X)	102.0	(X)	(X)	102.0	(X)	(X)
15 to 64 years	112.7	(X)	(X)	117.3	(X)	(X)	124.7	(X)	(X)
15 to 44 years	99.5	(X)	(X)	114.6	(X)	(X)	123.3	(X)	(X)
15 to 24 years	93.9	(X)	(X)	96.4	(X)	(X)	97.0	(X)	(X)
25 to 44 years	100.1	(X)	(X)	118.5	(X)	(X)	130.5	(X)	(X)
45 to 64 years	123.0	(X)	(X)	121.4	(X)	(X)	127.4	(X)	(X)

Table 7. Continued

		2000*			1990*			1980*	
Subject	Total	Male	Female	Total	Male	Female	Total	Male	Female
65 years and over	104.9	(X)	(X)	107.7	(X)	(X)	104.7	(X)	(X)
18 years and over [2]	111.3	(X)	(X)	(NA)	(X)	(X)	123.2	(X)	(X)
21 years and over [2]	111.5	(X)	(X)	(NA)	(X)	(X)	124.3	(X)	(X)
Age data not available [1]	169.9	(X)	(X)	188.6	(X)	(X)	238.8	(X)	(X)
		1910			1900			1890	
Subject	Total	Male	Female	Total	Male	Female	Total	Male	Female
AGE									
Total	13,515,886	7,667,748	5,848,138	10,341,276	5,630,190	4,711,086	9,249,547	5,067,130	4,182,417
Age data available [1]	13,319,334	7,504,082	5,815,252	10,314,214	5,611,941	4,702,273	9,097,250	4,935,228	4,162,022
Under 5 years	102,507	51,940	50,567	52,641	26,696	25,945	86,629	44,040	42,589
5 to 9 years	298,509	150,652	147,857	147,723	73,999	73,724	248,351	126,070	122,281
10 to 14 years	358,330	181,303	177,027	312,591	158,238	154,353	396,379	201,159	195,220
15 to 19 years	673,761	351,754	322,007	568,508	277,243	291,265	521,295	257,658	263,637
20 to 24 years	1,430,381	823,920	606,461	931,178	465,989	465,189	917,374	476,224	441,150
25 to 29 years	1,662,696	990,576	672,120	1,111,478	601,812	509,666	1,072,239	602,545	469,694
30 to 34 years	1,505,715	888,668	617,047	1,189,552	674,974	514,578	942,320	549,099	393,221
35 to 39 years	1,408,093	812,007	596,086	1,197,357	691,211	506,146	870,592	493,471	377,121
40 to 44 years	1,303,475	751,519	551,956	984,186	574,293	409,893	859,954	475,106	384,848
45 to 49 years	1,146,360	656,455	489,905	854,474	481,780	372,694	787,815	433,466	354,349
50 to 54 years	925,055	526,256	398,799	813,870	449,875	363,995	709,220	382,987	326,233
55 to 59 years	693,520	380,110	313,410	648,671	350,498	298,173	525,131	278,485	246,646
60 to 64 years	627,583	331,914	295,669	549,000	289,456	259,544	477,647	254,101	223,546
65 to 69 years	488,397	255,416	232,981	412,288	214,792	197,496	311,574	166,745	144,829
70 to 74 years	336,967	172,751	164,216	282,915	148,537	134,378	199,006	106,364	92,642
75 to 79 years	208,212	105,412	102,800	159,161	83,099	76,062	101,215	53,167	48,048
80 to 84 years	101,290	50,262	51,028	69,208	35,462	33,746	46,853	23,343	23,510
85 years and over	48,483	23,167	25,316	29,413	13,987	15,426	23,656	11,198	12,458

Table 7. Continued

Subject		2000*			1990*			1980*	
	Total	Male	Female	Total	Male	Female	Total	Male	Female
Age data not available [1]	196,552	163,666	32,886	27,062	18,249	8,813	152,297	131,902	20,395
Median age (years)	37.2	36.9	37.6	38.5	38.8	38.1	37.1	37.1	37
BROAD AGE GROUPS									
Total	13,515,886	7,667,748	5,848,138	10,341,276	5,630,190	4,711,086	9,249,547	5,067,130	4,182,417
Age data available [1]	13,319,334	7,504,082	5,815,252	10,314,214	5,611,941	4,702,273	9,097,250	4,935,228	4,162,022
Under 15 years	759,346	383,895	375,451	512,955	258,933	254,022	731,359	371,269	360,090
15 to 64 years	11,376,639	6,513,179	4,863,460	8,848,274	4,857,131	3,991,143	7,683,587	4,203,142	3,480,445
15 to 44 years	7,984,121	4,618,444	3,365,677	5,982,259	3,285,522	2,696,737	5,183,774	2,854,103	2,329,671
15 to 24 years	2,104,142	1,175,674	928,468	1,499,686	743,232	756,454	1,438,669	733,882	704,787
25 to 44 years	5,879,979	3,442,770	2,437,209	4,482,573	2,542,290	1,940,283	3,745,105	2,120,221	1,624,884
45 to 64 years	3,392,518	1,894,735	1,497,783	2,866,015	1,571,609	1,294,406	2,499,813	1,349,039	1,150,774
65 years and over	1,183,349	607,008	576,341	952,985	495,877	457,108	682,304	360,817	321,487
18 years and over [2]	12,265,760	6,973,431	5,292,329	9,513,147	5,211,261	4,301,886	8,093,146	4,427,754	3,665,392
21 years and over [2]	11,627,714	6,627,111	5,000,603	9,057,861	4,992,037	4,065,824	7,678,076	4,225,730	3,452,346
Age data not available [1]	196,552	163,666	32,886	27,062	18,249	8,813	152,297	131,902	20,395
PERCENT DISTRIBUTION									
Age data available [1]	100.0	100.0	100.0	100.0	100.0	100.0	100.0	100.0	100.0
Under 15 years	5.7	5.1	6.5	5.0	4.6	5.4	8.0	7.5	8.7
15 to 64 years	85.4	86.8	83.6	85.8	86.5	84.9	84.5	85.2	83.6
15 to 44 years	59.9	61.5	57.9	58.0	58.5	57.3	57.0	57.8	56.0
15 to 24 years	15.3	15.7	16.0	14.5	13.2	16.1	15.8	14.9	16.9
25 to 44 years	44.1	45.9	41.9	43.5	45.3	41.3	41.2	43.0	39.0
45 to 64 years	25.5	25.2	25.8	27.8	28.0	27.5	27.5	27.3	27.6
65 years and over	8.9	8.1	9.9	9.2	8.8	9.7	7.5	7.3	7.7
18 years and over [2]	92.1	92.9	91.0	92.2	92.9	91.5	89.0	89.7	88.1

Table 7. Continued

		2000*			1990*			1980*	
Subject	Total	Male	Female	Total	Male	Female	Total	Male	Female
21 years and over [2]	87.3	88.3	86.0	87.8	89.0	86.5	84.4	85.6	82.9
MALES PER 100 FEMALES									
Total	131.1	(X)	(X)	119.5	(X)	(X)	121.2	(X)	(X)
Age data available [1]	129.0	(X)	(X)	119.3	(X)	(X)	118.6	(X)	(X)
Under 15 years	102.2	(X)	(X)	101.9	(X)	(X)	103.1	(X)	(X)
15 to 64 years	133.9	(X)	(X)	121.7	(X)	(X)	120.8	(X)	(X)
15 to 44 years	137.2	(X)	(X)	121.8	(X)	(X)	122.5	(X)	(X)
15 to 24 years	126.6	(X)	(X)	98.3	(X)	(X)	104.1	(X)	(X)
25 to 44 years	141.3	(X)	(X)	131.0	(X)	(X)	130.5	(X)	(X)
45 to 64 years	126.5	(X)	(X)	121.4	(X)	(X)	117.2	(X)	(X)
65 years and over	105.3	(X)	(X)	108.5	(X)	(X)	112.2	(X)	(X)
18 years and over [2]	131.8	(X)	(X)	121.1	(X)	(X)	120.8	(X)	(X)
21 years and over [2]	132.5	(X)	(X)	122.8	(X)	(X)	122.4	(X)	(X)
Age data not available [1]	497.7	(X)	(X)	207.1	(X)	(X)	646.7	(X)	(X)

		1880			1870	
Subject AGE	**Total**	**Male**	**Female**	**Total**	**Male**	**Female**
Total	6,679,943	3,630,943	3,049,377	5,567,229	3,006,943	2,560,286
Age data available [1]	6,559,679	3,521,635	3,038,044	5,564,473	3,004,548	2,559,925
Under 5 years	62,371	31,256	31,115	84,316	42,529	41,787
5 to 9 years	122,697	61,803	60,894	175,026	88,754	86,272
10 to 14 years	238,439	120,740	117,699	207,447	106,139	101,308
15 to 19 years	378,812	184,320	194,492	332,342	162,942	169,400
20 to 24 years	528,255	274,038	254,217	622,089	317,832	304,257
25 to 29 years	671,116	365,094	306,022	722,123	391,721	330,402
30 to 34 years	762,631	419,769	342,862	701,637	379,445	322,192
35 to 39 years	789,265	432,957	356,308	676,283	367,113	309,170
40 to 44 years	712,890	384,931	327,959	607,720	334,598	273,122

Table 7. Continued

Subject	2000* Total	2000* Male	2000* Female	1990* Total	1990* Male	1990* Female
45 to 49 years	630,941	340,863	290,078	455,755	263,473	192,282
50 to 54 years	577,087	318,045	259,042	371,772	217,493	154,279
55 to 59 years	373,114	206,820	166,294	204,307	116,216	88,091
60 to 64 years	310,463	170,841	139,622	181,782	99,394	82,388
65 to 69 years	181,361	98,028	83,333	97,543	52,493	45,050
70 to 74 years	114,609	59,590	55,019	69,627	36,579	33,048
75 to 79 years	60,696	31,106	29,590	29,958	15,616	14,342
80 to 84 years	31,086	15,156	15,930	24,746	12,211	12,535
85 years and over	13,846	6,278	7,568	(NA)	(NA)	(NA)
Age data not available [1]	120,264	108,931	11,333	2,756	2,395	361
Median age (years)	38.3	38.5	38	34.6	35.2	33.8
BROAD AGE GROUPS						
Total	6,679,943	3,630,566	3,049,377	5,567,229	3,006,943	2,560,286
Age data available [1]	6,559,679	3,521,635	3,038,044	5,564,473	3,004,548	2,559,925
Under 15 years	423,507	213,799	209,708	466,789	237,422	229,367
15 to 64 years	5,734,574	3,097,678	2,636,896	4,875,810	2,650,227	2,225,583
15 to 44 years	3,842,969	2,061,109	1,781,860	3,662,194	1,953,651	1,708,543
15 to 24 years	907,067	458,358	448,709	954,431	480,774	473,657
25 to 44 years	2,935,902	1,602,751	1,333,151	2,707,763	1,472,877	1,234,886
45 to 64 years	1,891,605	1,036,569	855,036	1,213,616	696,576	517,040
65 years and over	401,598	210,158	191,440	221,874	116,899	104,975
18 years and over [2]	5,929,939	3,207,478	2,722,461	4,933,840	2,686,877	2,246,963
21 years and over [2]	5,651,978	3,072,487	2,579,491	4,631,872	2,542,583	2,089,289
Age data not available [1]	120,264	108,931	11,333	2,756	2,395	361
PERCENT DISTRIBUTION						
Age data available [1]	100.0	100.0	100.0	100.0	100.0	100.0

Table 7. Continued

		2000*			1990*	
Subject	**Total**	**Male**	**Female**	**Total**	**Male**	**Female**
Under 15 years	6.5	6.1	6.9	8.4	7.9	9.0
15 to 64 years	87.4	88.0	86.8	87.6	88.2	86.9
15 to 44 years	58.6	58.5	58.7	65.8	65.0	66.7
15 to 24 years	13.8	13.0	14.8	17.2	16.0	18.5
25 to 44 years	44.8	45.5	43.9	48.7	49.0	48.2
45 to 64 years	28.8	29.4	28.1	21.8	23.2	20.2
65 years and over	6.1	6.0	6.3	4.0	3.9	4.1
18 years and over [2]	90.4	91.1	89.6	88.7	89.4	87.8
21 years and over [2]	86.2	87.2	84.9	83.2	84.6	81.6
MALES PER 100 FEMALES						
Total	119.1	(X)	(X)	117.4	(X)	(X)
Age data available [1]	115.9	(X)	(X)	117.4	(X)	(X)
Under 15 years	102.0	(X)	(X)	103.5	(X)	(X)
15 to 64 years	117.5	(X)	(X)	119.1	(X)	(X)
15 to 44 years	115.7	(X)	(X)	114.3	(X)	(X)
15 to 24 years	102.2	(X)	(X)	101.5	(X)	(X)
25 to 44 years	120.2	(X)	(X)	119.3	(X)	(X)
45 to 64 years	121.2	(X)	(X)	134.7	(X)	(X)
65 years and over	109.8	(X)	(X)	111.4	(X)	(X)
18 years and over [2]	117.8	(X)	(X)	119.6	(X)	(X)
21 years and over [2]	119.1	(X)	(X)	121.7	(X)	(X)
Age data not available [1]	961.2	(X)	(X)	663.4	(X)	(X)

Footnotes:

* Indicates sample data. - Represents zero. (X) Not applicable. (NA) Not available.

[1] See text for Table 7. For 1870 and 1900, age data not available include age not reported for all races. For 1880 and 1940 (when age not reported was allocated), age data not available include only the foreign-born population of races other than White. For 1890 and 1910-1930 age data not available include age not reported for the White foreign-born population and also the total foreign-born population of races other than White as follows: 1890 - 127,680 total, 115,272 males, and 12,408 females; 1910 - 170,341 total, 143,960 males, and 26,381 females; 1920 - 207,938 total, 147,113 males, and 60,825 females; 1930 - 220,745 total, 144,599 males, and 76,146 females. For 1950- 2000 age not reported was allocated.

[2] For additional data on the foreign-born population 18 years and over and 21 years and over, see Table 11. [3] For 1930, 75 years and over. [4] For 1870, 80 years and over. Internet Release Date: February 2, 2006

Table 8. Race and Hispanic Origin of the Population by Nativity: 1850 to 1990 (Leading dots indicate subparts)

(See text for sources, definitions, and explanations)

Year and nativity	Total	Race						Hispanic origin (of any race) [4]	White, not of ispanic[4]
		White	Races other than White						
			Total	Black	American Indian, Eskimo, and Aleut [1]	Asian and Pacific Islander [2]	Other race [3]		
1990*									
Total	248,709,873	199,827,064	48,882,809	29,930,524	2,015,143	7,226,986	9,710,156	21,900,089	188,424,773
Native	228,942,557	189,804,252	39,138,305	28,475,230	1,968,224	2,668,242	6,026,609	14,058,439	182,257,430
Foreign born	19,767,316	10,022,812	9,744,504	1,455,294	46,919	4,558,744	3,683,547	7,841,650	6,167,343
Percent	7.9	5.0	19.9	4.9	2.3	63.1	37.9	35.8	3.3
1980*									
Total	226,545,805	189,035,012	37,510,793	26,482,349	1,534,336	3,726,440	5,767,668	14,603,683	180,602,838
Native	212,465,899	179,711,056	32,754,833	25,666,629	1,496,146	1,543,801	4,048,257	10,430,832	173,648,776
Foreign born	14,079,906	9,323,945	4,755,960	815,720	38,190	2,182,639	1,719,411	4,172,851	6,954,062
Percent	6.2	4.9	12.7	3.1	2.5	58.6	29.8	28.6	3.9
1970*									
Total	203,210,158	178,119,221	25,090,937	22,539,362	760,572	1,526,401	264,602	9,072,602	169,653,095
Native	193,590,856	169,385,451	24,205,405	22,285,904	746,084	981,964	191,453	7,270,270	162,596,991
Foreign born	9,619,302	8,733,770	885,532	253,458	14,488	544,437	73,149	1,802,332	7,056,104
Percent	4.7	4.9	3.5	1.1	1.9	35.7	27.6	19.9	4.2
1960*[5]									
Total	179,325,671	158,837,671	20,448,000	18,848,619	546,228	890,868	202,281	(NA)	(NA)
Native	169,587,528	149,543,638	20,003,890	18,723,297	(NA)	607,119	(NA)	(NA)	(NA)
Foreign born	9,738,143	9,294,033	444,110	125,322	(NA)	283,749	(NA)	(NA)	(NA)
Percent	5.4	5.9	2.2	0.7	(NA)	31.9	(NA)	(NA)	(NA)
1960*[5]									
Total	178,466,732	158,460,691	20,006,041	(NA)	(NA)	(NA)	(NA)	(NA)	(NA)
Native	168,805,716	149,181,384	19,624,332	(NA)	(NA)	(NA)	(NA)	(NA)	(NA)
Foreign born	9,661,016	9,279,307	381,709	(NA)	(NA)	(NA)	(NA)	(NA)	(NA)
Percent	5.4	5.9	1.9	(NA)	(NA)	(NA)	(NA)	(NA)	(NA)

Table 8. (Continued)

Year and nativity	Total	Race						Hispanic origin (of any race) [4]	White, not of ispanic[4]
		White	Races other than White						
			Total	Black	American Indian, Eskimo, and Aleut [1]	Asian and Pacific Islander [2]	Other race [3]		
1950*[6]									
Total	150,216,110	134,478,365	15,737,745	15,044,598	342,226	320,141	48,368	(NA)	(NA)
Native	139,868,715	124,382,950	15,485,765	(NA)	(NA)	(NA)	(NA)	(NA)	(NA)
Foreign born	10,347,395	10,095,415	251,980	(NA)	(NA)	(NA)	(NA)	(NA)	(NA)
Percent	6.9	7.5	1.6	(NA)	(NA)	(NA)	(NA)	(NA)	(NA)
1940									
Total	131,669,275	118,214,870	13,454,405	12,865,518	333,969	254,918	(X)	1,861,400	116,353,470
Native	120,074,379	106,795,732	13,278,647	12,781,577	329,478	167,592	(X)	1,433,040	105,362,692
Foreign born	11,594,896	11,419,138	175,758	83,941	4,491	87,326	(X)	428,360	10,990,778
Percent	8.8	9.7	1.3	0.7	1.3	34.3	(X)	23.0	9.4
1930									
Total	122,775,046	110,286,740	12,488,306	11,891,143	332,397	264,766	(X)	(NA)	(NA)
Native	108,570,897	96,303,335	12,267,562	11,792,523	328,845	146,194	(X)	(NA)	(NA)
Foreign born	14,204,149	13,983,405	220,744	98,620	3,552	118,572	(X)	(NA)	(NA)
Percent	11.6	12.7	1.8	0.8	1.1	44.8	(X)	(NA)	(NA)
1920									
Total	105,710,620	94,820,915	10,889,705	10,463,131	244,437	182,137	(X)	(NA)	(NA)
Native	91,789,928	81,108,161	10,681,767	10,389,328	238,138	54,301	(X)	(NA)	(NA)
Foreign born	13,920,692	13,712,754	207,938	73,803	6,299	127,836	(X)	(NA)	(NA)
Percent	13.2	14.5	1.9	0.7	2.6	70.2	(X)	(NA)	(NA)
1910									
Total	91,972,266	81,731,957	10,240,309	9,827,763	265,683	146,863	(X)	(NA)	(NA)
Native	78,456,380	80,386,412	10,069,968	9,787,424	262,930	19,614	(X)	(NA)	(NA)

Table 8. (Continued)

Year and nativity	Total	Race						Hispanic origin (of any race) [4]	White, not of ispanic[4]
		White	Races other than White						
			Total	Black	American Indian, Eskimo, and Aleut [1]	Asian and Pacific Islander [2]	Other race [3]		
Foreign born	13,515,886	1,345,545	170,341	40,339	2,753	127,249	(X)	(NA)	(NA)
Percent	14.7	1.6	1.7	0.4	1.0	86.6	(X)	(NA)	(NA)
1900									
Total	75,994,575	66,809,196	9,185,379	8,833,994	237,196	114,189	(X)	(NA)	(NA)
Native	65,653,299	56,595,379	9,057,920	8,813,658	234,983	9,279	(X)	(NA)	(NA)
Foreign born	10,341,276	10,213,817	127,459	20,336	2,213	104,910	(X)	(NA)	(NA)
Percent	13.6	15.3	1.4	0.2	0.9	91.9	(X)	(NA)	(NA)
1890[7]									
Total	62,947,714	55,101,258	7,846,456	7,488,676	248,253	109,527	(X)	(NA)	(NA)
1890[7]									
Total	62,622,250	54,983,890	7,638,360	7,470,040	58,806	109,514	(X)	(NA)	(NA)
Native	53,372,703	45,862,023	7,510,680	7,450,061	57,571	3,048	(X)	(NA)	(NA)
Foreign born	9,249,547	9,121,867	127,680	19,979	1,235	106,466	(X)	(NA)	(NA)
Percent	14.8	16.6	1.7	0.3	2.1	97.2	(X)	(NA)	(NA)
1880									
Total	50,155,783	43,402,970	6,752,813	6,580,793	66,407	105,613	(X)	(NA)	(NA)
Native	43,475,840	36,843,291	6,632,549	6,566,776	64,587	1,186	(X)	(NA)	(NA)
Foreign born	6,679,943	6,559,679	120,264	14,017	1,820	104,427	(X)	(NA)	(NA)
Percent	13.3	15.1	1.8	0.2	2.7	98.9	(X)	(NA)	(NA)
1870									
Total	38,558,371	33,589,377	4,968,994	4,880,009	25,731	63,254	(X)	(NA)	(NA)
Native	32,991,142	28,095,665	4,895,477	4,870,364	24,595	518	(X)	(NA)	(NA)
Foreign born	5,567,229	5,493,712	73,517	9,645	1,136	62,736	(X)	(NA)	(NA)
Percent	14.4	16.4	1.5	0.2	4.4	99.2	(X)	(NA)	(NA)

Table 8. (Continued)

Year and nativity	Total	Race						Hispanic origin (of any race) [4]	White, not of ispanic[4]
		White	Races other than White						
			Total	Black	American Indian, Eskimo, and Aleut [1]	Asian and Pacific Islander [2]	Other race [3]		
1860[8]									
Total	31,443,321	26,922,537	4,520,784	4,441,830	44,021	34,933	(X)	(NA)	(NA)
Native	27,304,624	22,825,784	4,478,840	4,434,819	44,021	-	(X)	(NA)	(NA)
Foreign born	4,138,697	4,096,753	41,944	7,011	-	34,933	(X)	(NA)	(NA)
Percent	13.2	15.2	0.9	0.2	-	100.0	(X)	(NA)	(NA)
1850[8]									
Total	23,191,876	19,553,068	3,638,808	3,638,808	(X)	(X)	(X)	(NA)	(NA)
Native	20,947,274	17,312,533	3,634,741	3,634,741	(X)	(X)	(X)	(NA)	(NA)
Foreign born	2,244,602	2,240,535	4,067	4,067	(X)	(X)	(X)	(NA)	(NA)
Percent	9.7	11.5	0.1	0.1	(X)	(X)	(X)	(NA)	(NA)

* Indicates sample data.

\- Represents zero or rounds to zero.

(X) Not applicable.

(NA) Not available.

[1] For 1950 to 1970, Eskimo and Aleut included with "Other race."

[2] For 1950 and 1960, Hawaiian included with "Other race."

[3] The 1950 census was the first census in which the race question included a separate category for "Other race." See text for Table 8.

[4] Estimates for 1940 of the Hispanic origin population and of the White, not of Hispanic origin population are based on 5-percent sample data on the White population with mother tongue of Spanish. See text for Table 8.

[6] See text for Table 8 regarding minor inconsistencies in sample data by race for 1950. Internet Release Date: February 2, 2006

[5] The 1960 population of Alaska and Hawaii (858,940) is included In the first block of data for 1960 and is excluded in the second block of data for 1960. See text for Table 8 regarding minor inconsistencies in sample data by race for 1960.

[7] The 1890 population of the Indian Territory and on Indian Reservations (325,464), for which data on nativity are not available, is included in the first block of data for 1890 and excluded in the second block of data for 1890. See text for Table 8.

[8] Data by nativity for the total population in 1850 and 1860 assume, as was done in 1870 census reports, that the entire slave population in 1850 and 1860 was native, that the entire American Indian population in 1860 was native, and that the entire Asian population in 1860 was foreign born.

Table 9. Race and Hispanic Origin of the Foreign-Born Population: 1850 to 1990 (Leading dots indicate subparts)

(See text for sources, definitions, and explanations)

Year and nativity	Total	Race						Hispanic origin (of any race)	White, not of Hispanic origin [4]
		White	Races other than White						
			Total	Black	American Indian, Eskimo, and Aleut [1]	Asian and Pacific Islander [2]	Other race [3]		
FOREIGN-BORN POPULATION									
1990*	19,767,316	10,022,812	9,744,504	1,455,294	46,919	4,558,744	3,683,547	7,841,650	6,167,343
1980*	14,079,906	9,323,946	4,755,960	815,720	38,190	2,182,639	1,719,411	4,172,851	6,954,062
1970*	9,619,302	8,733,770	885,532	253,458	14,488	544,437	73,149	1,802,332	7,056,104
1960* [5]	9,738,143	9,294,033	444,110	125,322	(NA)	283,749	(NA)	(NA)	(NA)
1960* [5]	9,661,016	9,279,307	381,709	(NA)	(NA)	(NA)	(NA)	(NA)	(NA)
1950*	10,347,395	10,095,415	251,980	(NA)	(NA)	(NA)	(NA)	(NA)	(NA)
1940	11,594,896	11,419,138	175,758	83,941	4,491	87,326	(X)	428,360	10,990,778
1930	14,204,149	13,983,405	220,744	98,620	3,552	118,572	(X)	(NA)	(NA)
1920	13,920,692	13,712,754	207,938	73,803	6,299	127,836	(X)	(NA)	(NA)
1910	13,515,886	13,345,545	170,341	40,339	2,753	127,249	(X)	(NA)	(NA)
1900	10,341,276	10,213,817	127,459	20,336	2,213	104,910	(X)	(NA)	(NA)
1890	9,249,547	9,121,867	127,680	19,979	1,235	106,466	(X)	(NA)	(NA)
1880	6,679,943	6,559,679	120,264	14,017	1,820	104,427	(X)	(NA)	(NA)
1870	5,567,229	5,493,712	73,517	9,645	1,136	62,736	(X)	(NA)	(NA)
1860 [6]	4,138,697	4,096,753	41,944	7,011	-	34,933	(X)	(NA)	(NA)
1850 [6]	2,244,602	2,240,535	4,067	4,067	(X)	(X)	(X)	(NA)	(NA)
PERCENT DISTRIBUTION									
1990*	100.0	50.7	49.3	7.4	0.2	23.1	18.6	39.7	31.2
1980*	100.0	66.2	33.8	5.8	0.3	15.5	12.2	29.6	49.4
1970*	100.0	90.8	9.2	2.6	0.2	5.7	0.8	18.7	73.4

Table 9. (Continued)

Year and nativity	Total	Race						Hispanic origin (of any race)	White, not of Hispanic origin [4]
		White	Races other than White						
			Total	Black	American Indian, Eskimo, and Aleut [1]	Asian and Pacific Islander [2]	Other race [3]		
1960* [5]	100.0	95.4	4.6	1.3	(NA)	2.9	(NA)	(NA)	(NA)
1960* [5]	100.0	96.0	4.0	(NA)	(NA)	(NA)	(NA)	(NA)	(NA)
1950*	100.0	97.6	2.4	(NA)	(NA)	(NA)	(NA)	(NA)	(NA)
1940	100.0	98.5	1.5	0.7	-	0.8	(X)	3.7	94.8
1930	100.0	98.4	1.6	0.7	-	0.8	(X)	(NA)	(NA)
1920	100.0	98.5	1.5	0.5	-	0.9	(X)	(NA)	(NA)
1910	100.0	98.7	1.3	0.3	-	0.9	(X)	(NA)	(NA)
1900	100.0	98.8	1.2	0.2	-	1.0	(X)	(NA)	(NA)
1890	100.0	98.6	1.4	0.2	-	1.2	(X)	(NA)	(NA)
1880	100.0	98.2	1.8	0.2	-	1.6	(X)	(NA)	(NA)
1870	100.0	98.7	1.3	0.2	-	1.1	(X)	(NA)	(NA)
1860 [6]	100.0	99.0	1.0	0.2	-	0.8	(X)	(NA)	(NA)
1850 [6]	100.0	99.8	0.2	0.2	(X)	(X)	(X)	(NA)	(NA)

Footnotes:

* Indicates sample data.

- Represents zero or rounds to zero.

(X) Not applicable.

(NA) Not available.

[1] For 1950 to 1970, Eskimo and Aleut included with "Other race."

[2] For 1950 and 1960, Hawaiian included with "Other race."

[3] The 1950 census was the first census in which the race question included a separate category for "Other race." See text for Table 8.

[4] Estimates for 1940 of the Hispanic origin population and of the White, not of Hispanic origin population are based on 5-percent sample data on the White population with mother tongue of Spanish. See text for Table 8.

[5] The 1960 foreign-born population of Alaska and Hawaii (77,127) is included in the first line of data for 1960 and is excluded in the second line of data for 1960.

[6] Data by nativity for the total population in 1850 and 1860 assume, as was done in 1870 census reports, that the entire slave population in 1850 and 1860 was native, that the entire American Indian population in 1860 was native, and that the entire Asian population in 1860 was foreign born. Internet Release Date: February 2, 2006

Table 10. Race and Hispanic Origin of the Population by Nativity and of the Foreign-Born Population: 1990 and 2000 (Leading dots indicate subparts)

(See text for sources, definitions, and explanations)

Race, Hispanic origin, and year	Total	Native	Foreign-born		Percent of foreign-born population
			Number	Percent	
TOTAL					
2000*	281,421,906	250,314,017	31,107,889	11.1	100.0
1990*	248,709,873	228,942,557	19,767,316	7.9	100.0
WHITE					
2000* - alone	211,353,725	197,977,521	13,376,204	6.3	43.0
2000* - alone or in combination[1]	217,140,902	202,594,457	14,546,445	6.7	46.8
1990*	199,827,064	189,804,252	10,022,812	5.0	50.7
BLACK OR AFRICAN AMERICAN					
2000* - alone	34,361,740	32,261,875	2,099,865	6.1	6.8
2000* - alone or in combination[1].	36,213,467	33,792,201	2,421,266	6.7	7.8
1990*	29,930,524	28,475,230	1,455,294	4.9	7.4
AMERICAN INDIAN AND ALASKA NATIVE					
2000* - alone	2,447,989	2,316,908	131,081	5.4	0.4
2000* - alone or in combination[1]	4,315,865	4,078,328	237,537	5.5	0.8
1990*	2,015,143	1,968,224	46,919	2.3	0.2
ASIAN					
2000* - alone	10,171,820	3,159,618	7,012,202	68.9	22.5
2000* - alone or in combination[1]	11,859,446	4,425,895	7,433,551	62.7	23.9
1990*	6,876,394	2,363,047	4,513,347	65.6	22.8
NATIVE HAWAIIAN AND OTHER PACIFIC ISLANDER					
2000* - alone	378,782	303,305	75,477	19.9	0.2
2000* - alone or in combination[1]	860,965	699,364	161,601	18.8	0.5
1990*	350,592	305,195	45,397	12.9	0.2
SOME OTHER RACE					
2000* - alone	15,436,924	8,735,644	6,701,280	43.4	21.5
2000* - alone or in combination[1]	18,850,054	10,782,184	8,067,870	42.8	25.9
1990*	9,710,156	6,026,609	3,683,547	37.9	18.6
TWO OR MORE RACES					
2000*	7,270,926	5,559,146	1,711,780	23.5	5.5
1990*	(X)	(X)	(X)	(X)	(X)
HISPANIC OR LATINO (of any race)					
2000*	35,238,481	21,080,664	14,157,817	40.2	45.5
1990*	21,900,089	14,058,439	7,841,650	35.8	39.7
WHITE, NOT HISPANIC OR LATINO					
2000* - alone	194,514,140	187,673,608	6,840,532	3.5	22.0
2000* - alone or in combination[1]	198,456,538	191,057,760	7,398,778	3.7	23.8
1990*	188,424,773	182,257,430	6,167,343	3.3	31.2

Footnotes: (X) Not applicable.

[1]Alone or in combination with one or more other races. See text for Table 10. Internet Release Date: February 2, 2006

Table 11. Length of Residence in the United States of the Foreign-Born Population: 1900 to 1930 and 1970 to 2000 (Leading dots indicate subparts)

(See text for sources, definitions, and explanations)

Length of residence, 1970 to 2000				
Years	2000*	1990*	1980*	1970*
NUMBER				
.. Total	31,107,889	19,767,316	14,079,906	9,739,723
Length reported	31,107,889	19,767,316	14,079,906	9,314,597
. Under 5 years	7,581,941	4,875,524	3,335,024	1,721,155
. 5 to 9 years	5,596,335	3,788,103	2,225,339	1,136,028
. 10 to 14 years	4,689,664	2,752,855	1,807,814	976,504
. 15 to 19 years	3,775,098	2,116,560	1,327,088	790,836
. 20 years and over	9,464,851	6,234,274	5,384,641	4,690,074
.. 20 to 24 years [1]	2,686,566	1,591,123	1,911,384	585,770
.. 25 to 29 years [2]	2,000,186	1,201,442	(NA)	323,449
.. 30 to 34 years [3]	1,484,167	1,599,021	3,473,257	(NA)
.. 35 to 39 years [4]	1,052,661	(NA)	(NA)	766,150
.. 40 to 44 years [5]	803,149	1,842,688	(NA)	(NA)
.. 45 to 49 years [6]	568,317	(NA)	(NA)	1,182,985
.. 50 to 54 years	379,716	(NA)	(NA)	(NA)
.. 55 years and over	490,089	(NA)	(NA)	1,831,720
Length not reported	-	-	-	425,126
PERCENT DISTRIBUTION				
. Length reported	100.0	100.0	100.0	100.0
Under 5 years	24.4	24.7	23.7	18.5
5 to 9 years	18.0	19.2	15.8	12.2
10 to 14 years	15.1	13.9	12.8	10.5
15 to 19 years	12.1	10.7	9.4	8.5
20 years and over	30.4	31.5	38.2	50.4
Median (years)	12.5	12.2	14.1	20.3

Length of residence, 1930	
Years	1930
NUMBER	
Total	14,204,149
Length reported	13,618,533
Under 5 years	1,085,214
5 to 9 years	1,738,185
10 to 14 years	730,309
15 to 18 years	1,811,637
19 years and over	8,253,188
19 to 28 years	3,823,694
29 years and over	4,429,494
Length not reported	585,616
PERCENT DISTRIBUTION	
Length reported	100.0
Under 5 years	8.0
5 to 9 years	12.8
10 to 14 years	5.4
15 to 18 years	13.3
19 years and over	60.6
Median (years)	20.9

Table 11. (Continued)

Length of residence, 1900 to 1920			
Years	**1920**	**1910**	**1900**
NUMBER			
.. Total	13,920,692	13,515,886	10,341,276
Length reported	12,656,332	12,175,067	9,328,623
. Under 4 years	593,099	2,570,123	1,003,866
. 4 to 8 years	2,257,864	2,036,022	1,359,231
. 9 to 13 years	2,229,868	1,063,699	1,596,930
. 14 to 18 years	1,814,264	1,157,513	1,566,448
. 19 years and over	5,761,237	5,347,710	3,802,148
Length not reported	1,264,360	1,340,819	1,012,653
PERCENT DISTRIBUTION			
. Length reported	100.0	100.0	100.0
Under 4 years	4.7	21.1	10.8
4 to 8 years	17.8	16.7	14.6
9 to 13 years	17.6	8.7	17.1
14 up to 18 years	14.3	9.5	16.8
19 years and over	45.5	43.9	40.8
Median (years)	17.4	15.8	16.2

Footnotes:

* Indicates sample data.

- Represents zero.

(NA) Not available.

[1] For 1980, 20 to 29 years.

[2] For 1970, 25 to 34 years.

[3] For 1990, 30 to 39 years. For 1980, 30 years and over.

[4] For 1970, 35 to 44 years.

[5] For 1990, 40 years and over.

[6] For 1970, 45 to 54 years.

Internet Release Date: February 2, 2006

Table 12. Citizenship Status of the Foreign-Born Population: 1890 to 1950 and 1970 to 2000 (Leading dots indicate subparts)

-(See text for sources, definitions, and explanations)

Population universe and year	Total	Citizenship status reported [1]				Citizenship status not reported [1]
		Total	Naturalized citizen		Not a citizen	
			Number	Percent		
TOTAL (all ages)						
2000*	31,107,889	31,107,889	12,542,626	40.3	18,565,263	-
1990*	19,767,316	19,767,316	7,996,998	40.5	11,770,318	-
1980*	14,079,906	14,079,906	7,110,475	50.5	6,969,431	-
1970*	9,739,723	9,739,723	6,198,173	63.6	3,541,550	-
1950*	10,347,395	9,615,610	7,562,970	78.7	2,052,640	731,785
1940	11,594,896	10,759,917	7,280,265	67.7	3,479,652	834,979
1930	14,204,149	13,704,296	7,919,536	57.8	5,784,760	499,853
1920	13,920,692	13,119,216	6,489,883	49.5	6,629,333	801,476
18 YEARS AND OVER						
Both sexes						
2000*	27,901,599	27,901,599	11,999,425	43.0	15,902,174	-
1990*	17,674,856	17,674,856	7,656,964	43.3	10,017,892	-
1980*	12,360,336	12,360,336	6,666,541	53.9	5,693,795	-
1970*	8,787,355	8,787,355	5,900,350	67.1	2,887,005	-
Male						
2000*	13,818,539	13,818,539	5,554,311	40.2	8,264,228	-
1990*	8,584,582	8,584,582	3,543,661	41.3	5,040,921	-
1980*	5,698,044	5,698,044	3,012,853	52.9	2,685,191	-
1970*	3,994,062	3,994,062	2,770,610	69.4	1,223,452	-
Female						
2000*	14,083,060	14,083,060	6,445,114	45.8	7,637,946	-
1990*	9,090,274	9,090,274	4,113,303	45.2	4,976,971	-
1980*	6,662,292	6,662,292	3,653,688	54.8	3,008,604	-
1970*	4,793,293	4,793,293	3,129,740	65.3	1,663,553	-
21 YEARS AND OVER						
Both sexes						
2000*	26,597,286	26,597,286	11,766,252	44.2	14,831,034	-
1990*	16,791,311	16,791,311	7,463,506	44.4	9,327,805	-
1980*	11,733,838	11,733,838	6,484,569	55.3	5,249,269	-
1970*	8,520,398	8,520,398	5,795,027	68.0	2,725,371	-
1950*	10,020,450	9,346,345	7,466,445	79.9	1,879,900	674,105
1940	11,292,821	10,495,035	7,159,643	68.2	3,335,392	797,786
1930	13,336,353	12,865,112	7,681,681	59.7	5,183,431	471,241
1920	12,686,393	11,946,255	6,218,801	52.1	5,727,454	740,138

Table 12. (Continued)

Population universe and year	Total	Citizenship status reported [1]				Citizenship status not reported [1]
Male						
2000*	13,088,312	13,088,312	5,435,470	41.5	7,652,842	-
1990*	8,095,967	8,095,967	3,439,722	42.5	4,656,245	-
1980*	5,363,748	5,363,748	2,920,723	54.5	2,443,025	-
1970*	3,864,834	3,864,834	2,719,383	70.4	1,145,451	-
1950*	5,092,230	4,772,195	3,981,895	83.4	790,300	320,035
1940	5,969,588	5,593,358	4,076,207	72.9	1,517,151	376,230
1930	7,218,977	6,987,874	4,247,704	60.8	2,740,170	231,103
1920	7,063,594	6,699,518	3,320,226	49.6	3,379,292	364,076
1910	6,780,214	6,000,250	3,038,303	50.6	2,961,947	779,964
1900	5,010,286	4,275,297	2,848,807	66.6	1,426,490	734,989
1890	4,348,459	3,971,266	2,545,753	64.1	1,425,513	377,193
Female						
2000*	13,508,974	13,508,974	6,330,782	46.9	7,178,192	-
1990*	8,695,344	8,695,344	4,023,784	46.3	4,671,560	-
1980*	6,370,090	6,370,090	3,563,846	55.9	2,806,244	-
1970*	4,655,564	4,655,564	3,075,644	66.1	1,579,920	-
1950*	4,928,220	4,574,150	3,484,550	76.2	1,089,600	354,070
1940	5,323,233	4,901,677	3,083,436	62.9	1,818,241	421,556
1930	6,117,376	5,877,238	3,433,977	58.4	2,443,261	240,138
1920	5,622,799	5,246,737	2,898,575	55.2	2,348,162	376,062

Footnotes:

* Indicates sample data.

- Represents zero.

(NA) Not available.

[1]Since 1970, data on citizenship have been imputed if not reported. Internet Release Date: February 2, 2006

Table 13. Nativity and Parentage of the Population: 1890 to 1930, 1960, and 1970 (Leading dots indicate subparts)

(See text for sources, definitions, and explanations)

Year	Total population	Native population							Foreign- born population
		Total	Native parentage	Foreign or mixed parentage					
				Total	Foreign parentage	Mixed parentage			
						Total	Father foreign born	Mother foreign born	
NUMBER									
1970*	203,210,158	193,590,856	169,634,926	23,955,930	(NA)	(NA)	(NA)	(NA)	9,619,302
1960*	179,325,675	169,587,520	145,275,233	24,312,287	14,105,139	10,207,148	6,451,715	3,755,433	9,738,155
1930	122,775,046	108,570,897	82,488,768	26,082,129	17,535,071	8,547,058	5,579,987	2,967,071	14,204,149
1920	105,710,620	91,789,928	68,994,682	22,795,246	15,764,366	7,030,880	4,564,295	2,466,585	13,920,692
1910	91,972,266	78,456,380	59,491,427	18,964,953	12,949,181	6,015,772	3,946,435	2,069,337	13,515,886
1900	75,994,575	65,653,299	49,956,178	15,697,121	10,650,802	5,046,319	3,368,228	1,678,091	10,341,276
1890 [1]	62,622,250	53,372,703	41,840,305	11,532,398	8,113,742	3,418,656	2,378,729	1,039,927	9,249,547
PERCENT DISTRIBUTION									
1970*	100.0	95.3	83.5	11.8	(NA)	(NA)	(NA)	(NA)	4.7
1960*	100.0	94.6	81.0	13.6	7.9	5.7	3.6	2.1	5.4
1930	100.0	88.4	67.2	21.2	14.3	7.0	4.5	2.4	11.6
1920	100.0	86.8	65.3	21.6	14.9	6.7	4.3	2.3	13.2
1910	100.0	85.3	64.7	20.6	14.1	6.5	4.3	2.2	14.7
1900	100.0	86.4	65.7	20.7	14.0	6.6	4.4	2.2	13.6
1890 [1]	100.0	85.2	66.8	18.4	13.0	5.5	3.8	1.7	14.8

Table 13. (Continued)

Year	Total population	Native stock	Foreign stock
NUMBER			
1970*	203,210,158	169,634,926	33,575,232
1960*	179,325,675	145,275,233	34,050,442
1930	122,775,046	82,488,768	40,286,278
1920	105,710,620	68,994,682	36,715,938
1910	91,972,266	59,491,427	32,480,839
1900	75,994,575	49,956,178	26,038,397
1890 [1]	62,622,250	41,840,305	20,781,945
PERCENT DISTRIBUTION			
1970*	100.0	83.5	16.5
1960*	100.0	81.0	19.0
1930	100.0	67.2	32.8
1920	100.0	65.3	34.7
1910	100.0	64.7	35.3
1900	100.0	65.7	34.3
1890 [1]	100.0	66.8	33.2

Footnotes:

* Indicates sample data.

(NA) Not available.

[1]See text for Table 13 regarding data for 1890. Internet Release Date: February 2, 2006

Table 14. Nativity of the Population, for Regions, Divisions, and States: 1850 to 2000 (Leading dots indicate subparts)

(See text for sources, definitions, and explanations)

Region, division, and state	2000*				1990*			
	Total	Native	Foreign born		Total	Native	Foreign born	
			Number	Percent			Number	Percent
United States	281,421,906	250,314,017	31,107,889	11.1	248,709,873	228,942,557	19,767,316	7.9
REGION AND DIVISION								
Northeast	53,594,378	46,365,310	7,229,068	13.5	50,809,229	45,578,205	5,231,024	10.3
New England	13,922,517	12,546,200	1,376,317	9.9	13,206,943	12,163,706	1,043,237	7.9
Middle Atlantic	39,671,861	33,819,110	5,852,751	14.8	37,602,286	33,414,499	4,187,787	11.1
Midwest	64,392,776	60,882,839	3,509,937	5.5	59,668,632	57,537,339	2,131,293	3.6
East North Central	45,155,037	42,382,826	2,772,211	6.1	42,008,942	40,225,794	1,783,148	4.2
West North Central	19,237,739	18,500,013	737,726	3.8	17,659,690	17,311,545	348,145	2.0
South	100,236,820	91,628,379	8,608,441	8.6	85,445,930	80,863,637	4,582,293	5.4
South Atlantic	51,769,160	46,748,638	5,020,522	9.7	43,566,853	40,843,908	2,722,945	6.3
East South Central	17,022,810	16,655,855	366,955	2.2	15,176,284	15,019,135	157,149	1.0
West South Central	31,444,850	28,223,886	3,220,964	10.2	26,702,793	25,000,594	1,702,199	6.4
West	63,197,932	51,437,489	11,760,443	18.6	52,786,082	44,963,376	7,822,706	14.8
Mountain	18,172,295	16,429,665	1,742,630	9.6	13,658,776	12,943,864	714,912	5.2
Pacific	45,025,637	35,007,824	10,017,813	22.2	39,127,306	32,019,512	7,107,794	18.2
STATE								
New England								
Maine	1,274,923	1,238,232	36,691	2.9	1,227,928	1,191,632	36,296	3.0
New Hampshire	1,235,786	1,181,632	54,154	4.4	1,109,252	1,068,059	41,193	3.7
Vermont	608,827	585,582	23,245	3.8	562,758	545,214	17,544	3.1

Table 14. (Continued)

Region, division, and state	2000*				1990*			
	Total	Native	Foreign born		Total	Native	Foreign born	
			Number	Percent			Number	Percent
Massachusetts	6,349,097	5,576,114	772,983	12.2	6,016,425	5,442,692	573,733	9.5
Rhode Island	1,048,319	929,042	119,277	11.4	1,003,464	908,376	95,088	9.5
Connecticut	3,405,565	3,035,598	369,967	10.9	3,287,116	3,007,733	279,383	8.5
Middle Atlantic								
New York	18,976,457	15,108,324	3,868,133	20.4	17,990,455	15,138,594	2,851,861	15.9
New Jersey	8,414,350	6,938,023	1,476,327	17.5	7,730,188	6,763,578	966,610	12.5
Pennsylvania	12,281,054	11,772,763	508,291	4.1	11,881,643	11,512,327	369,316	3.1
East North Central								
Ohio	11,353,140	11,013,861	339,279	3.0	10,847,115	10,587,442	259,673	2.4
Indiana	6,080,485	5,893,951	186,534	3.1	5,544,159	5,449,896	94,263	1.7
Illinois	12,419,293	10,890,235	1,529,058	12.3	11,430,602	10,478,330	952,272	8.3
Michigan	9,938,444	9,414,855	523,589	5.3	9,295,297	8,939,904	355,393	3.8
Wisconsin	5,363,675	5,169,924	193,751	3.6	4,891,769	4,770,222	121,547	2.5
West North Central								
Minnesota	4,919,479	4,659,016	260,463	5.3	4,375,099	4,262,060	113,039	2.6
Iowa	2,926,324	2,835,239	91,085	3.1	2,776,755	2,733,439	43,316	1.6
Missouri	5,595,211	5,444,015	151,196	2.7	5,117,073	5,033,440	83,633	1.6
North Dakota	642,200	630,086	12,114	1.9	638,800	629,412	9,388	1.5
South Dakota	754,844	741,349	13,495	1.8	696,004	688,273	7,731	1.1
Nebraska	1,711,263	1,636,625	74,638	4.4	1,578,385	1,550,187	28,198	1.8
Kansas	2,688,418	2,553,683	134,735	5.0	2,477,574	2,414,734	62,840	2.5
South Atlantic								
Delaware	783,600	738,702	44,898	5.7	666,168	643,893	22,275	3.3
Maryland	5,296,486	4,778,171	518,315	9.8	4,781,468	4,467,974	313,494	6.6
District of Columbia	572,059	498,498	73,561	12.9	606,900	548,013	58,887	9.7
Virginia	7,078,515	6,508,236	570,279	8.1	6,187,358	5,875,549	311,809	5.0

Table 14. (Continued)

Region, division, and state	2000*				1990*			
	Total	Native	Foreign born		Total	Native	Foreign born	
			Number	Percent			Number	Percent
West Virginia	1,808,344	1,788,954	19,390	1.1	1,793,477	1,777,765	15,712	0.9
North Carolina	8,049,313	7,619,313	430,000	5.3	6,628,637	6,513,560	115,077	1.7
South Carolina	4,012,012	3,896,034	115,978	2.9	3,486,703	3,436,739	49,964	1.4
Georgia	8,186,453	7,609,180	577,273	7.1	6,478,216	6,305,090	173,126	2.7
Florida	15,982,378	13,311,550	2,670,828	16.7	12,937,926	11,275,325	1,662,601	12.9
East South Central								
Kentucky	4,041,769	3,961,498	80,271	2.0	3,685,296	3,651,177	34,119	0.9
Tennessee	5,689,283	5,530,279	159,004	2.8	4,877,185	4,818,071	59,114	1.2
Alabama	4,447,100	4,359,328	87,772	2.0	4,040,587	3,997,054	43,533	1.1
Mississippi	2,844,658	2,804,750	39,908	1.4	2,573,216	2,552,833	20,383	0.8
West South Central								
Arkansas	2,673,400	2,599,710	73,690	2.8	2,350,725	2,325,858	24,867	1.1
Louisiana	4,468,976	4,353,091	115,885	2.6	4,219,973	4,132,566	87,407	2.1
Oklahoma	3,450,654	3,318,907	131,747	3.8	3,145,585	3,080,096	65,489	2.1
Texas	20,851,820	17,952,178	2,899,642	13.9	16,986,510	15,462,074	1,524,436	9.0
Mountain								
Montana	902,195	885,799	16,396	1.8	799,065	785,286	13,779	1.7
Idaho	1,293,953	1,229,873	64,080	5.0	1,006,749	977,844	28,905	2.9
Wyoming	493,782	482,577	11,205	2.3	453,588	445,941	7,647	1.7
Colorado	4,301,261	3,931,358	369,903	8.6	3,294,394	3,151,960	142,434	4.3
New Mexico	1,819,046	1,669,440	149,606	8.2	1,515,069	1,434,555	80,514	5.3
Arizona	5,130,632	4,474,449	656,183	12.8	3,665,228	3,387,023	278,205	7.6
Utah	2,233,169	2,074,505	158,664	7.1	1,722,850	1,664,250	58,600	3.4
Nevada	1,998,257	1,681,664	316,593	15.8	1,201,833	1,097,005	104,828	8.7
Pacific								
Washington	5,894,121	5,279,664	614,457	10.4	4,866,692	4,544,548	322,144	6.6

Table 14. (Continued)

Region, division, and state	2000*				1990*			
	Total	Native	Foreign born		Total	Native	Foreign born	
			Number	Percent			Number	Percent
Oregon	3,421,399	3,131,697	289,702	8.5	2,842,321	2,703,014	139,307	4.9
California	33,871,648	25,007,393	8,864,255	26.2	29,760,021	23,301,196	6,458,825	21.7
Alaska	626,932	589,762	37,170	5.9	550,043	525,229	24,814	4.5
Hawaii	1,211,537	999,308	212,229	17.5	1,108,229	945,525	162,704	14.7
Region, division, and state	**1980***				**1970***			
	Total	**Foreign born**			**Total**	**Foreign born**		
		Native	**Number**	**Percent**		**Native**	**Number**	**Percent**
United States	226,545,805	212,465,899	14,079,906	6.2	203,210,158	193,590,856	9,619,302	4.7
REGION AND DIVISION								
Northeast	49,135,283	44,629,360	4,505,923	9.2	49,044,015	44,924,334	4,119,681	8.4
New England	12,348,493	11,390,346	958,147	7.8	11,845,126	10,915,934	929,192	7.8
Middle Atlantic	36,786,790	33,239,014	3,547,776	9.6	37,198,889	34,008,400	3,190,489	8.6
Midwest	58,865,670	56,751,480	2,114,190	3.6	56,564,917	54,691,356	1,873,561	3.3
East North Central	41,682,217	39,912,085	1,770,132	4.2	40,246,817	38,663,247	1,583,570	3.9
West North Central	17,183,453	16,839,395	344,058	2.0	16,318,100	16,028,109	289,991	1.8
South	75,372,362	72,477,605	2,894,757	3.8	62,792,882	61,476,677	1,316,205	2.1
South Atlantic	36,959,123	35,230,206	1,728,917	4.7	30,671,188	29,792,434	878,754	2.9
East South Central	14,666,423	14,520,963	145,460	1.0	12,803,421	12,743,731	59,690	0.5
West South Central	23,746,816	22,726,436	1,020,380	4.3	19,318,273	18,940,512	377,761	2.0
West	43,172,490	38,607,454	4,565,036	10.6	34,808,344	32,498,489	2,309,855	6.6
Mountain	11,372,785	10,887,879	484,906	4.3	8,281,553	8,035,215	246,338	3.0
Pacific	31,799,705	27,719,575	4,080,130	12.8	26,526,791	24,463,274	2,063,517	7.8
STATE								
New England								
Maine	1,124,660	1,081,258	43,402	3.9	993,663	950,649	43,014	4.3

Table 14. (Continued)

Region, division, and state	1980*				1970*			
	Total	Foreign born			Total	Foreign born		
		Native	Number	Percent		Native	Number	Percent
New Hampshire	920,610	879,649	40,961	4.4	737,681	700,633	37,048	5.0
Vermont	511,456	490,461	20,995	4.1	444,330	425,848	18,482	4.2
Massachusetts	5,737,037	5,236,055	500,982	8.7	5,688,903	5,194,243	494,660	8.7
Rhode Island	947,154	863,153	84,001	8.9	948,844	874,470	74,374	7.8
Connecticut	3,107,576	2,839,770	267,806	8.6	3,031,705	2,770,091	261,614	8.6
Middle Atlantic								
New York	17,558,072	15,169,134	2,388,938	13.6	18,236,882	16,127,106	2,109,776	11.6
New Jersey	7,364,823	6,607,001	757,822	10.3	7,168,143	6,533,325	634,818	8.9
Pennsylvania	11,863,895	11,462,879	401,016	3.4	11,793,864	11,347,969	445,895	3.8
East North Central								
Ohio	10,797,630	10,495,445	302,185	2.8	10,650,903	10,334,407	316,496	3.0
Indiana	5,490,224	5,388,422	101,802	1.9	5,193,665	5,110,467	83,198	1.6
Illinois	11,426,518	10,602,822	823,696	7.2	11,109,450	10,480,552	628,898	5.7
Michigan	9,262,078	8,844,926	417,152	4.5	8,875,068	8,450,759	424,309	4.8
Wisconsin	4,705,767	4,580,470	125,297	2.7	4,417,731	4,287,062	130,669	3.0
West North Central								
Minnesota	4,075,970	3,968,496	107,474	2.6	3,804,971	3,706,915	98,056	2.6
Iowa	2,913,808	2,866,149	47,659	1.6	2,824,376	2,784,159	40,217	1.4
Missouri	4,916,686	4,831,070	85,616	1.7	4,676,495	4,610,751	65,744	1.4
North Dakota	652,717	637,899	14,818	2.3	617,761	599,324	18,437	3.0
South Dakota	690,768	681,169	9,599	1.4	665,507	654,608	10,899	1.6
Nebraska	1,569,825	1,538,824	31,001	2.0	1,482,412	1,453,616	28,796	1.9
Kansas	2,363,679	2,315,788	47,891	2.0	2,246,578	2,218,736	27,842	1.2
South Atlantic								
Delaware	594,338	575,509	18,829	3.2	548,093	532,445	15,648	2.9
Maryland	4,216,975	4,021,394	195,581	4.6	3,922,391	3,798,046	124,345	3.2

Table 14. (Continued)

Region, division, and state	1980*				1970*			
	Total	Foreign born			Total	Foreign born		
		Native	Number	Percent		Native	Number	Percent
District of Columbia	638,333	597,774	40,559	6.4	756,492	722,930	33,562	4.4
Virginia	5,346,818	5,169,500	177,318	3.3	4,648,479	4,576,198	72,281	1.6
West Virginia	1,949,644	1,927,664	21,980	1.1	1,744,236	1,727,574	16,662	1.0
North Carolina	5,881,766	5,803,408	78,358	1.3	5,082,036	5,053,416	28,620	0.6
South Carolina	3,121,820	3,075,740	46,080	1.5	2,590,509	2,576,145	14,364	0.6
Georgia	5,463,105	5,371,625	91,480	1.7	4,589,569	4,556,581	32,988	0.7
Florida	9,746,324	8,687,592	1,058,732	10.9	6,789,383	6,249,099	540,284	8.0
East South Centra								
Kentucky	3,660,777	3,626,215	34,562	0.9	3,218,697	3,202,144	16,553	0.5
Tennessee	4,591,120	4,542,751	48,369	1.1	3,923,726	3,904,702	19,024	0.5
Alabama	3,893,888	3,854,886	39,002	1.0	3,444,148	3,428,160	15,988	0.5
Mississippi	2,520,638	2,497,111	23,527	0.9	2,216,850	2,208,725	8,125	0.4
West South Central								
Arkansas	2,286,435	2,264,064	22,371	1.0	1,923,240	1,914,953	8,287	0.4
Louisiana	4,205,900	4,120,398	85,502	2.0	3,640,442	3,600,900	39,542	1.1
Oklahoma	3,025,290	2,968,996	56,294	1.9	2,559,175	2,539,015	20,160	0.8
Texas	14,229,191	13,372,978	856,213	6.0	11,195,416	10,885,644	309,772	2.8
Mountain								
Montana	786,690	768,371	18,319	2.3	694,409	674,775	19,634	2.8
Idaho	943,935	920,531	23,404	2.5	712,567	699,995	12,572	1.8
Wyoming	469,557	459,950	9,607	2.0	332,416	325,427	6,989	2.1
Colorado	2,889,964	2,775,834	114,130	3.9	2,207,259	2,146,948	60,311	2.7
New Mexico	1,302,894	1,250,489	52,405	4.0	1,015,998	993,488	22,510	2.2
Arizona	2,718,215	2,555,409	162,806	6.0	1,770,893	1,694,323	76,570	4.3
Utah	1,461,037	1,410,586	50,451	3.5	1,059,273	1,029,700	29,573	2.8
Nevada	800,493	746,709	53,784	6.7	488,738	470,559	18,179	3.7

Table 14. (Continued)

Region, division, and state	1980*				1970*			
	Total	Foreign born			Total	Foreign born		
		Native	Number	Percent		Native	Number	Percent
Pacific								
Washington	4,132,156	3,893,096	239,060	5.8	3,409,161	3,253,141	156,020	4.6
Oregon	2,633,105	2,525,300	107,805	4.1	2,091,385	2,025,236	66,149	3.2
California	23,667,902	20,087,869	3,580,033	15.1	19,957,304	18,199,314	1,757,990	8.8
Alaska	401,851	385,635	16,216	4.0	300,382	292,619	7,763	2.6
Hawaii	964,691	827,675	137,016	14.2	768,559	692,964	75,595	9.8

Region, division, and state	1960*				1950*			
	Total	Native	Foreign born		Total	Native	Foreign born	
			Number	Percent			Number	Percent
United States	179,325,671	169,587,528	9,738,143	5.4	150,216,110	139,868,715	10,347,395	6.9
REGION AND DIVISION								
Northeast	44,681,702	40,106,959	4,574,743	10.2	39,341,610	34,054,445	5,287,165	13.4
New England	10,510,106	9,443,646	1,066,460	10.1	9,269,755	7,978,740	1,291,015	13.9
Middle Atlantic	34,171,596	30,663,313	3,508,283	10.3	30,071,855	26,075,705	3,996,150	13.3
Midwest	51,623,773	49,346,814	2,276,959	4.4	44,281,175	41,573,785	2,707,390	6.1
East North Central	36,228,690	34,351,633	1,877,057	5.2	30,269,515	28,122,685	2,146,830	7.1
West North Central	15,395,083	14,995,181	399,902	2.6	14,011,660	13,451,100	560,560	4.0
South	54,963,470	54,000,550	962,920	1.8	47,085,880	46,318,560	767,320	1.6
South Atlantic	25,960,258	25,409,832	550,426	2.1	21,130,905	20,750,510	380,395	1.8
East South Central	12,050,126	11,994,440	55,686	0.5	11,456,570	11,404,600	51,970	0.5
West South Central	16,953,086	16,596,278	356,808	2.1	14,498,405	14,163,450	334,955	2.3
West	28,056,726	26,133,205	1,923,521	6.9	19,507,445	17,921,925	1,585,520	8.1
Mountain	6,855,038	6,602,314	252,724	3.7	5,058,470	4,814,730	243,740	4.8
Pacific	21,201,688	19,530,891	1,670,797	7.9	14,448,975	13,107,195	1,341,780	9.3

Table 14. (Continued)

Region, division, and state	1980*				1970*			
	Total	Native	Foreign born		Total	Native	Foreign born	
			Number	Percent			Number	Percent
STATE								
New England								
Maine	969,265	908,862	60,403	6.2	908,850	834,375	74,475	8.2
New Hampshire	606,921	562,149	44,772	7.4	529,330	471,855	57,475	10.9
Vermont	389,881	366,545	23,336	6.0	375,335	346,935	28,400	7.6
Massachusetts	5,149,317	4,572,865	576,452	11.2	4,672,020	3,950,790	721,230	15.4
Rhode Island	859,488	773,514	85,974	10.0	788,170	674,775	113,395	14.4
Connecticut	2,535,234	2,259,711	275,523	10.9	1,996,050	1,700,010	296,040	14.8
Middle Atlantic								
New York	16,783,604	14,494,290	2,289,314	13.6	14,788,960	12,211,855	2,577,105	17.4
New Jersey	6,067,412	5,451,933	615,479	10.1	4,816,435	4,181,355	635,080	13.2
Pennsylvania	11,320,580	10,717,090	603,490	5.3	10,466,460	9,682,495	783,965	7.5
East North Central								
Ohio	9,707,136	9,310,522	396,614	4.1	7,908,250	7,467,775	440,475	5.6
Indiana	4,662,451	4,569,249	93,202	2.0	3,917,640	3,818,365	99,275	2.5
Illinois	10,081,653	9,395,555	686,098	6.8	8,680,600	7,894,310	786,290	9.1
Michigan	7,824,965	7,295,341	529,624	6.8	6,342,590	5,738,765	603,825	9.5
Wisconsin	3,952,485	3,780,966	171,519	4.3	3,420,435	3,203,470	216,965	6.3
West North Central								
Minnesota	3,413,864	3,269,986	143,878	4.2	2,972,150	2,761,580	210,570	7.1
Iowa	2,757,537	2,701,259	56,278	2.0	2,611,540	2,527,570	83,970	3.2
Missouri	4,320,774	4,243,018	77,756	1.8	3,943,310	3,851,890	91,420	2.3
North Dakota	632,446	602,539	29,907	4.7	617,705	569,500	48,205	7.8
South Dakota	680,514	661,937	18,577	2.7	649,710	619,000	30,710	4.7
Nebraska	1,411,330	1,371,092	40,238	2.9	1,319,015	1,261,415	57,600	4.4
Kansas	2,178,618	2,145,350	33,268	1.5	1,898,230	1,860,145	38,085	2.0

Table 14. (Continued)

Region, division, and state	1980*				1970*			
	Total	Foreign born			Total	Foreign born		
		Native	Number	Percent		Native	Number	Percent
South Atlantic								
Delaware	446,292	431,642	14,650	3.3	315,735	302,680	13,055	4.1
Maryland	3,100,687	3,006,509	94,178	3.0	2,333,245	2,248,080	85,165	3.7
District of Columbia	763,956	724,985	38,971	5.1	800,830	758,090	42,740	5.3
Virginia	3,954,429	3,906,244	48,185	1.2	3,312,565	3,276,875	35,690	1.1
West Virginia	1,860,421	1,836,558	23,863	1.3	1,999,835	1,965,925	33,910	1.7
North Carolina	4,556,155	4,534,177	21,978	0.5	4,052,795	4,037,545	15,250	0.4
South Carolina	2,382,594	2,371,454	11,140	0.5	2,114,355	2,107,235	7,120	0.3
Georgia	3,942,936	3,917,636	25,300	0.6	3,438,680	3,422,280	16,400	0.5
Florida	4,952,788	4,680,627	272,161	5.5	2,762,865	2,631,800	131,065	4.7
East South Central								
Kentucky	3,038,156	3,021,326	16,830	0.6	2,936,630	2,921,105	15,525	0.5
Tennessee	3,567,089	3,551,246	15,843	0.4	3,286,285	3,271,980	14,305	0.4
Alabama	3,266,740	3,251,785	14,955	0.5	3,056,210	3,042,805	13,405	0.4
Mississippi	2,178,141	2,170,083	8,058	0.4	2,177,445	2,168,710	8,735	0.4
West South Central								
Arkansas	1,786,272	1,778,815	7,457	0.4	1,905,705	1,896,210	9,495	0.5
Louisiana	3,257,022	3,226,465	30,557	0.9	2,677,370	2,647,695	29,675	1.1
Oklahoma	2,328,284	2,308,281	20,003	0.9	2,229,665	2,211,395	18,270	0.8
Texas	9,581,508	9,282,717	298,791	3.1	7,685,665	7,408,150	277,515	3.6
Mountain								
Montana	674,767	644,121	30,646	4.5	587,940	544,555	43,385	7.4
Idaho	667,191	651,649	15,542	2.3	587,440	567,595	19,845	3.4
Wyoming	330,066	320,403	9,663	2.9	289,315	275,925	13,390	4.6
Colorado	1,753,925	1,694,044	59,881	3.4	1,320,905	1,260,340	60,565	4.6
New Mexico	951,023	929,615	21,408	2.3	679,425	661,990	17,435	2.6

Table 14. (Continued)

Region, division, and state	1980*				1970*			
	Total	Foreign born			Total	Foreign born		
		Native	Number	Percent		Native	Number	Percent
Arizona	1,302,161	1,231,843	70,318	5.4	746,655	699,280	47,375	6.3
Utah	890,627	858,494	32,133	3.6	687,400	656,375	31,025	4.5
Nevada	285,278	272,145	13,133	4.6	159,390	148,670	10,720	6.7
Pacific								
Washington	2,853,214	2,674,556	178,658	6.3	2,373,870	2,177,340	196,530	8.3
Oregon	1,768,675	1,697,361	71,314	4.0	1,516,180	1,431,305	84,875	5.6
California	15,720,860	14,377,162	1,343,698	8.5	10,558,925	9,498,550	1,060,375	10.0
Alaska	226,167	217,940	8,227	3.6	(X)	(X)	(X)	(X)
Hawaii	632,772	563,872	68,900	10.9	(X)	(X)	(X)	(X)

Region, division, and state	1940				1930			
	Total	Native	Foreign born		Total	Native	Foreign born	
			Number	Percent			Number	Percent
United States	131,669,275	120,074,379	11,594,896	8.8	122,775,046	108,570,897	14,204,149	11.6
REGION AND DIVISION								
Northeast	35,976,777	29,874,231	6,102,546	17.0	34,427,091	27,225,417	7,201,674	20.9
New England	8,437,290	6,927,318	1,509,972	17.9	8,166,341	6,317,398	1,848,943	22.6
Middle Atlantic	27,539,487	22,946,913	4,592,574	16.7	26,260,750	20,908,019	5,352,731	20.4
Midwest	40,143,332	36,784,366	3,358,966	8.4	38,594,100	34,234,224	4,359,876	11.3
East North Central	26,626,342	24,046,979	2,579,363	9.7	25,297,185	22,021,462	3,275,723	12.9
West North Central	13,516,990	12,737,387	779,603	5.8	13,296,915	12,212,762	1,084,153	8.2
South	41,665,901	41,026,113	639,788	1.5	37,857,633	37,039,019	818,614	2.2
South Atlantic	17,823,151	17,521,183	301,968	1.7	15,793,589	15,474,892	318,697	2.0
East South Central	10,778,225	10,732,377	45,848	0.4	9,887,214	9,827,850	59,364	0.6
West South Central	13,064,525	12,772,553	291,972	2.2	12,176,830	11,736,277	440,553	3.6
West	13,883,265	12,389,669	1,493,596	10.8	11,896,222	10,072,237	1,823,985	15.3

Table 14. (Continued)

Region, division, and state	1940				1930			
	Total	Native	Foreign born		Total	Native	Foreign born	
			Number	Percent			Number	Percent
Mountain	4,150,003	3,881,844	268,159	6.5	3,701,789	3,317,466	384,323	10.4
Pacific	9,733,262	8,507,825	1,225,437	12.6	8,194,433	6,754,771	1,439,662	17.6
STATE								
New England								
Maine	847,226	763,233	83,993	9.9	797,423	696,695	100,728	12.6
New Hampshire	491,524	423,131	68,393	13.9	465,293	382,364	82,929	17.8
Vermont	359,231	327,478	31,753	8.8	359,611	316,510	43,101	12.0
Massachusetts	4,316,721	3,459,063	857,658	19.9	4,249,614	3,183,994	1,065,620	25.1
Rhode Island	713,346	574,468	138,878	19.5	687,497	515,568	171,929	25.0
Connecticut	1,709,242	1,379,945	329,297	19.3	1,606,903	1,222,267	384,636	23.9
Middle Atlantic								
New York	13,479,142	10,562,497	2,916,645	21.6	12,588,066	9,325,788	3,262,278	25.9
New Jersey	4,160,165	3,460,809	699,356	16.8	4,041,334	3,191,296	850,038	21.0
Pennsylvania	9,900,180	8,923,607	976,573	9.9	9,631,350	8,390,935	1,240,415	12.9
East North Central								
Ohio	6,907,612	6,386,839	520,773	7.5	6,646,697	5,997,477	649,220	9.8
Indiana	3,427,796	3,316,804	110,992	3.2	3,238,503	3,095,504	142,999	4.4
Illinois	7,897,241	6,924,846	972,395	12.3	7,630,654	6,388,207	1,242,447	16.3
Michigan	5,256,106	4,569,921	686,185	13.1	4,842,325	3,989,567	852,758	17.6
Wisconsin	3,137,587	2,848,569	289,018	9.2	2,939,006	2,550,707	388,299	13.2
West North Central								
Minnesota	2,792,300	2,496,927	295,373	10.6	2,563,953	2,173,163	390,790	15.2
Iowa	2,538,268	2,420,903	117,365	4.6	2,470,939	2,302,689	168,250	6.8
Missouri	3,784,664	3,670,131	114,533	3.0	3,629,367	3,476,282	153,085	4.2
North Dakota	641,935	567,458	74,477	11.6	680,845	574,974	105,871	15.5
South Dakota	642,961	598,837	44,124	6.9	692,849	626,788	66,061	9.5

Table 14. (Continued)

Region, division, and state	1940				1930			
	Total	Native	Foreign born		Total	Native	Foreign born	
			Number	Percent			Number	Percent
Nebraska	1,315,834	1,233,733	82,101	6.2	1,377,963	1,258,764	119,199	8.7
Kansas	1,801,028	1,749,398	51,630	2.9	1,880,999	1,800,102	80,897	4.3
South Atlantic								
Delaware	266,505	251,592	14,913	5.6	238,380	221,355	17,025	7.1
Maryland	1,821,244	1,738,653	82,591	4.5	1,631,526	1,535,196	96,330	5.9
District of Columbia	663,091	628,175	34,916	5.3	486,869	456,136	30,733	6.3
Virginia	2,677,773	2,654,335	23,438	0.9	2,421,851	2,397,484	24,367	1.0
West Virginia	1,901,974	1,860,075	41,899	2.2	1,729,205	1,677,340	51,865	3.0
North Carolina	3,571,623	3,562,411	9,212	0.3	3,170,276	3,161,307	8,969	0.3
South Carolina	1,899,804	1,894,825	4,979	0.3	1,738,765	1,733,407	5,358	0.3
Georgia	3,123,723	3,111,542	12,181	0.4	2,908,506	2,894,203	14,303	0.5
Florida	1,897,414	1,819,575	77,839	4.1	1,468,211	1,398,464	69,747	4.8
East South Central								
Kentucky	2,845,627	2,829,883	15,744	0.6	2,614,589	2,592,582	22,007	0.8
Tennessee	2,915,841	2,904,373	11,468	0.4	2,616,556	2,603,305	13,251	0.5
Alabama	2,832,961	2,820,797	12,164	0.4	2,646,248	2,630,187	16,061	0.6
Mississippi	2,183,796	2,177,324	6,472	0.3	2,009,821	2,001,776	8,045	0.4
West South Central								
Arkansas	1,949,387	1,941,461	7,926	0.4	1,854,482	1,843,850	10,632	0.6
Louisiana	2,363,880	2,335,907	27,973	1.2	2,101,593	2,064,517	37,076	1.8
Oklahoma	2,336,434	2,315,889	20,545	0.9	2,396,040	2,365,482	30,558	1.3
Texas	6,414,824	6,179,296	235,528	3.7	5,824,715	5,462,428	362,287	6.2
Mountain								
Montana	559,456	503,092	56,364	10.1	537,606	461,703	75,903	14.1
Idaho	524,873	500,161	24,712	4.7	445,032	412,748	32,284	7.3
Wyoming	250,742	233,635	17,107	6.8	225,565	202,222	23,343	10.3

Table 14. (Continued)

Region, division, and state	1940				1930			
	Total	Native	Foreign born		Total	Native	Foreign born	
			Number	Percent			Number	Percent
Colorado	1,123,296	1,051,732	71,564	6.4	1,035,791	935,916	99,875	9.6
New Mexico	531,818	516,416	15,402	2.9	423,317	399,265	24,052	5.7
Arizona	499,261	460,568	38,693	7.8	435,573	369,817	65,756	15.1
Utah	550,310	517,034	33,276	6.0	507,847	459,832	48,015	9.5
Nevada	110,247	99,206	11,041	10.0	91,058	75,963	15,095	16.6
Pacific								
Washington	1,736,191	1,525,812	210,379	12.1	1,563,396	1,308,138	255,258	16.3
Oregon	1,089,684	999,491	90,193	8.3	953,786	843,346	110,440	11.6
California	6,907,387	5,982,522	924,865	13.4	5,677,251	4,603,287	1,073,964	18.9
Alaska	(X)	(X)	(X)	(X)	(X)	(X)	(X)	(X)
Hawaii	(X)	(X)	(X)	(X)	(X)	(X)	(X)	(X)

Region, division, and state	1920				1910			
	Total	Native	Foreign born		Total	Native	Foreign born	
			Number	Percent			Number	Percent
United States	105,710,620	91,789,928	13,920,692	13.2	91,972,266	78,456,380	13,515,886	14.7
REGION AND DIVISION								
Northeast	29,662,053	22,815,690	6,846,363	23.1	25,868,573	19,192,290	6,676,283	25.8
New England	7,400,909	5,514,964	1,885,945	25.5	6,552,681	4,727,571	1,825,110	27.9
Middle Atlantic	22,261,144	17,300,726	4,960,418	22.3	19,315,892	14,464,719	4,851,173	25.1
Midwest	34,019,792	29,411,998	4,607,794	13.5	29,888,542	25,198,081	4,690,461	15.7
East North Central	21,475,543	18,243,402	3,232,141	15.1	18,250,621	15,176,855	3,073,766	16.8
West North Central	12,544,249	11,168,596	1,375,653	11.0	11,637,921	10,021,226	1,616,695	13.9
South	33,125,803	32,257,449	868,354	2.6	29,389,330	28,649,319	740,011	2.5
South Atlantic	13,990,272	13,659,735	330,537	2.4	12,194,895	11,894,901	299,994	2.5
East South Central	8,893,307	8,820,318	72,989	0.8	8,409,901	8,322,076	87,825	1.0

Table 14. (Continued)

Region, division, and state	1920				1910			
	Total	Native	Foreign born		Total	Native	Foreign born	
			Number	Percent			Number	Percent
West South Central	10,242,224	9,777,396	464,828	4.5	8,784,534	8,432,342	352,192	4.0
West	8,902,972	7,304,791	1,598,181	18.0	6,825,821	5,416,690	1,409,131	20.6
Mountain	3,336,101	2,868,481	467,620	14.0	2,633,517	2,180,195	453,322	17.2
Pacific	5,566,871	4,436,310	1,130,561	20.3	4,192,304	3,236,495	955,809	22.8
STATE								
New England								
Maine	768,014	660,200	107,814	14.0	742,371	631,809	110,562	14.9
New Hampshire	443,083	351,686	91,397	20.6	430,572	333,905	96,667	22.5
Vermont	352,428	307,870	44,558	12.6	355,956	306,035	49,921	14.0
Massachusetts	3,852,356	2,763,808	1,088,548	28.3	3,366,416	2,307,171	1,059,245	31.5
Rhode Island	604,397	429,208	175,189	29.0	542,610	363,469	179,141	33.0
Connecticut	1,380,631	1,002,192	378,439	27.4	1,114,756	785,182	329,574	29.6
Middle Atlantic								
New York	10,385,227	7,559,852	2,825,375	27.2	9,113,614	6,365,603	2,748,011	30.2
New Jersey	3,155,900	2,413,414	742,486	23.5	2,537,167	1,876,379	660,788	26.0
Pennsylvania	8,720,017	7,327,460	1,392,557	16.0	7,665,111	6,222,737	1,442,374	18.8
East North Central								
Ohio	5,759,394	5,078,942	680,452	11.8	4,767,121	4,168,747	598,374	12.6
Indiana	2,930,390	2,779,062	151,328	5.2	2,700,876	2,541,213	159,663	5.9
Illinois	6,485,280	5,274,696	1,210,584	18.7	5,638,591	4,433,277	1,205,314	21.4
Michigan	3,668,412	2,939,120	729,292	19.9	2,810,173	2,212,623	597,550	21.3
Wisconsin	2,632,067	2,171,582	460,485	17.5	2,333,860	1,820,995	512,865	22.0
West North Central								
Minnesota	2,387,125	1,900,330	486,795	20.4	2,075,708	1,532,113	543,595	26.2
Iowa	2,404,021	2,178,027	225,994	9.4	2,224,771	1,951,006	273,765	12.3
Missouri	3,404,055	3,217,220	186,835	5.5	3,293,335	3,063,556	229,779	7.0

Table 14. (Continued)

Region, division, and state	1920				1910			
	Total	Native	Foreign born		Total	Native	Foreign born	
			Number	Percent			Number	Percent
North Dakota	646,872	515,009	131,863	20.4	577,056	420,402	156,654	27.1
South Dakota	636,547	554,013	82,534	13.0	583,888	483,098	100,790	17.3
Nebraska	1,296,372	1,145,707	150,665	11.6	1,192,214	1,015,552	176,662	14.8
Kansas	1,769,257	1,658,290	110,967	6.3	1,690,949	1,555,499	135,450	8.0
South Atlantic								
Delaware	223,003	203,102	19,901	8.9	202,322	184,830	17,492	8.6
Maryland	1,449,661	1,346,482	103,179	7.1	1,295,346	1,190,402	104,944	8.1
District of Columbia	437,571	408,206	29,365	6.7	331,069	306,167	24,902	7.5
Virginia	2,309,187	2,277,482	31,705	1.4	2,061,612	2,034,555	27,057	1.3
West Virginia	1,463,701	1,401,596	62,105	4.2	1,221,119	1,163,901	57,218	4.7
North Carolina	2,559,123	2,551,851	7,272	0.3	2,206,287	2,200,195	6,092	0.3
South Carolina	1,683,724	1,677,142	6,582	0.4	1,515,400	1,509,221	6,179	0.4
Georgia	2,895,832	2,879,268	16,564	0.6	2,609,121	2,593,644	15,477	0.6
Florida	968,470	914,606	53,864	5.6	752,619	711,986	40,633	5.4
East South Central								
Kentucky	2,416,630	2,385,724	30,906	1.3	2,289,905	2,249,743	40,162	1.8
Tennessee	2,337,885	2,322,237	15,648	0.7	2,184,789	2,166,182	18,607	0.9
Alabama	2,348,174	2,330,147	18,027	0.8	2,138,093	2,118,807	19,286	0.9
Mississippi	1,790,618	1,782,210	8,408	0.5	1,797,114	1,787,344	9,770	0.5
West South Central								
Arkansas	1,752,204	1,738,067	14,137	0.8	1,574,449	1,557,403	17,046	1.1
Louisiana	1,798,509	1,752,082	46,427	2.6	1,656,388	1,603,622	52,766	3.2
Oklahoma	2,028,283	1,987,851	40,432	2.0	1,657,155	1,616,713	40,442	2.4
Texas	4,663,228	4,299,396	363,832	7.8	3,896,542	3,654,604	241,938	6.2
Mountain								
Montana	548,889	453,298	95,591	17.4	376,053	281,340	94,713	25.2

Table 14. (Continued)

Region, division, and state	1920				1910			
	Total	Native	Foreign born		Total	Native	Foreign born	
			Number	Percent			Number	Percent
Idaho	431,866	391,119	40,747	9.4	325,594	283,016	42,578	13.1
Wyoming	194,402	167,835	26,567	13.7	145,965	116,945	29,020	19.9
Colorado	939,629	820,491	119,138	12.7	799,024	669,437	129,587	16.2
New Mexico	360,350	330,542	29,808	8.3	327,301	304,155	23,146	7.1
Arizona	334,162	253,596	80,566	24.1	204,354	155,589	48,765	23.9
Utah	449,396	390,196	59,200	13.2	373,351	307,529	65,822	17.6
Nevada	77,407	61,404	16,003	20.7	81,875	62,184	19,691	24.1
Pacific								
Washington	1,356,621	1,091,329	265,292	19.6	1,141,990	885,749	256,241	22.4
Oregon	783,389	675,745	107,644	13.7	672,765	559,629	113,136	16.8
California	3,426,861	2,669,236	757,625	22.1	2,377,549	1,791,117	586,432	24.7
Alaska	(X)	(X)	(X)	(X)	(X)	(X)	(X)	(X)
Hawaii	(X)	(X)	(X)	(X)	(X)	(X)	(X)	(X)

Region, division, and state	1900				1890			
	Total	Native	Foreign born		Total	Native	Foreign born	
			Number	Percent			Number	Percent
United States	75,994,575	65,653,299	10,341,276	13.6	62,622,250	53,372,703	9,249,547	14.8
REGION AND DIVISION								
Northeast	21,046,695	16,283,899	4,762,796	22.6	17,401,545	13,513,368	3,888,177	22.3
New England	5,592,017	4,146,780	1,445,237	25.8	4,700,745	3,558,313	1,142,432	24.3
Middle Atlantic	15,454,678	12,137,119	3,317,559	21.5	12,700,800	9,955,055	2,745,745	21.6
Midwest	26,333,004	22,174,530	4,158,474	15.8	22,362,279	18,302,165	4,060,114	18.2
East North Central	15,985,581	13,360,355	2,625,226	16.4	13,471,840	10,960,916	2,510,924	18.6
West North Central	10,347,423	8,814,175	1,533,248	14.8	8,890,439	7,341,249	1,549,190	17.4
South	24,523,527	23,949,842	573,685	2.3	19,830,813	19,300,467	530,346	2.7

Table 14. (Continued)

Region, division, and state	1900				1890			
	Total	Native	Foreign born		Total	Native	Foreign born	
			Number	Percent			Number	Percent
South Atlantic	10,443,480	10,227,450	216,030	2.1	8,857,920	8,649,395	208,525	2.4
East South Central	7,547,757	7,457,189	90,568	1.2	6,428,770	6,326,656	102,114	1.6
West South Central	6,532,290	6,265,203	267,087	4.1	4,544,123	4,324,416	219,707	4.8
West	4,091,349	3,245,028	846,321	20.7	3,027,613	2,256,703	770,910	25.5
Mountain	1,674,657	1,372,688	301,969	18.0	1,156,326	899,047	257,279	22.2
Pacific	2,416,692	1,872,340	544,352	22.5	1,871,287	1,357,656	513,631	27.4
STATE								
New England								
Maine	694,466	601,136	93,330	13.4	661,086	582,125	78,961	11.9
New Hampshire	411,588	323,481	88,107	21.4	376,530	304,190	72,340	19.2
Vermont	343,641	298,894	44,747	13.0	332,422	288,334	44,088	13.3
Massachusetts	2,805,346	1,959,022	846,324	30.2	2,238,943	1,581,806	657,137	29.4
Rhode Island	428,556	294,037	134,519	31.4	345,506	239,201	106,305	30.8
Connecticut	908,420	670,210	238,210	26.2	746,258	562,657	183,601	24.6
Middle Atlantic								
New York	7,268,894	5,368,469	1,900,425	26.1	5,997,853	4,426,803	1,571,050	26.2
New Jersey	1,883,669	1,451,785	431,884	22.9	1,444,933	1,115,958	328,975	22.8
Pennsylvania	6,302,115	5,316,865	985,250	15.6	5,258,014	4,412,294	845,720	16.1
East North Central								
Ohio	4,157,545	3,698,811	458,734	11.0	3,672,316	3,213,023	459,293	12.5
Indiana	2,516,462	2,374,341	142,121	5.6	2,192,404	2,046,199	146,205	6.7
Illinois	4,821,550	3,854,803	966,747	20.1	3,826,351	2,984,004	842,347	22.0
Michigan	2,420,982	1,879,329	541,653	22.4	2,093,889	1,550,009	543,880	26.0
Wisconsin	2,069,042	1,553,071	515,971	24.9	1,686,880	1,167,681	519,199	30.8
West North Central								
Minnesota	1,751,394	1,246,076	505,318	28.9	1,301,826	834,470	467,356	35.9

Table 14. (Continued)

Region, division, and state	1900				1890			
	Total	Native	Foreign born		Total	Native	Foreign born	
			Number	Percent			Number	Percent
Iowa	2,231,853	1,925,933	305,920	13.7	1,911,896	1,587,827	324,069	17.0
Missouri	3,106,665	2,890,286	216,379	7.0	2,679,184	2,444,315	234,869	8.8
North Dakota	319,146	206,055	113,091	35.4	182,719	101,258	81,461	44.6
South Dakota	401,570	313,062	88,508	22.0	328,808	237,753	91,055	27.7
Nebraska	1,066,300	888,953	177,347	16.6	1,058,910	856,368	202,542	19.1
Kansas	1,470,495	1,343,810	126,685	8.6	1,427,096	1,279,258	147,838	10.4
South Atlantic								
Delaware	184,735	170,925	13,810	7.5	168,493	155,332	13,161	7.8
Maryland	1,188,044	1,094,110	93,934	7.9	1,042,390	948,094	94,296	9.0
District of Columbia	278,718	258,599	20,119	7.2	230,392	211,622	18,770	8.1
Virginia	1,854,184	1,834,723	19,461	1.0	1,655,980	1,637,606	18,374	1.1
West Virginia	958,800	936,349	22,451	2.3	762,794	743,911	18,883	2.5
North Carolina	1,893,810	1,889,318	4,492	0.2	1,617,947	1,614,245	3,702	0.2
South Carolina	1,340,316	1,334,788	5,528	0.4	1,151,149	1,144,879	6,270	0.5
Georgia	2,216,331	2,203,928	12,403	0.6	1,837,353	1,825,216	12,137	0.7
Florida	528,542	504,710	23,832	4.5	391,422	368,490	22,932	5.9
East South Central								
Kentucky	2,147,174	2,096,925	50,249	2.3	1,858,635	1,799,279	59,356	3.2
Tennessee	2,020,616	2,002,870	17,746	0.9	1,767,518	1,747,489	20,029	1.1
Alabama	1,828,697	1,814,105	14,592	0.8	1,513,017	1,498,240	14,777	1.0
Mississippi	1,551,270	1,543,289	7,981	0.5	1,289,600	1,281,648	7,952	0.6
West South Central								
Arkansas	1,311,564	1,297,275	14,289	1.1	1,128,179	1,113,915	14,264	1.3
Louisiana	1,381,625	1,328,722	52,903	3.8	1,118,587	1,068,840	49,747	4.4
Oklahoma [1]	790,391	769,853	20,538	2.6	61,834	59,094	2,740	4.4
Texas	3,048,710	2,869,353	179,357	5.9	2,235,523	2,082,567	152,956	6.8

Table 14. (Continued)

Region, division, and state	1900				1890			
	Total	Native	Foreign born		Total	Native	Foreign born	
			Number	Percent			Number	Percent
Mountain								
Montana	243,329	176,262	67,067	27.6	132,159	89,063	43,096	32.6
Idaho	161,772	137,168	24,604	15.2	84,385	66,929	17,456	20.7
Wyoming	92,531	75,116	17,415	18.8	60,705	45,792	14,913	24.6
Colorado	539,700	448,545	91,155	16.9	412,198	328,208	83,990	20.4
New Mexico	195,310	181,685	13,625	7.0	153,593	142,334	11,259	7.3
Arizona	122,931	98,698	24,233	19.7	59,620	40,825	18,795	31.5
Utah	276,749	222,972	53,777	19.4	207,905	154,841	53,064	25.5
Nevada	42,335	32,242	10,093	23.8	45,761	31,055	14,706	32.1
Pacific								
Washington	518,103	406,739	111,364	21.5	349,390	259,385	90,005	25.8
Oregon	413,536	347,788	65,748	15.9	313,767	256,450	57,317	18.3
California	1,485,053	1,117,813	367,240	24.7	1,208,130	841,821	366,309	30.3
Alaska	(X)	(X)	(X)	(X)	(X)	(X)	(X)	(X)
Hawaii	(X)	(X)	(X)	(X)	(X)	(X)	(X)	(X)

Region, division, and state	1880				1870			
	Total	Native	Foreign born		Total	Native	Foreign born	
			Number	Percent			Number	Percent
United States	50,155,783	43,475,840	6,679,943	13.3	38,558,371	32,991,142	5,567,229	14.4
REGION AND DIVISION								
Northeast	14,507,407	11,692,887	2,814,520	19.4	12,298,730	9,778,124	2,520,606	20.5
New England	4,010,529	3,216,917	793,612	19.8	3,487,924	2,839,923	648,001	18.6
Middle Atlantic	10,496,878	8,475,970	2,020,908	19.3	8,810,806	6,938,201	1,872,605	21.3
Midwest	17,364,111	14,447,282	2,916,829	16.8	12,981,111	10,647,826	2,333,285	18.0
East North Central	11,206,668	9,290,038	1,916,630	17.1	9,124,517	7,462,843	1,661,674	18.2

Table 14. (Continued)

Region, division, and state	1880				1870			
	Total	Native	Foreign born		Total	Native	Foreign born	
			Number	Percent			Number	Percent
West North Central	6,157,443	5,157,244	1,000,199	16.2	3,856,594	3,184,983	671,611	17.4
South	16,516,568	16,068,036	448,532	2.7	12,288,020	11,888,045	399,975	3.3
South Atlantic	7,597,197	7,422,939	174,258	2.3	5,853,610	5,686,766	166,844	2.9
East South Central	5,585,151	5,489,989	95,162	1.7	4,404,445	4,300,578	103,867	2.4
West South Central	3,334,220	3,155,108	179,112	5.4	2,029,965	1,900,701	129,264	6.4
West	1,767,697	1,267,635	500,062	28.3	990,510	677,147	313,363	31.6
Mountain	653,119	492,237	160,882	24.6	315,385	228,477	86,908	27.6
Pacific	1,114,578	775,398	339,180	30.4	675,125	448,670	226,455	33.5
STATE								
New England								
Maine	648,936	590,053	58,883	9.1	626,915	578,034	48,881	7.8
New Hampshire	346,991	300,697	46,294	13.3	318,300	288,689	29,611	9.3
Vermont	332,286	291,327	40,959	12.3	330,551	283,396	47,155	14.3
Massachusetts	1,783,085	1,339,594	443,491	24.9	1,457,351	1,104,032	353,319	24.2
Rhode Island	276,531	202,538	73,993	26.8	217,353	161,957	55,396	25.5
Connecticut	622,700	492,708	129,992	20.9	537,454	423,815	113,639	21.1
Middle Atlantic								
New York	5,082,871	3,871,492	1,211,379	23.8	4,382,759	3,244,406	1,138,353	26.0
New Jersey	1,131,116	909,416	221,700	19.6	906,096	717,153	188,943	20.9
Pennsylvania	4,282,891	3,695,062	587,829	13.7	3,521,951	2,976,642	545,309	15.5
East North Central								
Ohio	3,198,062	2,803,119	394,943	12.3	2,665,260	2,292,767	372,493	14.0
Indiana	1,978,301	1,834,123	144,178	7.3	1,680,637	1,539,163	141,474	8.4
Illinois	3,077,871	2,494,295	583,576	19.0	2,539,891	2,024,693	515,198	20.3
Michigan	1,636,937	1,248,429	388,508	23.7	1,184,059	916,049	268,010	22.6
Wisconsin	1,315,497	910,072	405,425	30.8	1,054,670	690,171	364,499	34.6

Table 14. (Continued)

Region, division, and state	1880				1870			
	Total	Native	Foreign born		Total	Native	Foreign born	
			Number	Percent			Number	Percent
West North Central								
Minnesota	780,773	513,097	267,676	34.3	439,706	279,009	160,697	36.5
Iowa	1,624,615	1,362,965	261,650	16.1	1,194,020	989,328	204,692	17.1
Missouri	2,168,380	1,956,802	211,578	9.8	1,721,295	1,499,028	222,267	12.9
North Dakota [2]	[2]	[2]	[2]	[2]	[2]	[2]	[2]	[2]
South Dakota [2]	135,177	83,382	51,795	38.3	14,181	9,366	4,815	34.0
Nebraska	452,402	354,988	97,414	21.5	122,993	92,245	30,748	25.0
Kansas	996,096	886,010	110,086	11.1	364,399	316,007	48,392	13.3
South Atlantic								
Delaware	146,608	137,140	9,468	6.5	125,015	115,879	9,136	7.3
Maryland	934,943	852,137	82,806	8.9	780,894	697,482	83,412	10.7
District of Columbia	177,624	160,502	17,122	9.6	131,700	115,446	16,254	12.3
Virginia	1,512,565	1,497,869	14,696	1.0	1,225,163	1,211,409	13,754	1.1
West Virginia	618,457	600,192	18,265	3.0	442,014	424,923	17,091	3.9
North Carolina	1,399,750	1,396,008	3,742	0.3	1,071,361	1,068,332	3,029	0.3
South Carolina	995,577	987,891	7,686	0.8	705,606	697,532	8,074	1.1
Georgia	1,542,180	1,531,616	10,564	0.7	1,184,109	1,172,982	11,127	0.9
Florida	269,493	259,584	9,909	3.7	187,748	182,781	4,967	2.6
East South Central								
Kentucky	1,648,690	1,589,173	59,517	3.6	1,321,011	1,257,613	63,398	4.8
Tennessee	1,542,359	1,525,657	16,702	1.1	1,258,520	1,239,204	19,316	1.5
Alabama	1,262,505	1,252,771	9,734	0.8	996,992	987,030	9,962	1.0
Mississippi	1,131,597	1,122,388	9,209	0.8	827,922	816,731	11,191	1.4
West South Central								
Arkansas	802,525	792,175	10,350	1.3	484,471	479,445	5,026	1.0
Louisiana	939,946	885,800	54,146	5.8	726,915	665,088	61,827	8.5

Table 14. (Continued)

Region, division, and state	1880				1870			
	Total	Native	Foreign born		Total	Native	Foreign born	
			Number	Percent			Number	Percent
Oklahoma [1]	(NA)	(NA)	(NA)	(NA)	(NA)	(NA)	(NA)	(NA)
Texas	1,591,749	1,477,133	114,616	7.2	818,579	756,168	62,411	7.6
Mountain								
Montana	39,159	27,638	11,521	29.4	20,595	12,616	7,979	38.7
Idaho	32,610	22,636	9,974	30.6	14,999	7,114	7,885	52.6
Wyoming	20,789	14,939	5,850	28.1	9,118	5,605	3,513	38.5
Colorado	194,327	154,537	39,790	20.5	39,864	33,265	6,599	16.6
New Mexico	119,565	111,514	8,051	6.7	91,874	86,254	5,620	6.1
Arizona	40,440	24,391	16,049	39.7	9,658	3,849	5,809	60.1
Utah	143,963	99,969	43,994	30.6	86,786	56,084	30,702	35.4
Nevada	62,266	36,613	25,653	41.2	42,491	23,690	18,801	44.2
Pacific								
Washington	75,116	59,313	15,803	21.0	23,955	18,931	5,024	21.0
Oregon	174,768	144,265	30,503	17.5	90,923	79,323	11,600	12.8
California	864,694	571,820	292,874	33.9	560,247	350,416	209,831	37.5
Alaska	(X)	(X)	(X)	(X)	(X)	(X)	(X)	(X)
Hawaii	(X)	(X)	(X)	(X)	(X)	(X)	(X)	(X)

Region, division, and state	1860				1850			
	Total	Native	Foreign born		Total	Native	Foreign born	
			Number	Percent			Number	Percent
United States	31,443,321	27,304,624	4,138,697	13.2	23,191,876	20,947,274	2,244,602	9.7
REGION AND DIVISION								
Northeast	10,594,268	8,570,363	2,023,905	19.1	8,626,851	7,301,308	1,325,543	15.4
New England	3,135,283	2,665,953	469,330	15.0	2,728,116	2,421,867	306,249	11.2
Middle Atlantic	7,458,985	5,904,410	1,554,575	20.8	5,898,735	4,879,441	1,019,294	17.3

Table 14. (Continued)

Region, division, and state	1860				1850			
	Total	Native	Foreign born		Total	Native	Foreign born	
			Number	Percent			Number	Percent
Midwest	9,096,716	7,553,358	1,543,358	17.0	5,403,595	4,753,220	650,375	12.0
East North Central	6,926,884	5,729,688	1,197,196	17.3	4,523,260	3,972,423	550,837	12.2
West North Central	2,169,832	1,823,670	346,162	16.0	880,335	780,797	99,538	11.3
South	11,133,361	10,740,929	392,432	3.5	8,982,612	8,740,947	241,665	2.7
South Atlantic	5,364,703	5,202,203	162,500	3.0	4,679,090	4,574,180	104,910	2.2
East South Central	4,020,991	3,919,056	101,935	2.5	3,363,271	3,313,901	49,370	1.5
West South Central	1,747,667	1,619,670	127,997	7.3	940,251	852,866	87,385	9.3
West	618,976	439,974	179,002	28.9	178,818	151,799	27,019	15.1
Mountain	174,923	150,716	24,207	13.8	72,927	68,732	4,195	5.8
Pacific	444,053	289,258	154,795	34.9	105,891	83,067	22,824	21.6
STATE								
New England								
Maine	628,279	590,826	37,453	6.0	583,169	551,344	31,825	5.5
New Hampshire	326,073	305,135	20,938	6.4	317,976	303,711	14,265	4.5
Vermont	315,098	282,355	32,743	10.4	314,120	280,405	33,715	10.7
Massachusetts	1,231,066	970,960	260,106	21.1	994,514	830,490	164,024	16.5
Rhode Island	174,620	137,226	37,394	21.4	147,545	123,643	23,902	16.2
Connecticut	460,147	379,451	80,696	17.5	370,792	332,274	38,518	10.4
Middle Atlantic								
New York	3,880,735	2,879,455	1,001,280	25.8	3,097,394	2,441,465	655,929	21.2
New Jersey	672,035	549,245	122,790	18.3	489,555	429,607	59,948	12.2
Pennsylvania	2,906,215	2,475,710	430,505	14.8	2,311,786	2,008,369	303,417	13.1
East North Central								
Ohio	2,339,511	2,011,262	328,249	14.0	1,980,329	1,762,136	218,193	11.0
Indiana	1,350,428	1,232,144	118,284	8.8	988,416	932,844	55,572	5.6
Illinois	1,711,951	1,387,308	324,643	19.0	851,470	739,578	111,892	13.1

Table 14. (Continued)

Region, division, and state	1860				1850			
	Total	Native	Foreign born		Total	Native	Foreign born	
			Number	Percent			Number	Percent
Michigan	749,113	600,020	149,093	19.9	397,654	342,951	54,703	13.8
Wisconsin	775,881	498,954	276,927	35.7	305,391	194,914	110,477	36.2
West North Central								
Minnesota	172,023	113,295	58,728	34.1	6,077	4,100	1,977	32.5
Iowa	674,913	568,836	106,077	15.7	192,214	171,245	20,969	10.9
Missouri	1,182,012	1,021,471	160,541	13.6	682,044	605,452	76,592	11.2
North Dakota [2]	[2]	[2]	[2]	[2]	(NA)	(NA)	(NA)	(NA)
South Dakota [2]	4,837	3,063	1,774	36.7	(NA)	(NA)	(NA)	(NA)
Nebraska	28,841	22,490	6,351	22.0	(NA)	(NA)	(NA)	(NA)
Kansas	107,206	94,515	12,691	11.8	(NA)	(NA)	(NA)	(NA)
South Atlantic								
Delaware	112,216	103,051	9,165	8.2	91,532	86,279	5,253	5.7
Maryland	687,049	609,520	77,529	11.3	583,034	531,825	51,209	8.8
District of Columbia	75,080	62,596	12,484	16.6	51,687	46,769	4,918	9.5
Virginia [3]	1,596,318	1,561,260	35,058	2.2	1,421,661	1,398,676	22,985	1.6
West Virginia [3]	[3]	[3]	[3]	[3]	[3]	[3]	[3]	[3]
North Carolina	992,622	989,324	3,298	0.3	869,039	866,458	2,581	0.3
South Carolina	703,708	693,722	9,986	1.4	668,507	659,800	8,707	1.3
Georgia	1,057,286	1,045,615	11,671	1.1	906,185	899,697	6,488	0.7
Florida	140,424	137,115	3,309	2.4	87,445	84,676	2,769	3.2
East South Central								
Kentucky	1,155,684	1,095,885	59,799	5.2	982,405	950,985	31,420	3.2
Tennessee	1,109,801	1,088,575	21,226	1.9	1,002,717	997,064	5,653	0.6
Alabama	964,201	951,849	12,352	1.3	771,623	764,114	7,509	1.0
Mississippi	791,305	782,747	8,558	1.1	606,526	601,738	4,788	0.8
West South Central								

Table 14. (Continued)

Region, division, and state	1860				1850			
	Total	Native	Foreign born		Total	Native	Foreign born	
			Number	Percent			Number	Percent
Arkansas	435,450	431,850	3,600	0.8	209,897	208,426	1,471	0.7
Louisiana	708,002	627,027	80,975	11.4	517,762	449,529	68,233	13.2
Oklahoma [1]	(NA)	(NA)	(NA)	(NA)	(NA)	(NA)	(NA)	(NA)
Texas	604,215	560,793	43,422	7.2	212,592	194,911	17,681	8.3
Mountain								
Montana	(NA)	(NA)	(NA)	(NA)	(NA)	(NA)	(NA)	(NA)
Idaho	(NA)	(NA)	(NA)	(NA)	(NA)	(NA)	(NA)	(NA)
Wyoming	(NA)	(NA)	(NA)	(NA)	(NA)	(NA)	(NA)	(NA)
Colorado	34,277	31,611	2,666	7.8	(NA)	(NA)	(NA)	(NA)
New Mexico	93,516	86,793	6,723	7.2	61,547	59,396	2,151	3.5
Arizona	(NA)	(NA)	(NA)	(NA)	(NA)	(NA)	(NA)	(NA)
Utah	40,273	27,519	12,754	31.7	11,380	9,336	2,044	18.0
Nevada	6,857	4,793	2,064	30.1	(NA)	(NA)	(NA)	(NA)
Pacific								
Washington	11,594	8,450	3,144	27.1	(NA)	(NA)	(NA)	(NA)
Oregon	52,465	47,342	5,123	9.8	13,294	12,272	1,022	7.7
California	379,994	233,466	146,528	38.6	92,597	70,795	21,802	23.5
Alaska	(X)	(X)	(X)	(X)	(X)	(X)	(X)	(X)
Hawaii	(X)	(X)	(X)	(X)	(X)	(X)	(X)	(X)

Footnotes:

* Indicates sample data.

(X) Not applicable. Alaska and Hawaii prior to 1960 are in this category.

(NA) Not available. Geographic area not enumerated.

[1]Data shown for 1900 for Oklahoma include Oklahoma Territory and the Indian Territory, which were merged and admitted as the state of Oklahoma in 1907. Population of Oklahoma Territory in 1900: total, 398,331; native, 382,651; foreign-born, 15,680; percent foreign-born, 3.9. Population of Indian Territory in 1900: total 392,060; native 387,202; foreign-born, 4,858; percent foreign-born, 1.2 (1900 census, Vol. 1, Part 1, Dubester # 252, Table 9, p. 482).

[2]Data shown for 1860 to 1880 for South Dakota are for the Dakota Territory and include North Dakota. South Dakota and North Dakota were formed from Dakota Territory and admitted as states in 1889.

[3]Data shown for 1850 and 1860 for Virginia include the present area of West Virginia, which was admitted as a separate state in 1863. Internet Release Date: February 2, 2006

Table 15. Foreign-Born Population by Historical Section and Subsection of the United States: 1850 to 2000 (Leading dots indicate subparts)

(See text for sources, definitions, and explanations)

Historical section and subsection [1]	Total	North			South			
		Total	Northeast	North Central	Total	Southeast	South Central	West
(Region as currently defined)[1]			(Northeast)	(Midwest)	(South)			(West)
FOREIGN-BORN POPULATION								
2000*	31,107,889	10,739,005	7,229,068	3,509,937	8,608,441	5,020,522	3,587,919	11,760,443
1990*	19,767,316	7,362,317	5,231,024	2,131,293	4,582,293	2,722,945	1,859,348	7,822,706
1980*	14,079,906	6,620,113	4,505,923	2,114,190	2,894,757	1,728,917	1,165,840	4,565,036
1970*	9,619,302	5,993,242	4,119,681	1,873,561	1,316,205	878,754	437,451	2,309,855
1960*	9,738,143	6,851,702	4,574,743	2,276,959	962,920	550,426	412,494	1,923,521
1950*	10,347,395	7,994,555	5,287,165	2,707,390	767,320	380,395	386,925	1,585,520
1940	11,594,896	9,461,512	6,102,546	3,358,966	639,788	301,968	337,820	1,493,596
1930	14,204,149	11,561,550	7,201,674	4,359,876	818,614	318,697	499,917	1,823,985
1920	13,920,692	11,454,157	6,846,363	4,607,794	868,354	330,537	537,817	1,598,181
1910	13,515,886	11,366,744	6,676,283	4,690,461	740,011	299,994	440,017	1,409,131
1900	10,341,276	8,921,270	4,762,796	4,158,474	573,685	216,030	357,655	846,321
1890	9,249,547	7,948,291	3,888,177	4,060,114	530,346	208,525	321,821	770,910
1880	6,679,943	5,731,349	2,814,520	2,916,829	448,532	174,258	274,274	500,062
1870	5,567,229	4,853,891	2,520,606	2,333,285	399,975	166,844	233,131	313,363
1860	4,138,697	3,567,263	2,023,905	1,543,358	392,432	162,500	229,932	179,002
1850	2,244,602	1,975,918	1,325,543	650,375	241,665	104,910	136,755	27,019

Table 15. (Continued)

Historical section and subsection [1]	Total	North			South			
		Total	Northeast	North Central	Total	Southeast	South Central	West
(Region as currently defined)[1]			(Northeast)	(Midwest)	(South)			(West)
PERCENT DISTRIBUTION								
2000*	100.0	34.5	23.2	11.3	27.7	16.1	11.5	37.8
1990*	100.0	37.2	26.5	10.8	23.2	13.8	9.4	39.6
1980*	100.0	47.0	32.0	15.0	20.6	12.3	8.3	32.4
1970*	100.0	62.3	42.8	19.5	13.7	9.1	4.5	24.0
1960*	100.0	70.4	47.0	23.4	9.9	5.7	4.2	19.8
1950*	100.0	77.3	51.1	26.2	7.4	3.7	3.7	15.3
1940	100.0	81.6	52.6	29.0	5.5	2.6	2.9	12.9
1930	100.0	81.4	50.7	30.7	5.8	2.2	3.5	12.8
1920	100.0	82.3	49.2	33.1	6.2	2.4	3.9	11.5
1910	100.0	84.1	49.4	34.7	5.5	2.2	3.3	10.4
1900	100.0	86.3	46.1	40.2	5.5	2.1	3.5	8.2
1890	100.0	85.9	42.0	43.9	5.7	2.3	3.5	8.3
1880	100.0	85.8	42.1	43.7	6.7	2.6	4.1	7.5
1870	100.0	87.2	45.3	41.9	7.2	3.0	4.2	5.6
1860	100.0	86.2	48.9	37.3	9.5	3.9	5.6	4.3
1850	100.0	88.0	59.1	29.0	10.8	4.7	6.1	1.2

Footnotes:

* Indicates sample data.

[1] See text for Table 15 concerning regions and historical sections and subsections. See Table 14 for states in each region, and in each historical ection or subsection. The Southeast subsection corresponds to the South Atlantic division. The South Central subsection corresponds to the East outh Central division and the West South Central division combined. Internet Release Date: February 2, 2006

Table 16. Nativity of the Population by Type of Residence: 1960 to 2000 (Leading dots indicate subparts)

(See text for sources, definitions, and explanations)

Year and type of residence [1]	Population				Percent distribution by type of residence		
	Total	Native	Foreign born		Total	Native	Foreign born
			Number	Percent			
2000* (as defined effective June 6, 2003)							
Total	281,421,906	250,314,017	31,107,889	11.1	100.0	100.0	100.0
Inside core-based statistical area	261,534,991	230,859,424	30,675,567	11.7	92.9	92.2	98.6
Inside metropolitan statistical area	232,579,940	202,912,859	29,667,081	12.8	82.6	81.1	95.4
Inside principal cities	92,445,101	76,738,919	15,706,182	17.0	32.8	30.7	50.5
Outside principal cities	140,134,836	126,173,940	13,960,896	10.0	49.8	50.4	44.9
1,000,000 or more population	149,245,561	125,230,619	24,014,942	16.1	53.0	50.0	77.2
Inside principal cities	59,429,528	46,671,632	12,757,896	21.5	21.1	18.6	41.0
Outside principal cities	89,816,033	78,558,987	11,257,046	12.5	31.9	31.4	36.2
5,000,000 or more population	55,643,200	42,103,586	13,539,614	24.3	19.8	16.8	43.5
Inside principal cities	24,632,577	17,097,984	7,534,593	30.6	8.8	6.8	24.2
Outside principal cities	31,010,623	25,005,602	6,005,021	19.4	11.0	10.0	19.3
1,000,000 to 4,999,999 population	93,602,361	83,127,033	10,475,328	11.2	33.3	33.2	33.7
Inside principal cities	34,796,951	29,573,648	5,223,303	15.0	12.4	11.8	16.8
Outside principal cities	58,805,410	53,553,385	5,252,025	8.9	20.9	21.4	16.9
Less than 1,000,000 population	83,334,379	77,682,240	5,652,139	6.8	29.6	31.0	18.2
Inside principal cities	33,015,576	30,067,287	2,948,289	8.9	11.7	12.0	9.5
Outside principal cities	50,318,803	47,614,953	2,703,850	5.4	17.9	19.0	8.7
Inside micropolitan statistical area	28,955,051	27,946,565	1,008,486	3.5	10.3	11.2	3.2
Inside principal cities	9,595,536	9,141,485	454,051	4.7	3.4	3.7	1.5
Outside principal cities	19,359,515	18,805,080	554,435	2.9	6.9	7.5	1.8

Table 16. (Continued)

Year and type of residence [1]	Population				Percent distribution by type of residence		
	Total	Native	Foreign born		Total	Native	Foreign born
			Number	Percent			
Outside core-based statistical area	19,886,915	19,454,593	432,322	2.2	7.1	7.8	1.4
2000* (as defined effective June 30, 1999)							
Total	281,421,906	250,314,017	31,107,889	11.1	100.0	100.0	100.0
Inside metropolitan area	225,981,711	196,614,669	29,367,042	13.0	80.3	78.5	94.4
In central city	85,399,835	71,339,356	14,060,479	16.5	30.3	28.5	45.2
Not in central city	140,581,876	125,275,313	15,306,563	10.9	50.0	50.0	49.2
1,000,000 or more population	161,517,900	136,209,886	25,308,014	15.7	57.4	54.4	81.4
In central city	58,487,504	46,573,992	11,913,512	20.4	20.8	18.6	38.3
Not in central city	103,030,396	89,635,894	13,394,502	13.0	36.6	35.8	43.1
5,000,000 or more population	84,064,275	67,140,949	16,923,326	20.1	29.9	26.8	54.4
In central city	31,187,885	22,813,145	8,374,740	26.9	11.1	9.1	26.9
Not in central city	52,876,390	44,327,804	8,548,586	16.2	18.8	17.7	27.5
1,000,000 to 4,999,999 population	77,453,625	69,068,937	8,384,688	10.8	27.5	27.6	27.0
In central city	27,299,619	23,760,847	3,538,772	13.0	9.7	9.5	11.4
Not in central city	50,154,006	45,308,090	4,845,916	9.7	17.8	18.1	15.6
Less than 1,000,000 population	64,463,811	60,404,783	4,059,028	6.3	22.9	24.1	13.0
In central city	26,912,331	24,765,364	2,146,967	8.0	9.6	9.9	6.9
Not in central city	37,551,480	35,639,419	1,912,061	5.1	13.3	14.2	6.1
Outside metropolitan area	55,440,195	53,699,348	1,740,847	3.1	19.7	21.5	5.6
1990*							
Total	248,709,873	228,942,557	19,767,316	7.9	100.0	100.0	100.0
Inside metropolitan area	192,726,330	174,089,700	18,636,630	9.7	77.5	76.0	94.3
In central city	77,844,025	68,119,147	9,724,878	12.5	31.3	29.8	49.2

Table 16. (Continued)

Year and type of residence [1]	Population				Percent distribution by type of residence		
	Total	Native	Foreign born		Total	Native	Foreign born
			Number	Percent			
Not in central city	114,882,305	105,970,553	8,911,752	7.8	46.2	46.3	45.1
Urban	88,439,931	80,279,433	8,160,498	9.2	35.6	35.1	41.3
Rural	26,442,374	25,691,120	751,254	2.8	10.6	11.2	3.8
Outside metropolitan area	55,983,543	54,852,857	1,130,686	2.0	22.5	24.0	5.7
Urban	20,850,368	20,228,707	621,661	3.0	8.4	8.8	3.1
Rural	35,133,175	34,624,150	509,025	1.4	14.1	15.1	2.6
1980*							
Total	226,545,805	212,465,899	14,079,906	6.2	100.0	100.0	100.0
Inside metropolitan area	169,430,577	156,510,392	12,920,185	7.6	74.8	73.7	91.8
Urban	145,451,315	133,154,205	12,297,110	8.5	64.2	62.7	87.3
In central city	67,854,918	61,249,295	6,605,623	9.7	30.0	28.8	46.9
Not in central city	77,596,397	71,904,910	5,691,487	7.3	34.3	33.8	40.4
Rural	23,979,262	23,356,187	623,075	2.6	10.6	11.0	4.4
Outside metropolitan area	57,115,228	55,955,507	1,159,721	2.0	25.2	26.3	8.2
Urban	21,603,323	20,985,468	617,855	2.9	9.5	9.9	4.4
Rural	35,511,905	34,970,039	541,866	1.5	15.7	16.5	3.8
1970*							
Total	203,210,158	193,590,856	9,619,302	4.7	100.0	100.0	100.0
Inside metropolitan area	139,416,185	130,947,233	8,468,952	6.1	68.6	67.6	88.0
In central city	63,790,354	58,982,208	4,808,146	7.5	31.4	30.5	50.0
Not in central city	75,625,831	71,965,025	3,660,806	4.8	37.2	37.2	38.1
Urban	59,210,598	55,932,053	3,278,545	5.5	29.1	28.9	34.1
Rural	16,415,233	16,032,972	382,261	2.3	8.1	8.3	4.0

Table 16. (Continued)

Year and type of residence [1]	Population				Percent distribution by type of residence		
	Total	Native	Foreign born		Total	Native	Foreign born
			Number	Percent			
Outside metropolitan area	63,793,973	62,643,623	1,150,350	1.8	31.4	32.4	12.0
Urban	26,331,167	25,697,531	633,636	2.4	13.0	13.3	6.6
Rural	37,462,806	36,946,092	516,714	1.4	18.4	19.1	5.4
1960*							
Total	179,325,671	169,587,528	9,738,143	5.4	100.0	100.0	100.0
Inside metropolitan area	112,883,757	104,725,327	8,158,430	7.2	62.9	61.8	83.8
In central city	58,010,482	52,895,696	5,114,786	8.8	32.3	31.2	52.5
Not in central city	54,873,275	51,829,631	3,043,644	5.5	30.6	30.6	31.3
Urban	41,560,998	38,973,479	2,587,519	6.2	23.2	23.0	26.6
Rural	13,312,277	12,856,152	456,125	3.4	7.4	7.6	4.7
Outside metropolitan area	66,441,914	64,862,201	1,579,713	2.4	37.1	38.2	16.2
Urban	25,712,303	24,904,456	807,847	3.1	14.3	14.7	8.3
Rural	40,729,611	39,957,745	771,866	1.9	22.7	23.6	7.9

Footnotes:

* Indicates sample data.

[1] See text for Table 16 regarding classification by type of residence. Internet Release Date: February 2, 2006

Table 17. Nativity of the Population for Metropolitan Statistical Areas With 1,000,000 or More Population and Their Component Metropolitan Divisions: 2000* (Leading dots indicate subparts)

(See text for sources, definitions, and explanations)

Metropolitan statistical area (rank in total population)[1] Metropolitan division[1]	Statistical area description	Total	Native	Foreign born	
				Number	Percent
Atlanta-Sandy Springs-Marietta, GA (11)#	Metropolitan Statistical Area	4,247,981	3,823,462	424,519	10.0
Austin-Round Rock, TX (40)	Metropolitan Statistical Area	1,249,763	1,096,929	152,834	12.2
Baltimore-Towson, MD (19)#	Metropolitan Statistical Area	2,552,994	2,406,866	146,128	5.7
Birmingham-Hoover, AL (48)#	.Metropolitan Statistical Area	1,052,238	1,030,014	22,224	2.1
Boston-Cambridge-Quincy, MA-NH (10)#	Metropolitan Statistical Area	4,391,344	3,789,282	602,062	13.7
. Boston-Quincy, MA	Metropolitan Division	1,812,937	1,530,582	282,355	15.6
. Cambridge-Newton-Framingham, MA	.Metropolitan Division	1,465,396	1,241,931	223,465	15.2
. Essex County, MA	Metropolitan Division	723,419	641,380	82,039	11.3
. Rockingham County-Strafford County, NH	Metropolitan Division	389,592	375,389	14,203	3.6
Buffalo-Niagara Falls, NY (42)	Metropolitan Statistical Area	1,170,111	1,118,730	51,381	4.4
Charlotte-Gastonia-Concord, NC-SC (37)#	.Metropolitan Statistical Area	1,330,448	1,238,458	91,990	6.9
Chicago-Naperville-Joliet, IL-IN-WI (3)#	.Metropolitan Statistical Area	9,098,316	7,634,195	1,464,121	16.1
. Chicago-Naperville-Joliet, IL	Metropolitan Division	7,628,412	6,297,970	1,330,442	17.4
. Gary, IN	Metropolitan Division	675,971	644,972	30,999	4.6
. Lake County-Kenosha, IL-WI	Metropolitan Division	793,933	691,253	102,680	12.9
Cincinnati-Middletown, OH-KY-IN (24)#	.Metropolitan Statistical Area	2,009,632	1,958,232	51,400	2.6
Cleveland-Elyria-Mentor, OH (23)#	Metropolitan Statistical Area	2,148,143	2,035,137	113,006	5.3
Columbus, OH (31)#	Metropolitan Statistical Area	1,612,694	1,540,741	71,953	4.5
Dallas-Fort Worth-Arlington, TX (5)#	Metropolitan Statistical Area	5,161,544	4,378,549	782,995	15.2
. Dallas-Plano-Irving, TX	Metropolitan Division	3,451,226	2,862,846	588,380	17.0
. Fort Worth-Arlington, TX	Metropolitan Division	1,710,318	1,515,703	194,615	11.4
Denver-Aurora, CO (22)#	Metropolitan Statistical Area	2,179,250	1,943,754	235,496	10.8
Detroit-Warren-Livonia, MI (9)#	Metropolitan Statistical Area	4,452,557	4,115,498	337,059	7.6

Table 17. (Continued)

Metropolitan statistical area (rank in total population)[1] Metropolitan division [1]	Statistical area description	Total	Native	Foreign born	
				Number	Percent
. Detroit-Livonia-Dearborn, MI	Metropolitan Division	2,061,162	1,923,393	137,769	6.7
. Warren-Farmington Hills-Troy, MI	Metropolitan Division	2,391,395	2,192,105	199,290	8.3
Hartford-West Hartford-East Hartford, CT (44)#	Metropolitan Statistical Area	1,148,618	1,030,684	117,934	10.3
Houston-Baytown-Sugar Land, TX (8)#	Metropolitan Statistical Area	4,715,407	3,817,186	898,221	19.0
Indianapolis, IN (34)#	Metropolitan Statistical Area	1,525,104	1,471,808	53,296	3.5
Jacksonville, FL (45)	Metropolitan Statistical Area	1,122,750	1,062,914	59,836	5.3
Kansas City, MO-KS (26)#	Metropolitan Statistical Area	1,836,038	1,754,966	81,072	4.4
Las Vegas-Paradise, NV (36)#	.Metropolitan Statistical Area	1,375,765	1,128,014	247,751	18.0
Los Angeles-Long Beach-Santa Ana, CA (21)#	Metropolitan Statistical Area	12,365,627	8,066,284	4,299,343	34.8
. Los Angeles-Long Beach-Glendale, CA	Metropolitan Division	9,519,338	6,069,894	3,449,444	36.2
. Santa Ana-Anaheim-Irvine, CA	Metropolitan Division	2,846,289	1,996,390	849,899	29.9
Louisville, KY-IN (43)#	.Metropolitan Statistical Area	1,161,975	1,131,305	30,670	2.6
Memphis, TN-MS-AR (41)	Metropolitan Statistical Area	1,205,204	1,167,062	38,142	3.2
Miami-Fort Lauderdale-Miami Beach, FL (6)	.Metropolitan Statistical Area	5,007,564	3,252,560	1,755,004	35.0
. Fort Lauderdale-Pompano Beach-Deerfield Beach, FL	Metropolitan Division	1,623,018	1,212,631	410,387	25.3
. Miami-Miami Beach-Kendall, FL	Metropolitan Division	2,253,362	1,105,597	1,147,765	50.9
. West Palm Beach-Boca Raton-Boynton Beach, FL	Metropolitan Division	1,131,184	934,332	196,852	17.4
Milwaukee-Waukesha-West Allis, WI (35)#	Metropolitan Statistical Area	1,500,741	1,419,167	81,574	5.4
Minneapolis-St. Paul-Bloomington, MN-WI (16)#	.Metropolitan Statistical Area	2,968,806	2,758,462	210,344	7.1
Nashville-Davidson--Murfreesboro, TN (39)#	.Metropolitan Statistical Area	1,311,789	1,253,250	58,539	4.5
New Orleans-Metairie-Kenner, LA (38)#	Metropolitan Statistical Area	1,316,510	1,252,385	64,125	4.9
New York-Northern New Jersey-Long Island, NY-NJ-PA (1)# [2]	Metropolitan Statistical Area	18,323,002	13,476,680	4,846,322	26.4
. Edison, NJ	Metropolitan Division	2,173,869	1,841,212	332,657	15.3
. Nassau-Suffolk, NY [2]	Metropolitan Division	2,753,913	2,356,974	396,939	14.4

Table 17. (Continued)

Metropolitan statistical area (rank in total population)[1] Metropolitan division [1]	Statistical area description	Total	Native	Foreign born	
				Number	Percent
. Newark-Union, NJ-PA	Metropolitan Division	2,098,843	1,708,953	389,890	18.6
. New York-Wayne-White Plains, NY-NJ	.Metropolitan Division	11,296,377	7,569,541	3,726,836	33.0
Oklahoma City, OK (47)#	Metropolitan Statistical Area	1,095,421	1,033,553	61,868	5.6
Orlando, FL (30)#	Metropolitan Statistical Area	1,644,561	1,447,442	197,119	12.0
Philadelphia-Camden-Wilmington, PA-NJ-DE-MD (4)#	Metropolitan Statistical Area	5,687,147	5,295,318	391,829	6.9
. Camden, NJ	Metropolitan Division	1,186,999	1,116,402	70,597	5.9
Philadelphia, PA	Metropolitan Division	3,849,647	3,564,443	285,204	7.4
. Wilmington, DE-MD-NJ	Metropolitan Division	650,501	614,473	36,028	5.5
Phoenix-Mesa-Scottsdale, AZ (14)	Metropolitan Statistical Area	3,251,876	2,794,393	457,483	14.1
Pittsburgh, PA (20)#	Metropolitan Statistical Area	2,431,087	2,368,309	62,778	2.6
Portland-Vancouver-Beaverton, OR (25)	Metropolitan Statistical Area	1,927,881	1,719,459	208,422	10.8
Providence-New Bedford-Fall River, RI-MA (32)	Metropolitan Statistical Area	1,582,997	1,400,907	182,090	11.5
Richmond, VA (46)	Metropolitan Statistical Area	1,096,957	1,050,809	46,148	4.2
Riverside-San Bernardino-Ontario, CA (13)#	Metropolitan Statistical Area	3,254,821	2,642,462	612,359	18.8
Rochester, NY (49)#	.Metropolitan Statistical Area	1,037,831	976,342	61,489	5.9
Sacramento--Arden-Arcade--Roseville, CA (27)#	Metropolitan Statistical Area	1,796,857	1,536,746	260,111	14.5
St. Louis, MO-IL (18)#	Metropolitan Statistical Area	2,698,687	2,617,141	81,546	3.0
San Antonio, TX (29)	Metropolitan Statistical Area	1,711,703	1,544,161	167,542	9.8
San Diego-Carlsbad-San Marcos, CA (17)	Metropolitan Statistical Area	2,813,833	2,207,579	606,254	21.5
San Francisco-Oakland-Fremont, CA (12)#	Metropolitan Statistical Area	4,123,740	2,995,777	1,127,963	27.4
. Oakland-Fremont-Hayward, CA	Metropolitan Division	2,392,557	1,819,413	573,144	24.0
. San Francisco-San Mateo-Redwood City	Metropolitan Division	1,731,183	1,176,364	554,819	32.0
San Jose-Sunnyvale-Santa Clara, CA (28)#	Metropolitan Statistical Area	1,735,819	1,152,663	583,156	33.6
Seattle-Tacoma-Bellevue, WA (15)#	Metropolitan Statistical Area	3,043,878	2,660,054	383,824	12.6
. Seattle-Bellevue-Everett, WA	Metropolitan Division	2,343,058	2,015,759	327,299	14.0

Table 17. (Continued)

Metropolitan statistical area (rank in total population)[1] Metropolitan division [1]	Statistical area description	Total	Native	Foreign born	
				Number	Percent
. Tacoma, WA	.Metropolitan Division	700,820	644,295	56,525	8.1
Tampa-St. Petersburg-Clearwater, FL (21)	Metropolitan Statistical Area	2,395,997	2,162,090	233,907	9.8
Virginia Beach-Norfolk-Newport News, VA-NC (33)	Metropolitan Statistical Area	1,576,370	1,505,967	70,403	4.5
Washington-Arlington-Alexandria, DC-VA-MD-WV (7)#	Metropolitan Statistical Area	4,796,183	3,966,873	829,310	17.3
. Bethesda-Frederick-Gaithersburg, MD	Metropolitan Division	1,068,618	827,843	240,775	22.5
. Washington-Arlington-Alexandria, DC-VA-MD-WV	Metropolitan Division	3,727,565	3,139,030	588,535	15.8

Footnotes:

* Indicates sample data.

Part of a combined statistical area. See Table 18.

[1] As defined effective June 6, 2003. See text for Table 16.

[2] Title changed subsequent to the June 6, 2003 Office of Management and Budget definition. Internet Release Date: February 2, 2006

Table 18. Nativity of the Population for Combined Statistical Areas With 1,000,000 or More Population and Their Component Metropolitan and Micropolitan Statistical Areas: 2000* (Leading dots indicate subparts)

(See text for sources, definitions, and explanations)

Combined statistical area [1] Metropolitan statistical area [1] Micropolitan statistical area [1]	Statistical area description	Total	Native	Foreign born	
				Number	Percent
Albany-Schenectady-Amsterdam, NY	Combined Statistical Area	1,118,095	1,070,293	47,802	4.3
. Albany-Schenectady-Troy, NY	Metropolitan Statistical Area	825,875	786,190	39,685	4.8
. Amsterdam, NY	Micropolitan Statistical Area	49,708	48,134	1,574	3.2
. Glens Falls, NY	.Metropolitan Statistical Area	124,345	121,651	2,694	2.2
. Gloversville, NY	Micropolitan Statistical Area	55,073	54,003	1,070	1.9
. Hudson, NY	Micropolitan Statistical Area	63,094	60,315	2,779	4.4
Atlanta-Sandy Springs-Gainesville, GA-AL	Combined Statistical Area	4,548,344	4,097,001	451,343	9.9
. Atlanta-Sandy Springs-Marietta, GA	Metropolitan Statistical Area	4,247,981	3,823,462	424,519	10.0
. Cedartown, GA	Micropolitan Statistical Area	38,127	35,825	2,302	6.0
. Gainesville, GA	Metropolitan Statistical Area	139,277	116,775	22,502	16.2
. LaGrange, GA	Micropolitan Statistical Area	58,779	57,614	1,165	2.0
. Thomaston, GA	Micropolitan Statistical Area	27,597	27,036	561	2.0
. Valley, AL	Micropolitan Statistical Area	36,583	36,289	294	0.8
Birmingham-Hoover-Cullman, AL	Combined Statistical Area	1,129,721	1,106,167	23,554	2.1
. Birmingham-Hoover, AL	Metropolitan Statistical Area	1,052,238	1,030,014	22,224	2.1
. Cullman, AL	Micropolitan Statistical Area	77,483	76,153	1,330	1.7
Boston-Worcester-Manchester, MA-NH	Combined Statistical Area	5,715,698	5,023,007	692,691	12.1
. Boston-Cambridge-Quincy, MA-NH	Metropolitan Statistical Area	4,391,344	3,789,282	602,062	13.7
. Concord, NH	Micropolitan Statistical Area	136,225	131,874	4,351	3.2
. Laconia, NH	Micropolitan Statistical Area	56,325	54,903	1,422	2.5
. Manchester-Nashua, NH	Metropolitan Statistical Area	380,841	355,048	25,793	6.8
. Worcester, MA	Metropolitan Statistical Area	750,963	691,900	59,063	7.9

Table 18. (Continued)

Combined statistical area [1] Metropolitan statistical area [1] Micropolitan statistical area [1]	Statistical area description	Total	Native	Foreign born	
				Number	Percent
Charlotte-Gastonia-Salisbury, NC	Combined Statistical Area	1,897,034	1,788,349	108,685	5.7
. Albemarle, NC	Micropolitan Statistical Area	58,100	56,595	1,505	2.6
. Charlotte-Gastonia-Concord, NC-SC	Metropolitan Statistical Area	1,330,448	1,238,458	91,990	6.9
. Chester, SC	Micropolitan Statistical Area	34,068	33,783	285	0.8
. Lancaster, SC	Micropolitan Statistical Area	61,351	60,524	827	1.3
. Lincolnton, NC	Micropolitan Statistical Area	63,780	60,703	3,077	4.8
. Salisbury, NC	Micropolitan Statistical Area	130,340	125,468	4,872	3.7
. Shelby, NC	Micropolitan Statistical Area	96,287	94,630	1,657	1.7
. Statesville-Mooresville, NC	.Micropolitan Statistical Area	122,660	118,188	4,472	3.6
Chicago-Naperville-Michigan City, IL-IN-WI	Combined Statistical Area	9,312,255	7,841,793	1,470,462	15.8
. Chicago-Naperville-Joliet, IL-IN-WI	Metropolitan Statistical Area	9,098,316	7,634,195	1,464,121	16.1
. Kankakee-Bradley, IL	Metropolitan Statistical Area	103,833	100,222	3,611	3.5
. Michigan City-La Porte, IN	.Metropolitan Statistical Area	110,106	107,376	2,730	2.5
Cincinnati-Middletown-Wilmington, OH-KY-IN	Combined Statistical Area	2,050,175	1,998,351	51,824	2.5
. Cincinnati-Middletown, OH-KY-IN	Metropolitan Statistical Area	2,009,632	1,958,232	51,400	2.6
. Wilmington, OH	Micropolitan Statistical Area	40,543	40,119	424	1.0
Cleveland-Akron-Elyria, OH	Combined Statistical Area	2,945,831	2,810,434	135,397	4.6
. Akron, OH	Metropolitan Statistical Area	694,960	674,188	20,772	3.0
. Ashtabula, OH	Micropolitan Statistical Area	102,728	101,109	1,619	1.6
. Cleveland-Elyria-Mentor, OH	.Metropolitan Statistical Area	2,148,143	2,035,137	113,006	5.3
Columbus-Marion-Chillicothe, OH	Combined Statistical Area	1,835,189	1,761,142	74,047	4.0
. Chillicothe, OH	.Micropolitan Statistical Area	73,345	72,807	538	0.7
. Columbus, OH	Metropolitan Statistical Area	1,612,694	1,540,741	71,953	4.5
. Marion, OH	Micropolitan Statistical Area	66,217	65,482	735	1.1

Table 18. (Continued)

Combined statistical area [1] Metropolitan statistical area [1] Micropolitan statistical area [1]	Statistical area description	Total	Native	Foreign born	
				Number	Percent
. Mount Vernon, OH	.Micropolitan Statistical Area	54,500	53,940	560	1.0
. Washington, OH	Micropolitan Statistical Area	28,433	28,172	261	0.9
Dallas-Fort Worth, TX	Combined Statistical Area	5,346,119	4,555,373	790,746	14.8
. Athens, TX	Micropolitan Statistical Area	73,277	70,463	2,814	3.8
. Dallas-Fort Worth-Arlington, TX	Metropolitan Statistical Area	5,161,544	4,378,549	782,995	15.2
. Gainesville, TX	Micropolitan Statistical Area	36,363	34,353	2,010	5.5
. Granbury, TX	Micropolitan Statistical Area	47,909	46,183	1,726	3.6
. Mineral Wells, TX	Micropolitan Statistical Area	27,026	25,825	1,201	4.4
Dayton-Springfield-Greenville, OH	Combined Statistical Area	1,085,094	1,062,079	23,015	2.1
. Dayton, OH	Metropolitan Statistical Area	848,153	827,516	20,637	2.4
. Greenville, OH	Micropolitan Statistical Area	53,309	52,939	370	0.7
. Springfield, OH	Metropolitan Statistical Area	144,742	143,018	1,724	1.2
. Urbana, OH	Micropolitan Statistical Area	38,890	38,606	284	0.7
Denver-Aurora-Boulder, CO	Combined Statistical Area	2,449,044	2,187,644	261,400	10.7
. Boulder, CO	Metropolitan Statistical Area	269,794	243,890	25,904	9.6
. Denver-Aurora, CO	.Metropolitan Statistical Area	2,179,250	1,943,754	235,496	10.8
Detroit-Warren-Flint, MI	Combined Statistical Area	5,357,538	4,975,199	382,339	7.1
. Ann Arbor, MI	Metropolitan Statistical Area	322,895	289,731	33,164	10.3
. Detroit-Warren-Livonia, MI	Metropolitan Statistical Area	4,452,557	4,115,498	337,059	7.6
. Flint, MI	Metropolitan Statistical Area	436,141	426,788	9,353	2.1
. Monroe, MI	Metropolitan Statistical Area	145,945	143,182	2,763	1.9
Grand Rapids-Muskegon-Holland, MI	Combined Statistical Area	1,254,661	1,196,564	58,097	4.6
. Allegan, MI	.Micropolitan Statistical Area	105,665	102,579	3,086	2.9
. Grand Rapids-Wyoming, MI	Metropolitan Statistical Area	740,482	700,297	40,185	5.4

Table 18. (Continued)

Combined statistical area [1] Metropolitan statistical area [1] Micropolitan statistical area [1]	Statistical area description	Total	Native	Foreign born	
				Number	Percent
. Holland-Grand Haven, MI	Metropolitan Statistical Area	238,314	226,647	11,667	4.9
. Muskegon-Norton Shores, MI	.Metropolitan Statistical Area	170,200	167,041	3,159	1.9
Greensboro--Winston-Salem--High Point, NC	Combined Statistical Area	1,283,856	1,214,352	69,504	5.4
. Greensboro-High Point, NC	.Metropolitan Statistical Area	643,430	606,225	37,205	5.8
. Lexington-Thomasville, NC	Micropolitan Statistical Area	147,246	141,998	5,248	3.6
. Mount Airy, NC	Micropolitan Statistical Area	71,219	67,464	3,755	5.3
. Winston-Salem, NC	Metropolitan Statistical Area	421,961	398,665	23,296	5.5
Hartford-West Hartford-Willimantic, CT	Combined Statistical Area	1,257,709	1,135,107	122,602	9.7
. Hartford-West Hartford-East Hartford, CT	Metropolitan Statistical Area	1,148,618	1,030,684	117,934	10.3
. Willimantic, CT	.Micropolitan Statistical Area	109,091	104,423	4,668	4.3
Houston-Baytown-Huntsville, TX	Combined Statistical Area	4,815,122	3,910,385	904,737	18.8
. Bay City, TX	.Micropolitan Statistical Area	37,957	34,197	3,760	9.9
. Houston-Baytown-Sugar Land, TX	Metropolitan Statistical Area	4,715,407	3,817,186	898,221	19.0
. Huntsville, TX	Micropolitan Statistical Area	61,758	59,002	2,756	4.5
Indianapolis-Anderson-Columbus, IN	Combined Statistical Area	1,843,588	1,785,016	58,572	3.2
. Anderson, IN	.Metropolitan Statistical Area	133,358	131,771	1,587	1.2
. Columbus, IN	Metropolitan Statistical Area	71,435	68,752	2,683	3.8
. Crawfordsville, IN	Micropolitan Statistical Area	37,629	37,083	546	1.5
. Indianapolis, IN	Metropolitan Statistical Area	1,525,104	1,471,808	53,296	3.5
. New Castle, IN	.Micropolitan Statistical Area	48,508	48,249	259	0.5
. North Vernon, IN	.Micropolitan Statistical Area	27,554	27,353	201	0.7
Kansas City-Overland Park-Kansas City, MO-KS	Combined Statistical Area	1,901,070	1,818,428	82,642	4.3
. Atchison, KS	Micropolitan Statistical Area	16,774	16,662	112	0.7
. Kansas City, MO-KS	.Metropolitan Statistical Area	1,836,038	1,754,966	81,072	4.4

Table 18. (Continued)

Combined statistical area [1] Metropolitan statistical area [1] Micropolitan statistical area [1]	Statistical area description	Total	Native	Foreign born	
				Number	Percent
. Warrensburg, MO	Micropolitan Statistical Area	48,258	46,800	1,458	3.0
Las Vegas-Paradise-Pahrump, NV	Combined Statistical Area	1,408,250	1,158,870	249,380	17.7
. Las Vegas-Paradise, NV	Metropolitan Statistical Area	1,375,765	1,128,014	247,751	18.0
. Pahrump, NV	Micropolitan Statistical Area	32,485	30,856	1,629	5.0
Los Angeles-Long Beach-Riverside, CA	Combined Statistical Area	16,373,645	11,306,030	5,067,615	30.9
. Los Angeles-Long Beach-Santa Ana, CA	Metropolitan Statistical Area	12,365,627	8,066,284	4,299,343	34.8
. Oxnard-Thousand Oaks-Ventura, CA	Metropolitan Statistical Area	753,197	597,284	155,913	20.7
. Riverside-San Bernardino-Ontario, CA	Metropolitan Statistical Area	3,254,821	2,642,462	612,359	18.8
Louisville-Elizabethtown-Scottsburg, KY-IN	Combined Statistical Area	1,292,482	1,257,390	35,092	2.7
. Elizabethtown, KY	Metropolitan Statistical Area	107,547	103,220	4,327	4.0
. Louisville, KY-IN	Metropolitan Statistical Area	1,161,975	1,131,305	30,670	2.6
. Scottsburg, IN	Micropolitan Statistical Area	22,960	22,865	95	0.4
Milwaukee-Racine-Waukesha, WI	.Combined Statistical Area	1,689,572	1,600,288	89,284	5.3
. Milwaukee-Waukesha-West Allis, WI	Metropolitan Statistical Area	1,500,741	1,419,167	81,574	5.4
. Racine, WI	Metropolitan Statistical Area	188,831	181,121	7,710	4.1
Minneapolis-St. Paul-St. Cloud, MN-WI	Combined Statistical Area	3,271,888	3,053,671	218,217	6.7
. Faribault-Northfield, MN	Micropolitan Statistical Area	56,665	53,968	2,697	4.8
. Hutchinson, MN	Micropolitan Statistical Area	34,898	34,114	784	2.2
. Minneapolis-St. Paul-Bloomington, MN-WI	Metropolitan Statistical Area	2,968,806	2,758,462	210,344	7.1
. Red Wing, MN	Micropolitan Statistical Area	44,127	43,615	512	1.2
. St. Cloud, MN	Metropolitan Statistical Area	167,392	163,512	3,880	2.3
Nashville-Davidson--Murfreesboro--Columbia, TN	.Combined Statistical Area	1,381,287	1,321,302	59,985	4.3
. Columbia, TN	.Micropolitan Statistical Area	69,498	68,052	1,446	2.1
. Nashville-Davidson--Murfreesboro, TN	Metropolitan Statistical Area	1,311,789	1,253,250	58,539	4.5

Table 18. (Continued)

Combined statistical area [1] Metropolitan statistical area [1] Micropolitan statistical area [1]	Statistical area description	Total	Native	Foreign born	
				Number	Percent
New Orleans-Metairie-Bogalusa, LA	Combined Statistical Area	1,360,436	1,296,125	64,311	4.7
. Bogalusa, LA	Micropolitan Statistical Area	43,926	43,740	186	0.4
. New Orleans-Metairie-Kenner, LA	.Metropolitan Statistical Area	1,316,510	1,252,385	64,125	4.9
New York-Newark-Bridgeport, NY-NJ-CT-PA	Combined Statistical Area	21,361,797	16,170,675	5,191,122	24.3
. Bridgeport-Stamford-Norwalk, CT	Metropolitan Statistical Area	882,567	733,529	149,038	16.9
. Kingston, NY	.Metropolitan Statistical Area	177,749	167,281	10,468	5.9
. New Haven-Milford, CT	Metropolitan Statistical Area	824,008	749,581	74,427	9.0
. New York-Northern New Jersey-Long Island, NY-NJ-PA [2]	Metropolitan Statistical Area	18,323,002	13,476,680	4,846,322	26.4
. Poughkeepsie-Newburgh-Middletown, NY	Metropolitan Statistical Area	621,517	569,207	52,310	8.4
. Torrington, CT	Micropolitan Statistical Area	182,193	172,295	9,898	5.4
. Trenton-Ewing, NJ	Metropolitan Statistical Area	350,761	302,102	48,659	13.9
Oklahoma City-Shawnee, OK	Combined Statistical Area	1,160,942	1,098,359	62,583	5.4
. Oklahoma City, OK	Metropolitan Statistical Area	1,095,421	1,033,553	61,868	5.6
. Shawnee, OK	Micropolitan Statistical Area	65,521	64,806	715	1.1
Orlando-The Villages, FL	Combined Statistical Area	1,697,906	1,497,849	200,057	11.8
. Orlando, FL	Metropolitan Statistical Area	1,644,561	1,447,442	197,119	12.0
. The Villages, FL	Micropolitan Statistical Area	53,345	50,407	2,938	5.5
Philadelphia-Camden-Vineland, PA-NJ-DE-MD	Combined Statistical Area	5,833,585	5,432,749	400,836	6.9
. Philadelphia-Camden-Wilmington, PA-NJ-DE-MD	Metropolitan Statistical Area	5,687,147	5,295,318	391,829	6.9
. Vineland-Millville-Bridgeton, NJ	Metropolitan Statistical Area	146,438	137,431	9,007	6.2
Pittsburgh-New Castle, PA	Combined Statistical Area	2,525,730	2,461,691	64,039	2.5
. New Castle, PA	Micropolitan Statistical Area	94,643	93,382	1,261	1.3
. Pittsburgh, PA	Metropolitan Statistical Area	2,431,087	2,368,309	62,778	2.6

Table 18. (Continued)

Combined statistical area [1] Metropolitan statistical area [1] Micropolitan statistical area [1]	Statistical area description	Total	Native	Foreign born	
				Number	Percent
Raleigh-Durham-Cary, NC	Combined Statistical Area	1,314,589	1,201,161	113,428	8.6
. Dunn, NC	Micropolitan Statistical Area	91,025	86,848	4,177	4.6
. Durham, NC	Metropolitan Statistical Area	426,493	386,772	39,721	9.3
. Raleigh-Cary, NC	Metropolitan Statistical Area	797,071	727,541	69,530	8.7
Rochester-Batavia-Seneca Falls, NY	Combined Statistical Area	1,131,543	1,067,933	63,610	5.6
. Batavia, NY	Micropolitan Statistical Area	60,370	59,065	1,305	2.2
. Rochester, NY	Metropolitan Statistical Area	1,037,831	976,342	61,489	5.9
. Seneca Falls, NY	Micropolitan Statistical Area	33,342	32,526	816	2.4
Sacramento--Arden-Arcade--Truckee, CA	Combined Statistical Area	1,930,149	1,663,614	266,535	13.8
. Gardnerville Ranchos, NV	Micropolitan Statistical Area	41,259	38,900	2,359	5.7
. Sacramento--Arden-Arcade--Roseville, CA	Metropolitan Statistical Area	1,796,857	1,536,746	260,111	14.5
. Truckee-Grass Valley, CA	Micropolitan Statistical Area	92,033	87,968	4,065	4.4
St. Louis-St. Charles-Farmington, MO-IL	Combined Statistical Area	2,754,328	2,672,289	82,039	3.0
. Farmington, MO	Micropolitan Statistical Area	55,641	55,148	493	0.9
. St. Louis, MO-IL	Metropolitan Statistical Area	2,698,687	2,617,141	81,546	3.0
Salt Lake City-Ogden-Clearfield, UT	Combined Statistical Area	1,454,259	1,334,483	119,776	8.2
. Brigham City, UT	Micropolitan Statistical Area	42,745	41,476	1,269	3.0
. Ogden-Clearfield, UT	Metropolitan Statistical Area	442,656	421,228	21,428	4.8
. Salt Lake City, UT	Metropolitan Statistical Area	968,858	871,779	97,079	10.0
San Jose-San Francisco-Oakland, CA	Combined Statistical Area	7,092,596	5,180,266	1,912,330	27.0
. Napa, CA	Metropolitan Statistical Area	124,279	101,792	22,487	18.1
. San Francisco-Oakland-Fremont, CA	Metropolitan Statistical Area	4,123,740	2,995,777	1,127,963	27.4
. San Jose-Sunnyvale-Santa Clara, CA	Metropolitan Statistical Area	1,735,819	1,152,663	583,156	33.6
. Santa Cruz-Watsonville, CA	Metropolitan Statistical Area	255,602	209,100	46,502	18.2

Table 18. (Continued)

Combined statistical area [1] Metropolitan statistical area [1] Micropolitan statistical area [1]	Statistical area description	Total	Native	Foreign born	
				Number	Percent
. Santa Rosa-Petaluma, CA	Metropolitan Statistical Area	458,614	392,888	65,726	14.3
. Vallejo-Fairfield, CA	Metropolitan Statistical Area	394,542	328,046	66,496	16.9
Seattle-Tacoma-Olympia, WA	Combined Statistical Area	3,604,165	3,187,635	416,530	11.6
. Bremerton-Silverdale, WA	Metropolitan Statistical Area	231,969	218,789	13,180	5.7
. Oak Harbor, WA	Micropolitan Statistical Area	71,558	66,945	4,613	6.4
. Olympia, WA	Metropolitan Statistical Area	207,355	194,617	12,738	6.1
. Seattle-Tacoma-Bellevue, WA	Metropolitan Statistical Area	3,043,878	2,660,054	383,824	12.6
. Shelton, WA	Micropolitan Statistical Area	49,405	47,230	2,175	4.4
Washington-Baltimore-Northern Virginia, DC-MD-VA-WV	Combined Statistical Area	7,538,385	6,557,379	981,006	13.0
. Baltimore-Towson, MD	Metropolitan Statistical Area	2,552,994	2,406,866	146,128	5.7
. Lexington Park, MD	Micropolitan Statistical Area	86,211	83,779	2,432	2.8
. Washington-Arlington-Alexandria, DC-VA-MD-WV	Metropolitan Statistical Area	4,796,183	3,966,873	829,310	17.3
. Winchester, VA-WV	Metropolitan Statistical Area	102,997	99,861	3,136	3.0

Footnotes:

* Indicates sample data.

[1] As defined effective June 6, 2003.

[2] Title changed subsequent to the June 6, 2003 Office of Management and Budget definition. Internet Release Date: February 2, 2006

Table 19. Nativity of the Population for Metropolitan Statistical Areas (MSAs) and Consolidated Metropolitan Statistical Areas (CMSAs) With 1,000,000 or More Population: 2000* (Leading dots indicate subparts)

(See text for sources, definitions, and explanations)

Metropolitan area (rank in total population) [1]	Total	Native	Foreign born	
			Number	Percent
Atlanta, GA MSA (11)	4,112,198	3,689,093	423,105	10.3
Austin--San Marcos, TX MSA (37)	1,249,763	1,096,929	152,834	12.2
Boston--Worcester--Lawrence, MA--NH--ME--CT CMSA (7)	5,819,101	5,098,041	721,060	12.4
Boston, MA--NH PMSA	3,406,835	2,898,556	508,279	14.9
Brockton, MA PMSA	255,459	232,222	23,237	9.1
Fitchburg--Leominster, MA PMSA	142,285	131,959	10,326	7.3
Lawrence, MA--NH PMSA	396,230	353,534	42,696	10.8
Lowell, MA--NH PMSA	301,686	267,238	34,448	11.4
Manchester, NH PMSA	198,378	185,311	13,067	6.6
Nashua, NH PMSA	190,949	177,797	13,152	6.9
New Bedford, MA PMSA	175,198	149,822	25,376	14.5
Portsmouth--Rochester, NH--ME PMSA	240,692	232,409	8,283	3.4
Worcester, MA--CT PMSA	511,389	469,193	42,196	8.3
Buffalo--Niagara Falls, NY MSA (42)	1,170,111	1,118,730	51,381	4.4
Charlotte--Gastonia--Rock Hill, NC--SC MSA (33)	1,499,293	1,399,533	99,760	6.7
Chicago--Gary--Kenosha, IL--IN--WI CMSA (3)	9,157,540	7,690,600	1,466,940	16.0
Chicago,IL PMSA	8,272,768	6,846,790	1,425,978	17.2
Gary, IN PMSA	631,362	601,155	30,207	4.8
Kankakee, IL PMSA	103,833	100,222	3,611	3.5
Kenosha, WI PMSA	149,577	142,433	7,144	4.8
Cincinnati--Hamilton, OH--KY--IN CMSA (23)	1,979,202	1,927,966	51,236	2.6
Cincinnati, OH--KY--IN PMSA	1,646,395	1,604,306	42,089	2.6
Hamilton--Middletown, OH PMSA	332,807	323,660	9,147	2.7
Cleveland--Akron, OH CMSA (16)	2,945,831	2,810,434	135,397	4.6
Akron, OH PMSA	694,960	674,188	20,772	3.0
Cleveland--Lorain--Elyria, OH PMSA	2,250,871	2,136,246	114,625	5.1

Table 19. (Continued)

Metropolitan area (rank in total population) [1]	Total	Native	Foreign born	
			Number	Percent
Columbus, OH MSA (32)	1,540,157	1,468,740	71,417	4.6
Dallas--Fort Worth, TX CMSA (9)	5,221,801	4,437,159	784,642	15.0
Dallas, TX PMSA	3,519,176	2,928,007	591,169	16.8
Fort Worth--Arlington, TX PMSA	1,702,625	1,509,152	193,473	11.4
Denver--Boulder--Greeley, CO CMSA (19)	2,581,506	2,304,379	277,127	10.7
Boulder--Longmont, CO PMSA	291,288	264,009	27,279	9.4
Denver, CO PMSA	2,109,282	1,876,186	233,096	11.1
Greeley, CO PMSA	180,936	164,184	16,752	9.3
Detroit--Ann Arbor--Flint, MI CMSA (8)	5,456,428	5,072,458	383,970	7.0
Ann Arbor, MI PMSA	578,736	539,196	39,540	6.8
Detroit, MI PMSA	4,441,551	4,106,444	335,107	7.5
Flint, MI PMSA	436,141	426,788	9,353	2.1
Grand Rapids--Muskegon--Holland, MI MSA (47)	1,088,514	1,032,448	56,066	5.2
Greensboro--Winston-Salem--High Point, NC MSA (36)	1,251,509	1,179,944	71,565	5.7
Hartford, CT MSA (41)	1,183,110	1,062,755	120,355	10.2
Houston--Galveston--Brazoria, TX CMSA (10)	4,669,571	3,773,627	895,944	19.2
Brazoria, TX PMSA	241,767	221,170	20,597	8.5
Galveston--Texas City, TX PMSA	250,158	229,480	20,678	8.3
Houston, TX PMSA	4,177,646	3,322,977	854,669	20.5
Indianapolis, IN MSA (28)	1,607,486	1,553,143	54,343	3.4
Jacksonville, FL MSA (45)	1,100,491	1,040,905	59,586	5.4
Kansas City, MO--KS MSA (25)	1,776,062	1,695,523	80,539	4.5
Las Vegas, NV--AZ MSA (31)	1,563,282	1,304,788	258,494	16.5
Los Angeles--Riverside--Orange County, CA CMSA (2)	16,373,645	11,306,030	5,067,615	30.9
Los Angeles--Long Beach, CA PMSA	9,519,338	6,069,894	3,449,444	36.2
Orange County, CA PMSA	2,846,289	1,996,390	849,899	29.9
Riverside--San Bernardino, CA PMSA	3,254,821	2,642,462	612,359	18.8
Ventura, CA PMSA	753,197	597,284	155,913	20.7

Table 19. (Continued)

Metropolitan area (rank in total population) [1]	Total	Native	Foreign born	
			Number	Percent
Louisville, KY--IN MSA (49)	1,025,598	997,665	27,933	2.7
Memphis, TN--AR--MS MSA (43)	1,135,614	1,097,944	37,670	3.3
Miami--Fort Lauderdale, FL CMSA (12)	3,876,380	2,318,228	1,558,152	40.2
Fort Lauderdale, FL PMSA	1,623,018	1,212,631	410,387	25.3
Miami, FL PMSA	2,253,362	1,105,597	1,147,765	50.9
Milwaukee--Racine, WI CMSA (26)	1,689,572	1,600,288	89,284	5.3
Milwaukee--Waukesha, WI PMSA	1,500,741	1,419,167	81,574	5.4
Racine, WI PMSA	188,831	181,121	7,710	4.1
Minneapolis--St. Paul, MN--WI MSA (15)	2,968,806	2,758,462	210,344	7.1
Nashville, TN MSA (38)	1,231,311	1,173,697	57,614	4.7
New Orleans, LA MSA (34)	1,337,726	1,273,557	64,169	4.8
New York--Northern New Jersey--Long Island, NY--NJ--CT--PA CMSA (1)	21,199,865	16,017,610	5,182,255	24.4
Bergen--Passaic, NJ PMSA	1,373,167	1,020,575	352,592	25.7
Bridgeport, CT PMSA	459,479	402,314	57,165	12.4
Danbury, CT PMSA	217,980	186,012	31,968	14.7
Dutchess County, NY PMSA	280,150	256,550	23,600	8.4
Jersey City, NJ PMSA	608,975	374,378	234,597	38.5
Middlesex--Somerset--Hunterdon, NJ PMSA	1,169,641	926,235	243,406	20.8
Monmouth--Ocean, NJ PMSA	1,126,217	1,029,258	96,959	8.6
Nassau--Suffolk, NY PMSA	2,753,913	2,356,974	396,939	14.4
New Haven--Meriden, CT PMSA	542,069	495,952	46,117	8.5
New York, NY PMSA	9,314,235	6,174,588	3,139,647	33.7
Newark, NJ PMSA	2,032,989	1,647,182	385,807	19.0
Newburgh, NY--PA PMSA	387,669	356,667	31,002	8.0
Stamford--Norwalk, CT PMSA	353,556	281,493	72,063	20.4
Trenton, NJ PMSA	350,761	302,102	48,659	13.9
Waterbury, CT PMSA	229,064	207,330	21,734	9.5

Table 19. (Continued)

Metropolitan area (rank in total population) [1]	Total	Native	Foreign born	
			Number	Percent
Norfolk--Virginia Beach--Newport News, VA--NC MSA (30)	1,569,541	1,499,171	70,370	4.5
Oklahoma City, OK MSA (48)	1,083,346	1,021,536	61,810	5.7
Orlando, FL MSA (27)	1,644,561	1,447,442	197,119	12.0
Philadelphia--Wilmington--Atlantic City, PA--NJ--DE--MD CMSA (6)	6,188,463	5,754,544	433,919	7.0
Atlantic--Cape May, NJ PMSA	354,878	321,795	33,083	9.3
Philadelphia, PA--NJ PMSA	5,100,931	4,743,510	357,421	7.0
Vineland--Millville--Bridgeton, NJ PMSA	146,438	137,431	9,007	6.2
Wilmington--Newark, DE--MD PMSA	586,216	551,808	34,408	5.9
Phoenix--Mesa, AZ MSA (14)	3,251,876	2,794,393	457,483	14.1
Pittsburgh, PA MSA (21)	2,358,695	2,296,409	62,286	2.6
Portland--Salem, OR--WA CMSA (22)	2,265,223	2,017,155	248,068	11.0
Portland--Vancouver, OR--WA PMSA	1,918,009	1,709,934	208,075	10.8
Salem, OR PMSA	347,214	307,221	39,993	11.5
Providence--Fall River--Warwick, RI--MA MSA (39)	1,188,613	1,045,829	142,784	12.0
Raleigh--Durham--Chapel Hill, NC MSA (40)	1,187,941	1,079,138	108,803	9.2
Rochester, NY MSA (46)	1,098,201	1,035,407	62,794	5.7
Sacramento--Yolo, CA CMSA (24)	1,796,857	1,536,746	260,111	14.5
Sacramento, CA PMSA	1,628,197	1,402,257	225,940	13.9
Yolo, CA PMSA	168,660	134,489	34,171	20.3
St. Louis, MO--IL MSA (18)	2,603,607	2,522,662	80,945	3.1
Salt Lake City--Ogden, UT--MSA (35)	1,333,914	1,219,406	114,508	8.6
San Antonio, TX MSA (29)	1,592,383	1,430,459	161,924	10.2
San Diego, CA MSA (17)	2,813,833	2,207,579	606,254	21.5
San Francisco--Oakland-San Jose, CA CMSA (5)	7,039,362	5,137,058	1,902,304	27.0
Oakland, CA PMSA	2,392,557	1,819,413	573,144	24.0
San Francisco, CA PMSA	1,731,183	1,177,039	554,144	32.0
San Jose, CA PMSA	1,682,585	1,109,455	573,130	34.1

Table 19. (Continued)

Metropolitan area (rank in total population) [1]	Total	Native	Foreign born	
			Number	Percent
Santa Cruz--Watsonville, CA PMSA	255,602	209,100	46,502	18.2
Santa Rosa, CA PMSA	458,614	392,888	65,726	14.3
Vallejo--Fairfield--Napa, CA PMSA	518,821	429,838	88,983	17.2
Seattle--Tacoma-Bremerton, WA CMSA (13)	3,554,760	3,140,405	414,355	11.7
Bremerton, WA PMSA	231,969	218,789	13,180	5.7
Olympia, WA PMSA	207,355	194,617	12,738	6.1
Seattle--Bellevue--Everett, WA PMSA	2,414,616	2,082,704	331,912	13.7
Tacoma, WA PMSA	700,820	644,295	56,525	8.1
Tampa--St. Petersburg--Clearwater, FL MSA (20)	2,395,997	2,162,090	233,907	9.8
Washington--Baltimore, DC--MD--VA--WV CMSA (4)	7,608,070	6,627,449	980,621	12.9
Baltimore, MD PMSA	2,552,994	2,406,866	146,128	5.7
Hagerstown, MD PMSA	131,923	129,446	2,477	1.9
Washington, DC--MD--VA--WV PMSA	4,923,153	4,091,137	832,016	16.9
West Palm Beach--Boca Raton, FL MSA (44)	1,131,184	934,332	196,852	17.4

Footnotes:

* Indicated sample data.

[1]Metropolitan areas as defined effective June 30, 1993. See text for Table 16. Internet Release Date: February 2, 2006

Table 20. Nativity of the Population for Metropolitan Areas With 500,000 or More Population: 1960* (Leading dots indicate subparts)

(See text for sources, definitions, and explanations)

Metropolitan area (rank in total population)	Total	Native	Foreign born	
			Number	Percent
Akron, OH SMSA (45)	513,569	487,060	26,509	5.2
Albany-Schenectady-Troy, NY SMSA (36)	657,503	613,172	44,331	6.7
Atlanta, GA SMSA (22)	1,017,008	1,008,013	8,995	0.9
Baltimore, MD SMSA (12)	1,727,021	1,667,920	59,101	3.4
Birmingham, AL SMSA (38)	634,864	630,610	4,254	0.7
Boston, MA SMSA (7)	2,590,040	2,269,712	320,328	12.4
Buffalo, NY SMSA (14)	1,306,956	1,192,184	114,772	8.8
Chicago-Northwestern Indiana SCA (2)	6,794,453	6,155,341	639,112	9.4
. Chicago, IL SMSA	6,220,913	5,619,898	601,015	9.7
. Gary-Hammond-East Chicago, IN SMSA	573,540	535,443	38,097	6.6
Cincinnati, OH-KY SMSA (19)	1,071,624	1,045,273	26,351	2.5
Cleveland, OH SMSA (11)	1,796,595	1,621,461	175,134	9.7
Columbus, OH SMSA (34)	682,962	668,067	14,895	2.2
Dallas, TX SMSA (18)	1,083,601	1,067,257	16,344	1.5
Dayton, OH SMSA (32)	694,623	682,240	12,383	1.8
Denver, CO SMSA (24)	929,383	894,766	34,617	3.7
Detroit, MI SMSA (5)	3,764,131	3,399,556	364,575	9.7
Fort Worth, TX SMSA (42)	573,676	567,315	6,361	1.1
Hartford, CT SMSA (44)	525,207	464,411	60,796	11.6
Honolulu, HI SMSA (49)	500,409	453,109	47,300	9.5
Houston TX SMSA (15)	1,243,158	1,214,670	28,488	2.3
Indianapolis, IN SMSA (31)	697,567	686,015	11,552	1.7
Kansas City, MO-KS SMSA (20)	1,040,454	1,017,966	22,488	2.2

Table 20. (Continued)

Metropolitan area (rank in total population)	Total	Native	Foreign born	
			Number	Percent
Los Angles-Long Beach, CA SMSA (2)	6,746,356	6,129,679	616,677	9.1
Louisville, KY-IN SMSA (30)	725,139	718,799	6,340	0.9
Memphis, TN SMSA (39)	627,019	621,933	5,086	0.8
Miami, FL SMSA (23)	935,047	822,459	112,588	12.0
Milwaukee, WI SMSA (16)	1,194,290	1,114,645	79,645	6.7
Minneapolis-St. Paul, MN SMSA (13)	1,482,030	1,411,330	70,700	4.8
New Orleans, LA SMSA (25)	868,480	850,412	18,068	2.1
New York-Northeastern New Jersey CSA (1)	14,760,759	12,426,576	2,334,183	15.8
. New York, NY SMSA	10,695,963	8,837,061	1,858,902	17.4
. Jersey City, NJ SMSA	610,734	522,024	88,710	14.5
. Newark, NJ SMSA	1,689,420	1,507,896	181,524	10.7
. Paterson-Clifton-Passaic, NJ SMSA	1,186,873	1,037,729	149,144	12.6
. Middlesex County, NJ	433,856	391,635	42,221	9.7
. Somerset County, NJ	143,913	130,231	13,682	9.5
Norfolk-Portsmouth, VA SMSA (41)	578,507	569,952	8,555	1.5
Oklahoma City, OK SMSA (46)	511,833	506,359	5,474	1.1
Philadelphia, PA-NJ SMSA (4)	4,343,524	4,046,290	297,234	6.8
Phoenix, AZ SMSA (35)	663,510	629,685	33,825	5.1
Pittsburgh, PA SMSA (8)	2,406,301	2,250,640	155,661	6.5
Portland, OR-WA SMSA (26)	821,885	776,336	45,549	5.5
Providence-Pawtucket, RI-MA SMSA (27)	816,148	730,896	85,252	10.4
Rochester, NY SMSA (40)	586,387	527,897	58,490	10.0
Sacramento, CA SMSA (48)	502,778	473,293	29,485	5.9
St. Louis, MO-IL SMSA (9)	2,060,614	2,002,609	58,005	2.8
San Antonio, TX SMSA (33)	687,475	644,216	43,259	6.3

Table 20. (Continued)

Metropolitan area (rank in total population)	Total	Native	Foreign born	
			Number	Percent
San Bernadino-Riverside, CA SMSA (28)	809,782	757,181	52,601	6.5
San Diego, CA SMSA (21)	1,033,011	967,748	65,263	6.3
San Francisco-Oakland, CA SMSA (6)	2,783,355	2,483,114	300,241	10.8
San Jose, CA SMSA (37)	642,315	591,070	51,245	8.0
Seattle, WA SMSA (17)	1,107,213	1,017,246	89,967	8.1
Syracuse, NY SMSA (43)	563,781	527,673	36,108	6.4
Tampa-St. Petersburg, FL SMSA (29)	772,453	722,378	50,075	6.5
Washington, DC-MD-VA SMSA * (10)	1,989,377	1,905,435	83,942	4.2
Youngstown-Warren, OH SMSA (47)	509,006	472,498	36,508	7.2

Footnote:

* Indicates sample data. Internet Release Date: February 2, 2006

Table 21. Nativity of the Population for Metropolitan Districts With 250,000 or More Population: 1940 (Leading dots indicate subparts)

(See text for sources, definitions, and explanations)

Metropolitan district (rank in total population)	Total	Native	Foreign born	
			Number	Percent
Akron, OH (36)	349,705	316,426	33,279	9.5
Albany-Schenectady-Troy, NY (27)	431,575	377,736	53,839	12.5
Allentown-Bethlehem-Easton, PA-NJ (41)	325,142	293,987	31,155	9.6
Atlanta, GA (25)	442,294	436,918	5,376	1.2
Baltimore, MD (11)	1,046,692	976,717	69,975	6.7
Birmingham, AL (29)	407,851	402,405	5,446	1.3
Boston, MA (5)	2,350,514	1,862,373	488,141	20.8
Buffalo-Niagara, NY (14)	857,719	718,589	139,130	16.2
Chicago, IL-IN (2)	4,499,126	3,665,424	833,702	18.5
Cincinnati, OH-KY-IN (16)	789,309	754,487	34,822	4.4
Cleveland, OH (10)	1,214,943	991,680	223,263	18.4
Columbus, OH (35)	365,796	352,131	13,665	3.7
Dallas, TX (33)	376,548	367,903	8,645	2.3
Dayton, OH (47)	271,513	260,400	11,113	4.1
Denver, CO (32)	384,372	355,893	28,479	7.4
Detroit, MI (6)	2,295,867	1,867,656	428,211	18.7
Fall River-New Bedford, MA-RI (46)	272,648	208,116	64,532	23.7
Hartford-New Britain, CT (22)	502,193	401,915	100,278	20.0
Houston TX (21)	510,397	491,598	18,799	3.7
Indianapolis, IN (23)	455,357	443,252	12,105	2.7
Kansas City, MO-Kansas City, KS (18)	634,093	604,934	29,159	4.6
Los Angles, CA (3)	2,904,596	2,536,898	367,698	12.7
Louisville, KY-IN (26)	434,408	426,993	7,415	1.7
Lowell-Lawrence-Haverhill, MA (38)	334,969	264,163	70,806	21.1
Memphis, TN-AR (39)	332,477	327,482	4,995	1.5
Miami, FL (50)	250,537	223,449	27,088	10.8
Milwaukee, WI (15)	790,336	683,919	106,417	13.5

Table 21. (Continued)

Metropolitan area (rank in total population)	Total	Native	Foreign born	
			Number	Percent
Minneapolis-St. Paul, MN (12)	911,077	800,384	110,693	12.2
New Haven, CT (43)	308,228	250,145	58,083	18.8
New Orleans, LA (20)	540,030	523,850	16,180	3.0
New York-Northeastern New Jersey, NY-NJ-CT (1)	11,690,520	8,764,546	2,925,974	25.0
Norfolk-Portsmouth-Newport News, VA (40)	330,396	323,007	7,389	2.2
Omaha, NE-Council Bluffs, IA (45)	287,698	261,174	26,524	9.2
Philadelphia, PA-NJ (4)	2,898,644	2,516,153	382,491	13.2
Pittsburgh, PA (7)	1,994,060	1,736,702	257,358	12.9
Portland, OR-WA (30)	406,406	356,898	49,508	12.2
Providence-Pawtucket, RI-MA (17)	711,500	570,456	141,044	19.8
Rochester, NY (28)	411,970	341,826	70,144	17.0
St. Louis, MO-IL (9)	1,367,977	1,281,242	86,735	6.3
San Antonio, TX (42)	319,010	286,849	32,161	10.1
San Diego, CA (49)	256,368	230,911	25,457	9.9
San Francisco-Oakland, CA (8)	1,428,525	1,170,722	257,803	18.0
Scranton-Wilkes Barre, PA (19)	629,581	542,194	87,387	13.9
Seattle, WA (24)	452,639	377,693	74,946	16.6
Springfield-Holyoke, MA-CT (31)	394,623	320,692	73,931	18.7
Syracuse, NY (48)	258,352	224,668	33,684	13.0
Toledo, OH (37)	341,663	313,310	28,353	8.3
Washington, DC-MD-VA (13)	907,816	865,769	42,047	4.6
Worcester, MA (44)	306,194	247,022	59,172	19.3
Youngstown, OH-PA (34)	372,428	317,152	55,276	14.8

Internet Release Date: February 2, 2006

Table 22. Nativity of the Population by Urban-Rural Residence and Size of Place: 1870 to 1940 and 1960 to 2000 (Leading dots indicate subparts)

(See text for sources, definitions, and explanations)

Year, type of residence, and size of place	Population				Percent distribution by type of residence		
	Total	Native	Foreign born		Total	Native	Foreign born
			Number	Percent			
2000*							
Total	281,421,906	250,314,017	31,107,889	11.1	100.0	100.0	100.0
Urban	222,358,309	192,752,092	29,606,217	13.3	79.0	77.0	95.2
In central place	132,540,981	111,814,254	20,726,727	15.6	47.1	44.7	66.6
Not in central place	89,817,328	80,937,838	8,879,490	9.9	31.9	32.3	28.5
In urbanized area	192,338,121	164,343,643	27,994,478	14.6	68.3	65.7	90.0
In central place	109,701,596	90,240,497	19,461,099	17.7	39.0	36.1	62.6
Not in central place	82,636,525	74,103,146	8,533,379	10.3	29.4	29.6	27.4
In urban cluster	30,020,188	28,408,449	1,611,739	5.4	10.7	11.3	5.2
In central place	22,839,385	21,573,757	1,265,628	5.5	8.1	8.6	4.1
Not in central place	7,180,803	6,834,692	346,111	4.8	2.6	2.7	1.1
Rural	59,063,597	57,561,925	1,501,672	2.5	21.0	23.0	4.8
2,500 or more	4,082,148	3,916,779	165,369	4.1	1.5	1.6	0.5
1,000 to 2,499	4,990,251	4,836,968	153,283	3.1	1.8	1.9	0.5
Less than 1,000	3,832,482	3,752,690	79,792	2.1	1.4	1.5	0.3
Other (not in place)	46,158,716	45,055,488	1,103,228	2.4	16.4	18.0	3.5
Rural nonfarm	56,076,066	54,628,803	1,447,263	2.6	19.9	21.8	4.7
Rural farm	2,987,531	2,933,122	54,409	1.8	1.1	1.2	0.2
1990*							
Total	248,709,873	228,942,557	19,767,316	7.9	100.0	100.0	100.0
Urban	187,051,543	168,546,897	18,504,646	9.9	75.2	73.6	93.6

Table 22. (Continued)

Year, type of residence, and size of place	Population				Percent distribution by type of residence		
	Total	Native	Foreign born		Total	Native	Foreign born
			Number	Percent			
Inside urbanized area	158,258,042	140,802,811	17,455,231	11.0	63.6	61.5	88.3
Central place	78,847,231	69,015,791	9,831,440	12.5	31.7	30.1	49.7
Urban fringe	79,410,811	71,787,020	7,623,791	9.6	31.9	31.4	38.6
Outside urbanized area	28,793,501	27,744,086	1,049,415	3.6	11.6	12.1	5.3
10,000 or more	13,826,325	13,260,584	565,741	4.1	5.6	5.8	2.9
2,500 to 9,999	14,967,176	14,483,502	483,674	3.2	6.0	6.3	2.4
Rural	61,658,330	60,395,660	1,262,670	2.0	24.8	26.4	6.4
1,000 to 2,499	7,047,131	6,881,223	165,908	2.4	2.8	3.0	0.8
Less than 1,000	3,802,263	3,758,824	43,439	1.1	1.5	1.6	0.2
Other (not in place)	50,808,936	49,755,613	1,053,323	2.1	20.4	21.7	5.3
Rural nonfarm	57,786,747	56,581,024	1,205,723	2.1	23.2	24.7	6.1
Rural farm	3,871,583	3,814,636	56,947	1.5	1.6	1.7	0.3
1980*							
Total	226,545,805	212,465,899	14,079,906	6.2	100.0	100.0	100.0
Urban	167,054,638	154,139,673	12,914,965	7.7	73.7	72.5	91.7
Inside urbanized area	139,182,696	127,164,565	12,018,131	8.6	61.4	59.9	85.4
Central place	67,035,742	60,610,967	6,424,775	9.6	29.6	28.5	45.6
Urban fringe	72,146,954	66,553,598	5,593,356	7.8	31.8	31.3	39.7
Outside urbanized area	27,871,942	26,975,108	896,834	3.2	12.3	12.7	6.4
10,000 or more	13,480,685	13,009,780	470,905	3.5	6.0	6.1	3.3
2,500 to 9,999	14,391,257	13,965,328	425,929	3.0	6.4	6.6	3.0
Rural	59,491,167	58,326,226	1,164,941	2.0	26.3	27.5	8.3
1,000 to 2,499	7,034,378	6,872,139	162,239	2.3	3.1	3.2	1.2

Table 22. (Continued)

Year, type of residence, and size of place	Population				Percent distribution by type of residence		
	Total	Native	Foreign born		Total	Native	Foreign born
			Number	Percent			
Other	52,456,789	51,454,087	1,002,702	1.9	23.2	24.2	7.1
Rural nonfarm	53,873,264	52,781,474	1,091,790	2.0	23.8	24.8	7.8
Rural farm	5,617,903	5,544,752	73,151	1.3	2.5	2.6	0.5
1970*							
Total	203,210,158	193,590,856	9,619,302	4.7	100.0	100.0	100.0
Urban	149,332,119	140,611,792	8,720,327	5.8	73.5	72.6	90.7
Inside urbanized area	118,440,006	110,468,396	7,971,610	6.7	58.3	57.1	82.9
Central cities	63,913,205	59,099,762	4,813,443	7.5	31.5	30.5	50.0
Urban fringe	54,526,801	51,368,634	3,158,167	5.8	26.8	26.5	32.8
Outside urbanized area	30,892,113	30,143,396	748,717	2.4	15.2	15.6	7.8
10,000 or more	16,617,734	16,199,308	418,426	2.5	8.2	8.4	4.3
2,500 to 9,999	14,274,379	13,944,088	330,291	2.3	7.0	7.2	3.4
Rural	53,878,039	52,979,064	898,975	1.7	26.5	27.4	9.3
Rural nonfarm	43,276,785	42,515,379	761,406	1.8	21.3	22.0	7.9
Rural farm	10,601,254	10,463,685	137,569	1.3	5.2	5.4	1.4
1960*							
Total	179,325,671	169,587,528	9,738,143	5.4	100.0	100.0	100.0
Urban	125,283,783	116,773,631	8,510,152	6.8	69.9	68.9	87.4
Inside urbanized area	95,821,832	88,275,983	7,545,849	7.9	53.4	52.1	77.5
Central cities	57,981,280	52,874,866	5,106,414	8.8	32.3	31.2	52.4
Urban fringe	37,840,552	35,401,117	2,439,435	6.4	21.1	20.9	25.1
Outside urbanized area	29,461,951	28,497,648	964,303	3.3	16.4	16.8	9.9
10,000 or more	16,188,314	15,617,145	571,169	3.5	9.0	9.2	5.9

Table 22. (Continued)

Year, type of residence, and size of place	Population				Percent distribution by type of residence		
	Total	Native	Foreign born		Total	Native	Foreign born
			Number	Percent			
2,500 to 9,999	13,273,637	12,880,503	393,134	3.0	7.4	7.6	4.0
Rural	54,041,888	52,813,897	1,227,991	2.3	30.1	31.1	12.6
Rural nonfarm	40,596,990	39,589,369	1,007,621	2.5	22.6	23.3	10.3
Rural farm	13,444,898	13,224,528	220,370	1.6	7.5	7.8	2.3
1940							
Total	131,669,275	120,074,379	11,594,896	8.8	100.0	100.0	100.0
Urban	74,423,702	65,146,995	9,276,707	12.5	56.5	54.3	80.0
100,000 or more	37,987,989	31,829,892	6,158,097	16.2	28.9	26.5	53.1
2,500 to 99,999	36,435,713	33,317,103	3,118,610	8.6	27.7	27.7	26.9
Rural	57,245,573	54,927,384	2,318,189	4.0	43.5	45.7	20.0
Rural nonfarm	27,029,385	25,644,685	1,384,700	5.1	20.5	21.4	11.9
Rural farm	30,216,188	29,282,699	933,489	3.1	22.9	24.4	8.1
1930							
Total	122,775,046	108,570,897	14,204,149	11.6	100.0	100.0	100.0
Urban	68,954,823	57,704,008	11,250,815	16.3	56.2	53.1	79.2
100,000 or more	36,325,736	28,872,338	7,453,398	20.5	29.6	26.6	52.5
2,500 to 99,999	32,629,087	28,831,670	3,797,417	11.6	26.6	26.6	26.7
Rural	53,820,223	50,866,889	2,953,334	5.5	43.8	46.9	20.8
Rural nonfarm	23,662,710	21,934,261	1,728,449	7.3	19.3	20.2	12.2
Rural farm	30,157,513	28,932,628	1,224,885	4.1	24.6	26.6	8.6
1920							
Total	105,710,620	91,789,928	13,920,692	13.2	100.0	100.0	100.0
Urban	54,304,603	43,803,661	10,500,942	19.3	51.4	47.7	75.4

Table 22. (Continued)

Year, type of residence, and size of place	Population				Percent distribution by type of residence		
	Total	Native	Foreign born		Total	Native	Foreign born
			Number	Percent			
100,000 or more	27,429,326	20,786,024	6,643,302	24.2	25.9	22.6	47.7
2,500 to 99,999	26,875,277	23,017,637	3,857,640	14.4	25.4	25.1	27.7
Rural	51,406,017	47,986,267	3,419,750	6.7	48.6	52.3	24.6
1910							
Total	91,972,266	78,456,380	13,515,886	14.7	100.0	100.0	100.0
Urban	42,623,383	32,877,686	9,745,697	22.9	46.3	41.9	72.1
100,000 or more	20,302,138	14,419,064	5,883,074	29.0	22.1	18.4	43.5
2,500 to 99,999	22,321,245	18,458,622	3,862,623	17.3	24.3	23.5	28.6
Rural	49,348,883	45,578,694	3,770,189	7.6	53.7	58.1	27.9
1900							
Total	75,994,575	65,653,299	10,341,276	13.6	100.0	100.0	100.0
Urban	30,583,411	23,724,333	6,859,078	22.4	40.2	36.1	66.3
100,000 or more	14,208,347	10,200,262	4,008,085	28.2	18.7	15.5	38.8
Less than 100,000	16,375,064	13,524,071	2,850,993	17.4	21.5	20.6	27.6
25,000 to 99,999	5,509,965	4,387,769	1,122,196	20.4	7.3	6.7	10.9
2,500 to 24,999	10,865,099	9,136,302	1,728,797	15.9	14.3	13.9	16.7
Rural	45,411,164	41,928,966	3,482,198	7.7	59.8	63.9	33.7
1890							
Total	62,622,250	53,372,703	9,249,547	14.8	100.0	100.0	100.0
Urban	22,559,367	16,880,232	5,679,135	25.2	36.0	31.6	61.4
100,000 or more	9,697,960	6,613,312	3,084,648	31.8	15.5	12.4	33.3
Less than 100,000	12,861,407	10,266,920	2,594,487	20.2	20.5	19.2	28.0
25,000 to 99,999	4,291,608	3,294,329	997,279	23.2	6.9	6.2	10.8

Table 22. (Continued)

Year, type of residence, and size of place	Population				Percent distribution by type of residence		
	Total	Native	Foreign born		Total	Native	Foreign born
			Number	Percent			
2,500 to 24,999	8,569,799	6,972,591	1,597,208	18.6	13.7	13.1	17.3
Rural	40,062,883	36,492,471	3,570,412	8.9	64.0	68.4	38.6
1880							
Total	50,155,783	43,475,840	6,679,943	13.3	100.0	100.0	100.0
100,000 or more	6,210,909	4,260,285	1,950,624	31.4	12.4	9.8	29.2
25,000 to 99,999	2,394,284	1,829,060	565,224	23.6	4.8	4.2	8.5
Remainder of population	41,550,590	37,386,495	4,164,095	10.0	82.8	86.0	62.3
1870							
Total	38,558,371	32,991,142	5,567,229	14.4	100.0	100.0	100.0
100,000 or more	4,129,989	2,657,925	1,472,064	35.6	10.7	8.1	26.4
25,000 to 99,999	1,698,357	1,195,776	502,581	29.6	4.4	3.6	9.0
Remainder of population	32,730,025	29,137,441	3,592,584	11.0	84.9	88.3	64.5

Footnote:

* Indicates sample data. Internet Release Date: February 2, 2006

Table 23. Nativity of the Population for the 50 Largest Urban Places: 1870 to 2000 (Leading dots indicate subparts)

(See text for sources, definitions, and explanations)

2000*					1990*				
Rank Place	Total	Native	Foreign born		Rank Place	Total	Native	Foreign born	
			Number	Percent				Number	Percent
1 New York city, NY	8,008,278	5,137,246	2,871,032	35.9	1 New York city, NY	7,322,564	5,239,633	2,082,931	28.4
2 Los Angeles city, CA	3,694,834	2,182,114	1,512,720	40.9	2 Los Angeles city, CA	3,485,398	2,148,733	1,336,665	38.4
3 Chicago city, IL	2,895,964	2,267,058	628,906	21.7	3 Chicago city, IL	2,783,726	2,314,539	469,187	16.9
4 Houston city, TX	1,954,848	1,438,743	516,105	26.4	4 Houston city, TX	1,630,672	1,340,298	290,374	17.8
5 Philadelphia city, PA	1,517,550	1,380,345	137,205	9.0	5 Philadelphia city, PA	1,585,577	1,480,763	104,814	6.6
6 Phoenix city, AZ	1,320,994	1,063,669	257,325	19.5	6 San Diego city, CA	1,110,549	878,411	232,138	20.9
7 San Diego city, CA	1,223,341	909,114	314,227	25.7	7 Detroit city, MI	1,027,974	993,484	34,490	3.4
8 Dallas city, TX	1,188,204	897,768	290,436	24.4	8 Dallas city, TX	1,006,831	880,969	125,862	12.5
9 San Antonio city, TX	1,144,554	1,010,879	133,675	11.7	9 Phoenix city, AZ	983,403	898,731	84,672	8.6
10 Detroit city, MI	951,270	905,729	45,541	4.8	10 San Antonio city, TX	935,927	848,378	87,549	9.4
11 San Jose city, CA	893,889	564,132	329,757	36.9	11 San Jose city, CA	782,225	575,184	207,041	26.5
12 Indianapolis city (balance), IN	782,414	746,347	36,067	4.6	12 Baltimore city, MD	736,014	712,547	23,467	3.2
13 San Francisco city, CA	776,733	491,192	285,541	36.8	13 Indianapolis city, IN	731,321	717,358	13,963	1.9
14 Jacksonville city, FL	735,503	691,842	43,661	5.9	14 San Francisco city, CA	723,959	477,925	246,034	34.0
15 Columbus city, OH	711,644	663,931	47,713	6.7	15 Jacksonville city, FL	635,230	613,467	21,763	3.4
16 Austin city, TX	656,302	547,296	109,006	16.6	16 Columbus city, OH	632,958	609,487	23,471	3.7
17 Baltimore city, MD	651,154	621,516	29,638	4.6	17 Milwaukee city, WI	628,088	598,421	29,667	4.7
18 Memphis city, TN	649,845	623,770	26,075	4.0	18 Memphis city, TN	610,337	602,039	8,298	1.4
19 Milwaukee city, WI	596,956	550,834	46,122	7.7	19 Washington city, DC	606,900	548,013	58,887	9.7
20 Boston city, MA	589,141	437,305	151,836	25.8	20 Boston city, MA	574,283	459,686	114,597	20.0
21 Washington city, DC	572,059	498,498	73,561	12.9	21 Seattle city, WA	516,259	448,523	67,736	13.1
22 El Paso city, TX	564,280	416,775	147,505	26.1	22 El Paso city, TX	515,342	394,910	120,432	23.4
23 Seattle city, WA	563,375	468,423	94,952	16.9	23 Cleveland city, OH	505,616	484,641	20,975	4.1
24 Denver city, CO	554,636	458,035	96,601	17.4	24 New Orleans city, LA	496,938	476,154	20,784	4.2
25 Nashville-Davidson (balance), TN..	545,549	506,613	38,936	7.1	25 Nashville-Davidson, TN	488,518	476,347	12,171	2.5

Table 23. (Continued)

2000*					1990*				
Rank Place	Total	Native	Foreign born		Rank Place	Total	Native	Foreign born	
			Number	Percent				Number	Percent
26 Charlotte city, NC	542,131	482,282	59,849	11.0	26 Denver city, CO	467,610	432,895	34,715	7.4
27 Fort Worth city, TX	535,420	448,300	87,120	16.3	27 Austin city, TX	465,577	425,951	39,626	8.5
28 Portland city, OR	529,025	460,049	68,976	13.0	28 Fort Worth city, TX	447,619	407,319	40,300	9.0
29 Oklahoma City city, OK	505,963	463,078	42,885	8.5	29 Oklahoma City city, OK	444,730	425,998	18,732	4.2
30 Tucson city, AZ	486,591	417,115	69,476	14.3	30 Portland city, OR	437,398	403,797	33,601	7.7
31 New Orleans city, LA	484,674	464,093	20,581	4.2	31 Kansas City city, MO	435,141	422,754	12,387	2.8
32 Las Vegas city, NV	478,868	388,212	90,656	18.9	32 Long Beach city, CA	429,433	325,283	104,150	24.3
33 Cleveland city, OH	478,393	457,021	21,372	4.5	33 Tucson city, AZ	405,390	361,993	43,397	10.7
34 Long Beach city, CA	461,381	329,213	132,168	28.6	34 St. Louis city, MO	396,685	386,651	10,034	2.5
35 Albuquerque city, NM	448,627	408,865	39,762	8.9	35 Charlotte city, NC	396,003	380,884	15,119	3.8
36 Kansas City city, MO	441,269	415,637	25,632	5.8	36 Atlanta city, GA	394,017	380,663	13,354	3.4
37 Fresno city, CA	427,224	340,287	86,937	20.3	37 Virginia Beach city, VA	393,069	372,552	20,517	5.2
38 Virginia Beach city, VA	425,257	396,981	28,276	6.6	38 Albuquerque city, NM	384,736	363,426	21,310	5.5
39 Atlanta city, GA	416,629	389,277	27,352	6.6	39 Oakland city, CA	372,242	298,718	73,524	19.8
40 Sacramento city, CA	407,075	324,459	82,616	20.3	40 Pittsburgh city, PA	369,879	352,933	16,946	4.6
41 Oakland city, CA	399,477	293,361	106,116	26.6	41 Sacramento city, CA	369,365	318,796	50,569	13.7
42 Mesa city, AZ	397,215	352,669	44,546	11.2	42 Minneapolis city, MN	368,383	345,759	22,624	6.1
43 Tulsa city, OK	393,051	367,386	25,665	6.5	43 Tulsa city, OK	367,193	356,183	11,010	3.0
44 Omaha city, NE	390,112	364,425	25,687	6.6	44 Honolulu CDP, HI	365,272	286,957	78,315	21.4
45 Minneapolis city, MN	382,452	326,977	55,475	14.5	45 Cincinnati city, OH	364,040	353,995	10,045	2.8
46 Honolulu CDP, HI	371,619	277,724	93,895	25.3	46 Miami city, FL	358,548	144,420	214,128	59.7
47 Miami city, FL	362,563	146,824	215,739	59.5	47 Fresno city, CA	354,202	293,467	60,735	17.1
48 Colorado Springs city, CO	360,798	335,534	25,264	7.0	48 Omaha city, NE	335,795	326,393	9,402	2.8
49 St. Louis city, MO	348,189	328,647	19,542	5.6	49 Toledo city, OH	332,943	323,680	9,263	2.8
50 Wichita city, KS	343,997	316,059	27,938	8.1	50 Buffalo city, NY	328,123	313,382	14,741	4.5

Table 23. (Continued)

2000*					1990*				
Rank Place	Total	Native	Foreign born		Rank Place	Total	Native	Foreign born	
			Number	Percent				Number	Percent
1 New York city, NY	7,071,639	5,401,440	1,670,199	23.6	1 New York city, NY	7,894,798	6,457,740	1,437,058	18.2
2 Chicago city, IL	3,005,078	2,569,846	435,232	14.5	2 Chicago city, IL	3,362,947	2,989,028	373,919	11.1
3 Los Angeles city, CA	2,966,850	2,162,032	804,818	27.1	3 Los Angeles city, CA	2,815,998	2,405,128	410,870	14.6
4 Philadelphia city, PA	1,688,210	1,580,259	107,951	6.4	4 Philadelphia city, PA	1,948,608	1,821,712	126,896	6.5
5 Houston city, TX	1,595,167	1,439,590	155,577	9.8	5 Detroit city, MI	1,511,322	1,391,975	119,347	7.9
6 Detroit city, MI	1,203,339	1,135,036	68,303	5.7	6 Houston city, TX	1,231,572	1,194,071	37,501	3.0
7 Dallas city, TX	904,074	849,162	54,912	6.1	7 Baltimore city, MD	905,757	877,047	28,710	3.2
8 San Diego city, CA	875,538	744,632	130,906	15.0	8 Dallas city, TX	844,280	826,854	17,426	2.1
9 Phoenix city, AZ	789,704	745,042	44,662	5.7	9 Washington city, DC	756,492	722,930	33,562	4.4
10 Baltimore city, MD	786,775	762,108	24,667	3.1	10 Cleveland city, OH	750,932	694,532	56,400	7.5
11 San Antonio city, TX	785,809	720,933	64,876	8.3	11 Indianapolis city, IN	744,768	733,895	10,873	1.5
12 Indianapolis city, IN	700,719	687,294	13,425	1.9	12 Milwaukee city, WI	717,110	677,534	39,576	5.5
13 San Francisco city, CA	678,974	486,770	192,204	28.3	13 San Francisco city, CA	715,673	561,166	154,507	21.6
14 Memphis city, TN	646,356	637,969	8,387	1.3	14 San Diego city, CA	696,474	643,497	52,977	7.6
15 Washington city, DC	638,333	597,774	40,559	6.4	15 San Antonio city, TX	654,468	615,779	38,689	5.9
16 Milwaukee city, WI	636,212	604,494	31,718	5.0	16 Boston city, MA	641,056	557,068	83,988	13.1
17 San Jose city, CA	629,442	538,528	90,914	14.4	17 Memphis city, TN	623,753	618,652	5,101	0.8
18 Cleveland city, OH	573,822	540,475	33,347	5.8	18 St. Louis city, MO	622,234	605,974	16,260	2.6
19 Columbus city, OH	564,866	548,411	16,455	2.9	19 New Orleans city, LA	593,467	575,358	18,109	3.1
20 Boston city, MA	562,994	475,938	87,056	15.5	20 Phoenix city, AZ	581,466	559,810	21,656	3.7
21 New Orleans city, LA	557,515	535,806	21,709	3.9	21 Columbus city, OH	539,469	528,275	11,194	2.1
22 Jacksonville city, FL	540,920	525,436	15,484	2.9	22 Seattle city, WA	530,860	482,437	48,423	9.1
23 Seattle city, WA	493,846	438,230	55,616	11.3	23 Jacksonville city, FL	528,865	519,169	9,696	1.8
24 Denver city, CO	492,365	461,653	30,712	6.2	24 Pittsburgh city, PA	520,146	488,871	31,275	6.0
25 Nashville-Davidson, TN	455,663	448,000	7,663	1.7	25 Denver city, CO	514,678	493,752	20,926	4.1
26 St. Louis city, MO	453,085	441,207	11,878	2.6	26 Kansas City city, MO	507,247	496,995	10,252	2.0
27 Kansas City city, MO	448,154	435,415	12,739	2.8	27 Atlanta city, GA	497,046	491,194	5,852	1.2

Table 23. (Continued)

2000*					1990*				
Rank Place	Total	Native	Foreign born		Rank Place	Total	Native	Foreign born	
			Number	Percent				Number	Percent
28 El Paso city, TX	425,259	334,352	90,907	21.4	28 Buffalo city, NY	462,781	427,529	35,252	7.6
29 Atlanta city, GA	425,022	415,245	9,777	2.3	29 Cincinnati city, OH	452,376	440,039	12,337	2.7
30 Pittsburgh city, PA	423,938	401,743	22,195	5.2	30 Nashville-Davidson, TN	448,003	444,315	3,688	0.8
31 Oklahoma City city, OK	403,243	391,791	11,452	2.8	31 San Jose city, CA	447,025	413,063	33,962	7.6
32 Cincinnati city, OH	385,457	374,833	10,624	2.8	32 Minneapolis city, MN	434,408	413,533	20,875	4.8
33 Fort Worth city, TX	385,166	366,854	18,312	4.8	33 Fort Worth city, TX	393,516	387,577	5,939	1.5
34 Minneapolis city, MN	370,951	352,691	18,260	4.9	34 Toledo city, OH	384,067	371,601	12,466	3.2
35 Portland city, OR	366,423	340,440	25,983	7.1	35 Newark city, NJ	382,374	342,270	40,104	10.5
36 Honolulu CDP, HI	365,048	297,010	68,038	18.6	36 Portland city, OR	381,927	360,847	21,080	5.5
37 Long Beach city, CA	361,334	309,923	51,411	14.2	37 Oklahoma City city, OK	366,756	362,877	3,879	1.1
38 Tulsa city, OK	360,919	351,570	9,349	2.6	38 Oakland city, CA	361,607	329,368	32,239	8.9
39 Buffalo city, NY	357,870	335,845	22,025	6.2	39 Louisville city, KY	361,496	358,058	3,438	1.0
40 Toledo city, OH	354,635	343,625	11,010	3.1	40 Long Beach city, CA	358,622	334,370	24,252	6.8
41 Miami city, FL	346,865	160,585	186,280	53.7	41 Omaha city, NE	347,790	337,053	10,737	3.1
42 Austin city, TX	345,544	328,840	16,704	4.8	42 Miami city, FL	335,062	194,855	140,207	41.8
43 Oakland city, CA	339,337	296,758	42,579	12.5	43 Tulsa city, OK	331,768	328,269	3,499	1.1
44 Albuquerque city, NM	331,767	316,711	15,056	4.5	44 Honolulu CDP, HI	324,869	289,644	35,225	10.8
45 Tucson city, AZ	330,537	304,331	26,206	7.9	45 El Paso city, TX	322,261	277,919	44,342	13.8
46 Newark city, NJ	329,248	281,509	47,739	14.5	46 St. Paul city, MN	310,004	297,966	12,038	3.9
47 Charlotte city, NC	314,447	305,705	8,742	2.8	47 Norfolk city, VA	307,951	300,477	7,474	2.4
48 Omaha city, NE	314,267	304,103	10,164	3.2	48 Birmingham city, AL	300,559	298,440	2,119	0.7
49 Louisville city, KY	298,455	294,293	4,162	1.4	49 Rochester city, NY	296,233	265,003	31,230	10.5
50 Birmingham city, AL	284,413	281,182	3,231	1.1	50 Tampa city, FL	277,748	261,381	16,367	5.9

Table 23. (Continued)

1960*					1950*				
Rank Place	Total	Native	Foreign born		Rank Place	Total	Native	Foreign born	
			Number	Percent				Number	Percent
1 New York city, NY	7,783,314	6,224,624	1,558,690	20.0	1 New York city, NY	7,887,380	6,026,450	1,860,930	23.6
2 Chicago city, IL	3,550,404	3,112,012	438,392	12.3	2 Chicago city, IL	3,611,580	3,078,610	532,970	14.8
3 Los Angeles city, CA	2,481,456	2,169,779	311,677	12.6	3 Philadelphia city, PA	2,068,095	1,830,300	237,795	11.5
4 Philadelphia city, PA	2,002,509	1,824,082	178,427	8.9	4 Los Angeles city, CA	1,965,150	1,702,210	262,940	13.4
5 Detroit city, MI	1,670,144	1,468,431	201,713	12.1	5 Detroit city, MI	1,846,660	1,568,400	278,260	15.1
6 Baltimore city, MD	939,024	899,337	39,687	4.2	6 Baltimore city, MD	945,940	893,295	52,645	5.6
7 Houston city, TX	938,219	913,920	24,299	2.6	7 Cleveland city, OH	912,840	779,960	132,880	14.6
8 Cleveland city, OH	876,050	779,466	96,584	11.0	8 St. Louis city, MO	853,490	811,435	42,055	4.9
9 Washington city, DC	763,956	724,985	38,971	5.1	9 Washington city, DC	800,830	758,090	42,740	5.3
10 St. Louis city, MO	750,026	723,547	26,479	3.5	10 Boston city, MA	800,590	651,590	149,000	18.6
11 Milwaukee city, WI	741,324	684,310	57,014	7.7	11 San Francisco city, CA	775,075	638,065	137,010	17.7
12 San Francisco city, CA	740,316	597,785	142,531	19.3	12 Pittsburgh city, PA	675,465	609,895	65,570	9.7
13 Boston city, MA	697,938	587,974	109,964	15.8	13 Milwaukee city, WI	636,005	572,815	63,190	9.9
14 Dallas city, TX	679,684	666,964	12,720	1.9	14 Houston city, TX	594,585	577,030	17,555	3.0
15 New Orleans city, LA	627,525	612,945	14,580	2.3	15 Buffalo city, NY	577,825	507,320	70,505	12.2
16 Pittsburgh city, PA	604,332	559,079	45,253	7.5	16 New Orleans city, LA	568,680	553,335	15,345	2.7
17 San Antonio city, TX	588,042	548,258	39,784	6.8	17 Minneapolis city, MN	519,245	470,455	48,790	9.4
18 San Diego city, CA	573,224	532,797	40,427	7.1	18 Cincinnati city, OH	502,010	481,485	20,525	4.1
19 Seattle city, WA	557,087	497,367	59,720	10.7	19 Seattle city, WA	466,110	406,845	59,265	12.7
20 Buffalo city, NY	532,759	477,739	55,020	10.3	20 Kansas City city, MO	456,710	440,660	16,050	3.5
21 Cincinnati city, OH	502,550	485,950	16,600	3.3	21 Newark city, NJ	437,540	365,730	71,810	16.4
22 Memphis city, TN	497,524	493,112	4,412	0.9	22 Dallas city, TX	432,970	424,620	8,350	1.9
23 Denver city, CO	493,887	470,134	23,753	4.8	23 Indianapolis city, IN	426,945	418,015	8,930	2.1
24 Atlanta city, GA	487,275	482,680	4,595	0.9	24 Denver city, CO	415,760	392,650	23,110	5.6
25 Minneapolis city, MN	482,872	448,424	34,448	7.1	25 San Antonio city, TX	407,335	374,340	32,995	8.1
26 Indianapolis city, IN	476,258	467,642	8,616	1.8	26 Memphis city, TN	394,985	390,650	4,335	1.1
27 Kansas City city, MO	476,500	463,329	13,171	2.8	27 Oakland city, CA	383,200	342,455	40,745	10.6
28 Columbus city, OH	471,316	460,264	11,052	2.3	28 Portland city, OR	373,105	338,185	34,920	9.4

Table 23. (Continued)

1960*					1950*				
Rank Place	Total	Native	Foreign born		Rank Place	Total	Native	Foreign born	
			Number	Percent				Number	Percent
29 Phoenix city, AZ	439,170	419,732	19,438	4.4	29 Louisville city, KY	367,375	362,485	4,890	1.3
30 Newark city, NJ	405,220	355,261	49,959	12.3	30 Columbus city, OH	362,205	351,740	10,465	2.9
31 Louisville city, KY	390,639	386,683	3,956	1.0	31 San Diego city, CA	333,865	308,605	25,260	7.6
32 Portland city, OR	372,664	345,238	27,426	7.4	32 Atlanta city, GA	331,210	327,015	4,195	1.3
33 Oakland city, CA	367,548	332,369	35,179	9.6	33 Rochester city, NY	330,990	281,945	49,045	14.8
34 Fort Worth city, TX	356,729	351,913	4,816	1.4	34 Birmingham city, AL	325,745	321,925	3,820	1.2
35 Long Beach city, CA	344,153	322,700	21,453	6.2	35 St. Paul city, MN	310,220	285,755	24,465	7.9
36 Birmingham city, AL	340,887	338,260	2,627	0.8	36 Toledo city, OH	303,725	283,650	20,075	6.6
37 Oklahoma City city, OK	324,253	320,757	3,496	1.1	37 Jersey City city, NJ	299,130	257,740	41,390	13.8
38 Rochester city, NY	318,611	276,567	42,044	13.2	38 Fort Worth city, TX	277,585	273,465	4,120	1.5
39 Toledo city, OH	318,003	302,620	15,383	4.8	39 Akron city, OH	273,710	252,855	20,855	7.6
40 St. Paul city, MN	313,411	295,997	17,414	5.6	40 Long Beach city, CA	250,135	233,875	16,260	6.5
41 Norfolk city, VA	305,872	300,091	5,781	1.9	41 Omaha city, NE	249,740	232,210	17,530	7.0
42 Omaha city, NE	301,598	287,215	14,383	4.8	42 Miami city, FL	248,970	218,850	30,120	12.1
43 Honolulu CDP, HI	294,194	263,216	30,978	10.5	43 Providence city, RI	248,520	209,085	39,435	15.9
44 Miami city, FL	291,688	242,442	49,246	16.9	44 Dayton city, OH	243,050	234,985	8,065	3.3
45 Akron city, OH	290,351	272,988	17,363	6.0	45 Oklahoma City city, OK	242,085	239,380	2,705	1.1
46 El Paso city, TX	276,687	233,673	43,014	15.5	46 Richmond city, VA	229,655	225,800	3,855	1.7
47 Jersey City city, NJ	276,101	245,128	30,973	11.2	47 Syracuse city, NY	218,830	195,335	23,495	10.7
48 Tampa city, FL	274,970	258,986	15,984	5.8	48 Norfolk city, VA	214,360	209,290	5,070	2.4
49 Dayton city, OH	262,332	256,234	6,098	2.3	49 Jacksonville city, FL	204,275	199,995	4,280	2.1
50 Tulsa city, OK	261,685	258,738	2,947	1.1	50 Worcester city, MA	202,940	168,925	34,015	16.8

Table 23. (Continued)

1940					1930				
Rank Place	Total	Native	Foreign born		Rank Place	Total	Native	Foreign born	
			Number	Percent				Number	Percent
1 New York city, NY	7,454,995	5,316,338	2,138,657	28.7	1 New York city, NY	6,930,446	4,571,760	2,358,686	34.0
2 Chicago city, IL	3,396,808	2,721,661	675,147	19.9	2 Chicago city, IL	3,376,438	2,517,029	859,409	25.5
3 Philadelphia city, PA	1,931,334	1,638,788	292,546	15.1	3 Philadelphia city, PA	1,950,961	1,578,883	372,078	19.1
4 Detroit city, MI	1,623,452	1,300,764	322,688	19.9	4 Detroit city, MI	1,568,662	1,162,780	405,882	25.9
5 Los Angeles city, CA	1,504,277	1,277,240	227,037	15.1	5 Los Angeles city, CA	1,238,048	990,913	247,135	20.0
6 Cleveland city, OH	878,336	698,552	179,784	20.5	6 Cleveland city, OH	900,429	669,483	230,946	25.6
7 Baltimore city, MD	859,100	797,402	61,698	7.2	7 St. Louis city, MO	821,960	740,614	81,346	9.9
8 St. Louis city, MO	816,048	756,401	59,647	7.3	8 Baltimore city, MD	804,874	729,426	75,448	9.4
9 Boston city, MA	770,816	586,736	184,080	23.9	9 Boston city, MA	781,188	547,501	233,687	29.9
10 Pittsburgh city, PA	671,659	586,756	84,903	12.6	10 Pittsburgh city, PA	669,817	560,132	109,685	16.4
11 Washington city, DC	663,091	628,175	34,916	5.3	11 San Francisco city, CA	634,394	462,753	171,641	27.1
12 San Francisco city, CA	634,536	494,513	140,023	22.1	12 Milwaukee city, WI	578,249	467,638	110,611	19.1
13 Milwaukee city, WI	587,472	503,531	83,941	14.3	13 Buffalo city, NY	573,076	454,135	118,941	20.8
14 Buffalo city, NY	575,901	483,500	92,401	16.0	14 Washington city, DC	486,869	456,136	30,733	6.3
15 New Orleans city, LA	494,537	479,334	15,203	3.1	15 Minneapolis city, MN	464,356	383,233	81,123	17.5
16 Minneapolis city, MN	492,370	428,006	64,364	13.1	16 New Orleans city, LA	458,762	437,716	21,046	4.6
17 Cincinnati city, OH	455,610	429,712	25,898	5.7	17 Cincinnati city, OH	451,160	416,174	34,986	7.8
18 Newark city, NJ	429,760	338,889	90,871	21.1	18 Newark city, NJ	442,337	326,202	116,135	26.3
19 Kansas City city, MO	399,178	379,758	19,420	4.9	19 Kansas City city, MO	399,746	373,548	26,198	6.6
20 Indianapolis city, IN	386,972	376,344	10,628	2.7	20 Seattle city, WA	365,583	287,241	78,342	21.4
21 Houston city, TX	384,514	369,050	15,464	4.0	21 Indianapolis city, IN	364,161	350,307	13,854	3.8
22 Seattle city, WA	368,302	304,832	63,470	17.2	22 Rochester city, NY	328,132	253,293	74,839	22.8
23 Rochester city, NY	324,975	264,737	60,238	18.5	23 Jersey City city, NJ	316,715	246,027	70,688	22.3
24 Denver city, CO	322,412	297,430	24,982	7.7	24 Louisville city, KY	307,745	298,714	9,031	2.9
25 Louisville city, KY	319,077	312,832	6,245	2.0	25 Portland city, OR	301,815	251,587	50,228	16.6
26 Columbus city, OH	306,087	294,035	12,052	3.9	26 Houston city, TX	292,352	274,415	17,937	6.1
27 Portland city, OR	305,394	265,389	40,005	13.1	27 Toledo city, OH	290,718	256,717	34,001	11.7
28 Atlanta city, GA	302,288	297,934	4,354	1.4	28 Columbus city, OH	290,564	275,122	15,442	5.3

Table 23. (Continued)

1940					1930				
Rank Place	Total	Native	Foreign born		Rank Place	Total	Native	Foreign born	
			Number	Percent				Number	Percent
29 Oakland city, CA	302,163	257,622	44,541	14.7	29 Denver city, CO	287,861	255,004	32,857	11.4
30 Jersey City city, NJ	301,173	247,797	53,376	17.7	30 Oakland city, CA	284,063	230,032	54,031	19.0
31 Dallas city, TX	294,734	287,339	7,395	2.5	31 St. Paul city, MN	271,606	226,954	44,652	16.4
32 Memphis city, TN	292,942	288,431	4,511	1.5	32 Atlanta city, GA	270,366	265,574	4,792	1.8
33 St. Paul city, MN	287,736	254,020	33,716	11.7	33 Dallas city, TX	260,475	251,014	9,461	3.6
34 Toledo city, OH	282,349	257,493	24,856	8.8	34 Birmingham city, AL	259,678	253,764	5,914	2.3
35 Birmingham city, AL	267,583	263,127	4,456	1.7	35 Akron city, OH	255,040	223,346	31,694	12.4
36 San Antonio city, TX	253,854	225,558	28,296	11.1	36 Memphis city, TN	253,143	247,816	5,327	2.1
37 Providence city, RI	253,504	201,655	51,849	20.5	37 Providence city, RI	252,981	187,626	65,355	25.8
38 Akron city, OH	244,791	219,313	25,478	10.4	38 San Antonio city, TX	231,542	190,830	40,712	17.6
39 Omaha city, NE	223,844	201,455	22,389	10.0	39 Omaha city, NE	214,006	184,480	29,526	13.8
40 Dayton city, OH	210,718	201,357	9,361	4.4	40 Syracuse city, NY	209,326	174,176	35,150	16.8
41 Syracuse city, NY	205,967	178,335	27,632	13.4	41 Dayton city, OH	200,982	188,888	12,094	6.0
42 Oklahoma City city, OK	204,424	201,573	2,851	1.4	42 Worcester city, MA	195,311	144,150	51,161	26.2
43 San Diego city, CA	203,341	183,228	20,113	9.9	43 Oklahoma City city, OK	185,389	181,667	3,722	2.0
44 Worcester city, MA	193,694	153,634	40,060	20.7	44 Richmond city, VA	182,929	178,810	4,119	2.3
45 Richmond city, VA	193,042	189,555	3,487	1.8	45 Youngstown city, OH	170,002	136,771	33,231	19.5
46 Fort Worth city, TX	177,662	174,098	3,564	2.0	46 Grand Rapids city, MI	168,592	141,243	27,349	16.2
47 Jacksonville city, FL	173,065	168,970	4,095	2.4	47 Hartford city, CT	164,072	119,416	44,656	27.2
48 Miami city, FL	172,172	155,547	16,625	9.7	48 Fort Worth city, TX	163,447	158,514	4,933	3.0
49 Youngstown city, OH	167,720	141,002	26,718	15.9	49 New Haven city, CT	162,655	122,111	40,544	24.9
50 Nashville city, TN	167,402	165,846	1,556	0.9	50 Flint city, MI	156,492	135,028	21,464	13.7

Table 23. (Continued)

1920					1910				
Rank Place	Total	Native	Foreign born		Rank Place	Total	Native	Foreign born	
			Number	Percent				Number	Percent
1 New York city, NY	5,620,048	3,591,888	2,028,160	36.1	1 New York city, NY	4,766,883	2,822,526	1,944,357	40.8
2 Chicago city, IL	2,701,705	1,893,147	808,558	29.9	2 Chicago city, IL	2,185,283	1,401,855	783,428	35.9
3 Philadelphia city, PA	1,823,779	1,423,035	400,744	22.0	3 Philadelphia city, PA	1,549,008	1,164,301	384,707	24.8
4 Detroit city, MI	993,678	702,794	290,884	29.3	4 St. Louis city, MO	687,029	560,806	126,223	18.4
5 Cleveland city, OH	796,841	556,668	240,173	30.1	5 Boston city, MA	670,585	427,220	243,365	36.3
6 St. Louis city, MO	772,897	669,271	103,626	13.4	6 Cleveland city, OH	560,663	364,493	196,170	35.0
7 Boston city, MA	748,060	505,441	242,619	32.4	7 Baltimore city, MD	558,485	480,823	77,662	13.9
8 Baltimore city, MD	733,826	649,017	84,809	11.6	8 Pittsburgh city, PA	533,905	392,981	140,924	26.4
9 Pittsburgh city, PA	588,343	467,551	120,792	20.5	9 Detroit city, MI	465,766	308,232	157,534	33.8
10 Los Angeles city, CA	576,673	454,542	122,131	21.2	10 Buffalo city, NY	423,715	305,026	118,689	28.0
11 Buffalo city, NY	506,775	384,951	121,824	24.0	11 San Francisco city, CA	416,912	274,614	142,298	34.1
12 San Francisco city, CA	506,676	357,481	149,195	29.4	12 Milwaukee city, WI	373,857	262,328	111,529	29.8
13 Milwaukee city, WI	457,147	346,987	110,160	24.1	13 Cincinnati city, OH	363,591	306,732	56,859	15.6
14 Washington city, DC	437,571	408,206	29,365	6.7	14 Newark city, NJ	347,469	236,462	111,007	31.9
15 Newark city, NJ	414,524	296,975	117,549	28.4	15 New Orleans city, LA	339,075	310,742	28,333	8.4
16 Cincinnati city, OH	401,247	358,326	42,921	10.7	16 Washington city, DC	331,069	306,167	24,902	7.5
17 New Orleans city, LA	387,219	359,854	27,365	7.1	17 Los Angeles city, CA	319,198	253,065	66,133	20.7
18 Minneapolis city, MN	380,582	292,334	88,248	23.2	18 Minneapolis city, MN	301,408	215,309	86,099	28.6
19 Kansas City city, MO	324,410	296,827	27,583	8.5	19 Jersey City city, NJ	267,779	189,792	77,987	29.1
20 Seattle city, WA	315,312	234,336	80,976	25.7	20 Kansas City city, MO	248,381	222,915	25,466	10.3
21 Indianapolis city, IN	314,194	297,098	17,096	5.4	21 Seattle city, WA	237,194	169,738	67,456	28.4
22 Jersey City city, NJ	298,103	221,809	76,294	25.6	22 Indianapolis city, IN	233,650	213,808	19,842	8.5
23 Rochester city, NY	295,750	224,339	71,411	24.1	23 Providence city, RI	224,326	147,327	76,999	34.3
24 Portland city, OR	258,288	208,510	49,778	19.3	24 Louisville city, KY	223,928	206,455	17,473	7.8
25 Denver city, CO	256,491	218,261	38,230	14.9	25 Rochester city, NY	218,149	159,073	59,076	27.1
26 Toledo city, OH	243,164	204,868	38,296	15.7	26 St. Paul city, MN	214,744	158,087	56,657	26.4
27 Providence city, RI	237,595	167,700	69,895	29.4	27 Denver city, CO	213,381	173,632	39,749	18.6
28 Columbus city, OH	237,031	220,844	16,187	6.8	28 Portland city, OR	207,214	156,902	50,312	24.3

Table 23. (Continued)

1920					1910				
Rank Place	Total	Native	Foreign born		Rank Place	Total	Native	Foreign born	
			Number	Percent				Number	Percent
29 Louisville city, KY	234,891	223,224	11,667	5.0	29 Columbus city, OH	181,511	165,148	16,363	9.0
30 St. Paul city, MN	234,698	182,976	51,722	22.0	30 Toledo city, OH	168,497	136,353	32,144	19.1
31 Oakland city, CA	216,261	166,366	49,895	23.1	31 Atlanta city, GA	154,839	150,338	4,501	2.9
32 Akron city, OH	208,435	170,414	38,021	18.2	32 Oakland city, CA	150,174	109,328	40,846	27.2
33 Atlanta city, GA	200,616	195,827	4,789	2.4	33 Worcester city, MA	145,986	97,389	48,597	33.3
34 Omaha city, NE	191,601	155,956	35,645	18.6	34 Syracuse city, NY	137,249	106,401	30,848	22.5
35 Worcester city, MA	179,754	126,227	53,527	29.8	35 New Haven city, CT	133,605	90,616	42,989	32.2
36 Birmingham city, AL	178,806	172,666	6,140	3.4	36 Birmingham city, AL	132,685	126,955	5,730	4.3
37 Syracuse city, NY	171,717	139,334	32,383	18.9	37 Memphis city, TN	131,105	124,585	6,520	5.0
38 Richmond city, VA	171,667	166,954	4,713	2.7	38 Scranton city, PA	129,867	94,745	35,122	27.0
39 New Haven city, CT	162,537	116,413	46,124	28.4	39 Richmond city, VA	127,628	123,492	4,136	3.2
40 Memphis city, TN	162,351	156,507	5,844	3.6	40 Paterson city, NJ	125,600	80,115	45,485	36.2
41 San Antonio city, TX	161,379	124,555	36,824	22.8	41 Omaha city, NE	124,096	96,917	27,179	21.9
42 Dallas city, TX	158,976	150,175	8,801	5.5	42 Fall River city, MA	119,295	68,337	50,958	42.7
43 Dayton city, OH	152,559	139,394	13,165	8.6	43 Dayton city, OH	116,577	102,685	13,892	11.9
44 Bridgeport city, CT	143,555	96,773	46,782	32.6	44 Grand Rapids city, MI	112,571	84,184	28,387	25.2
45 Houston city, TX	138,276	126,188	12,088	8.7	45 Nashville city, TN	110,364	107,347	3,017	2.7
46 Hartford city, CT	138,036	97,124	40,912	29.6	46 Lowell city, MA	106,294	62,800	43,494	40.9
47 Scranton city, PA	137,783	109,196	28,587	20.7	47 Cambridge city, MA	104,839	69,511	35,328	33.7
48 Grand Rapids city, MI	137,634	109,207	28,427	20.7	48 Spokane city, WA	104,402	82,582	21,820	20.9
49 Paterson city, NJ	135,875	90,633	45,242	33.3	49 Bridgeport city, CT	102,054	65,790	36,264	35.5
50 Youngstown city, OH	132,358	98,413	33,945	25.6	50 Albany city, NY	100,253	82,035	18,218	18.2

Table 23. (Continued)

1900					1890				
Rank Place	Total	Native	Foreign born		Rank Place	Total	Native	Foreign born	
			Number	Percent				Number	Percent
1 New York city, NY	3,437,202	2,167,122	1,270,080	37.0	1 New York city, NY	1,515,301	875,358	639,943	42.2
2 Chicago city, IL	1,698,575	1,111,463	587,112	34.6	2 Chicago city, IL	1,099,850	649,184	450,666	41.0
3 Philadelphia city, PA	1,293,697	998,357	295,340	22.8	3 Philadelphia city, PA	1,046,964	777,484	269,480	25.7
4 St. Louis city, MO	575,238	463,882	111,356	19.4	4 Brooklyn city, NY	806,343	544,643	261,700	32.5
5 Boston city, MA	560,892	363,763	197,129	35.1	5 St. Louis city, MO	451,770	336,894	114,876	25.4
6 Baltimore city, MD	508,957	440,357	68,600	13.5	6 Boston city, MA	448,477	290,305	158,172	35.3
7 Cleveland city, OH	381,768	257,137	124,631	32.6	7 Baltimore city, MD	434,439	365,436	69,003	15.9
8 Buffalo city, NY	352,387	248,135	104,252	29.6	8 San Francisco city, CA	298,997	172,186	126,811	42.4
9 San Francisco city, CA	342,782	225,897	116,885	34.1	9 Cincinnati city, OH	296,908	225,500	71,408	24.1
10 Cincinnati city, OH	325,902	267,941	57,961	17.8	10 Cleveland city, OH	261,353	164,258	97,095	37.2
11 Pittsburgh city, PA	321,616	236,738	84,878	26.4	11 Buffalo city, NY	255,664	166,179	89,485	35.0
12 New Orleans city, LA	287,104	256,779	30,325	10.6	12 New Orleans city, LA	242,039	207,670	34,369	14.2
13 Detroit city, MI	285,704	189,201	96,503	33.8	13 Pittsburgh city, PA	238,617	165,328	73,289	30.7
14 Milwaukee city, WI	285,315	196,324	88,991	31.2	14 Washington city, DC	230,392	211,622	18,770	8.1
15 Washington city, DC	278,718	258,599	20,119	7.2	15 Detroit city, MI	205,876	124,167	81,709	39.7
16 Newark city, NJ	246,070	174,707	71,363	29.0	16 Milwaukee city, WI	204,468	124,892	79,576	38.9
17 Jersey City city, NJ	206,433	148,009	58,424	28.3	17 Newark city, NJ	181,830	126,259	55,571	30.6
18 Louisville city, KY	204,731	183,304	21,427	10.5	18 Minneapolis city, MN	164,738	104,180	60,558	36.8
19 Minneapolis city, MN	202,718	141,697	61,021	30.1	19 Jersey City city, NJ	163,003	109,645	53,358	32.7
20 Providence city, RI	175,597	119,742	55,855	31.8	20 Louisville city, KY	161,129	137,619	23,510	14.6
21 Indianapolis city, IN	169,164	152,042	17,122	10.1	21 Omaha city, NE	140,452	105,413	35,039	24.9
22 Kansas City city, MO	163,752	145,342	18,410	11.2	22 Rochester city, NY	133,896	94,121	39,775	29.7
23 St. Paul city, MN	163,065	116,246	46,819	28.7	23 St. Paul city, MN	133,156	79,979	53,177	39.9
24 Rochester city, NY	162,608	121,860	40,748	25.1	24 Kansas City city, MO	132,716	111,858	20,858	15.7
25 Denver city, CO	133,859	108,558	25,301	18.9	25 Providence city, RI	132,146	91,782	40,364	30.5
26 Toledo city, OH	131,822	104,000	27,822	21.1	26 Denver city, CO	106,713	81,249	25,464	23.9
27 Allegheny city, PA	129,896	99,680	30,216	23.3	27 Indianapolis city, IN	105,436	90,949	14,487	13.7
28 Columbus city, OH	125,560	113,232	12,328	9.8	28 Allegheny city, PA	105,287	79,152	26,135	24.8

Table 23. (Continued)

1900					1890				
Rank Place	Total	Native	Foreign born		Rank Place	Total	Native	Foreign born	
			Number	Percent				Number	Percent
29 Worcester city, MA	118,421	80,769	37,652	31.8	29 Albany city, NY	94,923	72,630	22,293	23.5
30 Syracuse city, NY	108,374	84,617	23,757	21.9	30 Columbus city, OH	88,150	75,662	12,488	14.2
31 New Haven city, CT	108,027	77,225	30,802	28.5	31 Syracuse city, NY	88,143	65,801	22,342	25.3
32 Paterson city, NJ	105,171	66,380	38,791	36.9	32 New Haven city, CT	81,298	58,304	22,994	28.3
33 Fall River city, MA	104,863	54,821	50,042	47.7	33 Worcester city, MA	84,655	57,952	26,703	31.5
34 St. Joseph city, MO	102,979	94,555	8,424	8.2	34 Toledo city, OH	81,434	59,245	22,189	27.2
35 Omaha city, NE	102,555	79,003	23,552	23.0	35 Richmond city, VA	81,388	77,915	3,473	4.3
36 Los Angeles city, CA	102,479	82,515	19,964	19.5	36 Paterson city, NJ	78,347	47,185	31,162	39.8
37 Memphis city, TN	102,320	97,210	5,110	5.0	37 Lowell city, MA	77,696	43,095	34,601	44.5
38 Scranton city, PA	102,026	73,053	28,973	28.4	38 Nashville city, TN	76,168	72,374	3,794	5.0
39 Lowell city, MA	94,969	53,995	40,974	43.1	39 Scranton city, PA	75,215	49,642	25,573	34.0
40 Albany city, NY	94,151	76,433	17,718	18.8	40 Fall River city, MA	74,398	36,664	37,734	50.7
41 Cambridge city, MA	91,886	61,420	30,466	33.2	41 Cambridge city, MA	70,028	46,177	23,851	34.1
42 Portland city, OR	90,426	64,550	25,876	28.6	42 Atlanta city, GA	65,533	63,662	1,871	2.9
43 Atlanta city, GA	89,872	87,341	2,531	2.8	43 Memphis city, TN	64,495	59,095	5,400	8.4
44 Grand Rapids city, MI	87,565	63,669	23,896	27.3	44 Wilmington city, DE	61,431	52,332	9,099	14.8
45 Dayton city, OH	85,333	75,280	10,053	11.8	45 Dayton city, OH	61,220	51,633	9,587	15.7
46 Richmond city, VA	85,050	82,185	2,865	3.4	46 Troy city, NY	60,956	43,691	17,265	28.3
47 Nashville city, TN	80,865	77,828	3,037	3.8	47 Grand Rapids city, MI	60,278	40,874	19,404	32.2
48 Seattle city, WA	80,671	58,668	22,003	27.3	48 Reading city, PA	58,661	53,929	4,732	8.1
49 Hartford city, CT	79,850	56,092	23,758	29.8	49 Camden city, NJ	58,313	50,580	7,733	13.3
50 Reading city, PA	78,961	73,021	5,940	7.5	50 Trenton city, NJ	57,458	43,410	14,048	24.4

Table 23. (Continued)

1880					1870				
Rank Place	Total	Native	Foreign born		Rank Place	Total	Native	Foreign born	
			Number	Percent				Number	Percent
1 New York city, NY	1,206,299	727,629	478,670	39.7	1 New York city, NY	942,292	523,198	419,094	44.5
2 Philadelphia city, PA	847,170	642,835	204,335	24.1	2 Philadelphia city, PA	674,022	490,398	183,624	27.2
3 Brooklyn city, NY	566,663	388,969	177,694	31.4	3 Brooklyn city, NY	396,099	251,381	144,718	36.5
4 Chicago city, IL	503,185	298,326	204,859	40.7	4 St. Louis city, MO	310,864	198,615	112,249	36.1
5 Boston city, MA	362,839	248,043	114,796	31.6	5 Chicago city, IL	298,977	154,420	144,557	48.4
6 St. Louis city, MO	350,518	245,505	105,013	30.0	6 Baltimore city, MD	267,354	210,870	56,484	21.1
7 Baltimore city, MD	332,313	276,177	56,136	16.9	7 Boston city, MA	250,526	162,540	87,986	35.1
8 Cincinnati city, OH	255,139	183,480	71,659	28.1	8 Cincinnati city, OH	216,239	136,627	79,612	36.8
9 San Francisco city, CA	233,959	129,715	104,244	44.6	9 New Orleans city, LA	191,418	142,943	48,475	25.3
10 New Orleans city, LA	216,090	174,933	41,157	19.0	10 San Francisco city, CA	149,473	75,754	73,719	49.3
11 Cleveland city, OH	160,146	100,737	59,409	37.1	11 Buffalo city, NY	117,714	71,477	46,237	39.3
12 Pittsburgh city, PA	156,389	111,784	44,605	28.5	12 Washington city, DC	109,199	95,442	13,757	12.6
13 Buffalo city, NY	155,134	103,866	51,268	33.0	13 Newark city, NJ	105,059	69,175	35,884	34.2
14 Washington city, DC	147,293	133,051	14,242	9.7	14 Louisville city, KY	100,753	75,085	25,668	25.5
15 Newark city, NJ	136,508	96,178	40,330	29.5	15 Cleveland city, OH	92,829	54,014	38,815	41.8
16 Louisville city, KY	123,758	100,602	23,156	18.7	16 Pittsburgh city, PA	86,076	58,254	27,822	32.3
17 Jersey City city, NJ	120,722	81,464	39,258	32.5	17 Jersey City city, NJ	82,546	50,711	31,835	38.6
18 Detroit city, MI	116,340	70,695	45,645	39.2	18 Detroit city, MI	79,577	44,196	35,381	44.5
19 Milwaukee city, WI	115,587	69,514	46,073	39.9	19 Milwaukee city, WI	71,440	37,667	33,773	47.3
20 Providence city, RI	104,857	76,782	28,075	26.8	20 Albany city, NY	69,422	47,215	22,207	32.0
21 Albany city, NY	90,758	66,993	23,765	26.2	21 Providence city, RI	68,904	51,727	17,177	24.9
22 Rochester city, NY	89,366	62,744	26,622	29.8	22 Rochester city, NY	62,386	41,202	21,184	34.0
23 Allegheny city, PA	78,682	59,245	19,437	24.7	23 Allegheny city, PA	53,180	37,872	15,308	28.8
24 Indianapolis city, IN	75,056	62,446	12,610	16.8	24 Richmond city, VA	51,038	47,260	3,778	7.4
25 Richmond city, VA	63,600	60,260	3,340	5.3	25 New Haven city, CT	50,840	36,484	14,356	28.2
26 New Haven city, CT	62,882	47,214	15,668	24.9	26 Charleston city, SC	48,956	44,064	4,892	10.0
27 Lowell city, MA	59,475	36,421	23,054	38.8	27 Indianapolis city, IN	48,244	37,587	10,657	22.1
28 Worcester city, MA	58,291	42,667	15,624	26.8	28 Troy city, NY	46,465	30,246	16,219	34.9

Table 23. (Continued)

1880					1870				
Rank Place	Total	Native	Foreign born		Rank Place	Total	Native	Foreign born	
			Number	Percent				Number	Percent
29 Troy city, NY	56,747	39,809	16,938	29.8	29 Syracuse city, NY	43,051	29,061	13,990	32.5
30 Kansas City city, MO	55,785	46,484	9,301	16.7	30 Worcester city, MA	41,105	29,159	11,946	29.1
31 Cambridge city, MA	52,669	37,001	15,668	29.7	31 Lowell city, MA	40,928	26,493	14,435	35.3
32 Syracuse city, NY	51,792	38,774	13,018	25.1	32 Memphis city, TN	40,226	33,446	6,780	16.9
33 Columbus city, OH	51,647	42,576	9,071	17.6	33 Cambridge city, MA	39,634	27,579	12,055	30.4
34 Paterson city, NJ	51,031	32,329	18,702	36.6	34 Hartford city, CT	37,180	26,363	10,817	29.1
35 Toledo city, OH	50,137	35,788	14,349	28.6	35 Scranton city, PA	35,092	19,205	15,887	45.3
36 Charleston city, SC	49,984	46,034	3,950	7.9	36 Reading city, PA	33,930	30,059	3,871	11.4
37 Fall River city, MA	48,961	25,386	23,575	48.2	37 Paterson city, NJ	33,579	20,711	12,868	38.3
38 Minneapolis city, MN	46,887	31,874	15,013	32.0	38 Kansas City city, MO	32,260	24,581	7,679	23.8
39 Scranton city, PA	45,850	29,993	15,857	34.6	39 Mobile city, AL	32,034	27,795	4,239	13.2
40 Nashville city, TN	43,350	40,325	3,025	7.0	40 Toledo city, OH	31,584	20,485	11,099	35.1
41 Reading city, PA	43,278	39,654	3,624	8.4	41 Portland city, ME	31,413	24,401	7,012	22.3
42 Wilmington city, DE	42,478	36,804	5,674	13.4	42 Columbus city, OH	31,274	23,663	7,611	24.3
43 Hartford city, CT	42,015	31,420	10,595	25.2	43 Wilmington city, DE	30,841	25,689	5,152	16.7
44 Camden city, NJ	41,659	37,164	4,495	10.8	44 Dayton city, OH	30,473	23,050	7,423	24.4
45 St. Paul city, MN	41,473	26,398	15,075	36.3	45 Lawrence city, MA	28,921	16,204	12,717	44.0
46 Lawrence city, MA	39,151	21,885	17,266	44.1	46 Utica city, NY	28,804	18,955	9,849	34.2
47 Dayton city, OH	38,678	31,432	7,246	18.7	47 Charlestown city, MA	28,323	21,399	6,924	24.4
48 Lynn city, MA	38,274	31,234	7,040	18.4	48 Savannah city, GA	28,235	24,564	3,671	13.0
49 Atlanta city, GA	37,409	35,993	1,416	3.8	49 Lynn city, MA	28,233	23,298	4,935	17.5
50 Denver city, CO	35,629	26,924	8,705	24.4	50 Fall River city, MA	26,766	15,288	11,478	42.9

Footnote:

* Indicates sample data. Internet Release Date: February 2, 2006

Table 24. Nativity of the Population for the 25 Largest Urban Places and for Selected Counties: 1860 (Leading dots indicate subparts)

(See text for sources, definitions, and explanations)

Place (rank in parentheses) and county	Total	Native	Foreign born	
			Number	Percent
New York city, NY (1)	813,669	429,952	383,717	47.2
Philadelphia city, PA (2)	565,529	396,099	169,430	30.0
Kings county, NY	279,122	170,045	109,077	39.1
. Brooklyn city, NY (3)	266,661	(NA)	(NA)	(NA)
Baltimore city, MD (4)	212,418	159,921	52,497	24.7
Boston city, MA (5)	177,841	114,050	63,791	35.9
New Orleans city, LA (6)	168,675	104,054	64,621	38.3
Cincinnati city, OH (7)	161,044	87,430	73,614	45.7
St. Louis county, MO	190,524	94,438	96,086	50.4
. St. Louis city, MO (8)	160,773	(NA)	(NA)	(NA)
Chicago city, IL (9)	109,260	54,636	54,624	50.0
Erie county, NY	141,971	87,067	54,904	38.7
. Buffalo city, NY (10)	81,129	(NA)	(NA)	(NA)
Essex county, NJ	98,877	65,071	33,806	34.2
. Newark city, NJ (11)	71,941	(NA)	(NA)	(NA)
Jefferson county, KY	89,404	63,281	26,123	29.2
. Louisville city, KY (12)	68,033	(NA)	(NA)	(NA)
Albany county, NY	113,917	79,629	34,288	30.1
. Albany city, NY (13)	62,367	(NA)	(NA)	(NA)
District of Columbia	75,080	62,596	12,484	16.6
. Washington city, DC (14)	61,122	(NA)	(NA)	(NA)
San Francisco city, CA (15)	56,802	28,348	28,454	50.1
Providence county, RI	107,799	80,394	27,405	25.4
. Providence city, RI (16)	50,666	(NA)	(NA)	(NA)
Allegheny county, PA	178,831	125,104	53,727	30.0
. Pittsburgh city, PA (17)	49,221	(NA)	(NA)	(NA)
Monroe county, NY	100,648	69,476	31,172	31.0
. Rochester city, NY (18)	48,204	(NA)	(NA)	(NA)
Wayne county, MI	75,547	46,249	29,298	38.8
. Detroit city, MI (19)	45,619	(NA)	(NA)	(NA)
Milwaukee county, WI	62,518	29,374	33,144	53.0
. Milwaukee city, WI (20)	45,246	(NA)	(NA)	(NA)
Cuyahoga county, OH	78,033	49,224	28,809	36.9
. Cleveland city, OH (21)	43,417	(NA)	(NA)	(NA)
Charleston county, SC	70,100	63,565	6,535	9.3
. Charleston city, SC (22)	40,522	(NA)	(NA)	(NA)
New Haven county, CT	97,345	74,966	22,379	23.0
. New Haven city, CT (23)	39,267	(NA)	(NA)	(NA)
Rensselaer county, NY	86,328	65,004	21,324	24.7
. Troy city, NY (24)	39,235	(NA)	(NA)	(NA)
Henrico county, VA	61,616	55,258	6,358	10.3
. Richmond city, VA (25)	37,910	(NA)	(NA)	(NA)

Footnote:

(NA) Not available. Internet Release Date: February 2, 2006

Table 25. Nativity of the Population for the 25 Largest Urban Places and for Selected Counties: 1850 (Leading dots indicate subparts)

(See text for sources, definitions, and explanations)

Place (rank in parentheses) and county[1]	Total	Native	Foreign born	
			Number	Percent
New York city, NY (1)	515,547	279,814	235,733	45.7
Baltimore city, MD (2)	169,054	133,562	35,492	21.0
Boston city, MA (3)	136,881	90,204	46,677	34.1
Philadelphia county, PA	408,762	287,063	121,699	29.8
. Philadelphia city, PA (4)	121,376	(NA)	(NA)	(NA)
. Spring Garden district, PA (9)	58,894	(NA)	(NA)	(NA)
. Northern Liberties district, PA (11)	47,223	(NA)	(NA)	(NA)
. Kensington district, PA (12)	46,774	(NA)	(NA)	(NA)
. Southwark district, PA (20)	38,799	(NA)	(NA)	(NA)
New Orleans city, LA (5)	116,375	67,774	48,601	41.8
Cincinnati city, OH (6)	115,435	60,894	54,541	47.2
Kings county, NY	138,882	82,681	56,201	40.5
. Brooklyn city, NY (7)	96,838	(NA)	(NA)	(NA)
. Williamsburg town, NY (23)	30,780	(NA)	(NA)	(NA)
St. Louis County, MO	104,978	52,009	52,969	50.5
. St. Louis city, MO (8)	77,860	39,463	38,397	49.3
Albany county, NY	93,279	65,835	27,444	29.4
. Albany city, NY (10)	50,763	34,172	16,591	32.7
Allegheny county, PA	138,290	94,876	43,414	31.4
. Pittsburgh city, PA (13)	46,601	(NA)	(NA)	(NA)
Jefferson county, KY	59,831	44,049	15,782	26.4
. Louisville city, KY (14)	43,194	30,733	12,461	28.8
Charleston county, SC	72,805	66,851	5,954	8.2
. Charleston city, SC (15)	42,985	38,342	4,643	10.8
Erie county, NY	100,993	63,520	37,473	37.1
. Buffalo city, NY (16)	42,261	(NA)	(NA)	(NA)
Providence county, RI	87,526	69,050	18,476	21.1
. Providence city, RI (17)	41,513	31,834	9,679	23.3
District of Columbia	51,687	46,769	4,918	9.5
. Washington city, DC (18)	40,001	35,719	4,282	10.7
Essex county, NJ	73,950	53,687	20,263	27.4
. Newark city, NJ (19)	38,894	26,572	12,322	31.7
Monroe county, NY	87,650	61,573	26,077	29.8
. Rochester city, NY (21)	36,403	(NA)	(NA)	(NA)
Middlesex county, MA	161,383	130,261	31,122	19.3
. Lowell city, MA (22)	33,383	(NA)	(NA)	(NA)
Chicago city, IL (24)	29,963	14,281	15,682	52.3
Rensselaer county, NY	73,363	58,862	14,501	19.8
. Troy city, NY (25)	28,785	(NA)	(NA)	(NA)

Footnotes:

(NA) Not available.

[1] 1850 census results for San Francisco were destroyed by fire. The population of San Francisco according to the 1852 state census was 34,776. Population of San Francisco county in 1852: total, 36,154; native, 16,851; foreign-born, 19,303; 53.4 percent foreign born. Internet Release Date: February 2, 2006

Table 26. Nativity of the Population for Urban Places Ever Among the 50 Largest Urban Places Since 1870: 1850 to 2000 (Leading dots indicate subparts)

(See text for sources, definitions, and explanations)

State, urban place and year (rank in total population)	Total	Native	Foreign born	
			Number	Percent
ALABAMA				
Birmingham				
2000* (71)	243,072	237,948	5,124	2.1
1990* (60)	265,852	262,671	3,181	1.2
1980* (50)	284,413	281,182	3,231	1.1
1970* (48)	300,559	298,440	2,119	0.7
1960* (36)	340,887	338,260	2,627	0.8
1950* (34)	325,745	321,925	3,820	1.2
1940 (35)	267,583	263,127	4,456	1.7
1930 (34)	259,678	253,764	5,914	2.3
1920 (36)	178,806	172,666	6,140	3.4
1910 (36)	132,685	126,955	5,730	4.3
1900 (99)	38,415	36,639	1,776	4.6
1890 (-)	26,178	24,526	1,652	6.3
Mobile				
2000* (91)	198,887	193,025	5,862	2.9
1990* (79)	196,278	192,165	4,113	2.1
1980* (72)	200,396	196,621	3,775	1.9
1970* (68)	190,122	188,825	1,297	0.7
1960* (58)	202,779	200,792	1,987	1.0
1950* (78)	129,030	127,050	1,980	1.5
1940 (-)	78,720	77,164	1,556	2.0
1930 (-)	68,202	66,062	2,140	3.1
1920 (-)	60,777	58,620	2,157	3.5
1910 (-)	51,521	49,216	2,305	4.5
1900 (98)	38,469	36,358	2,111	5.5
1890 (97)	31,076	28,921	2,155	6.9
1880 (68)	29,132	26,195	2,937	10.1
1870 (39)	32,034	27,795	4,239	13.2
1860 (27)	29,258	(NA)	(NA)	(NA)
1850 (32)	20,515	16,429	4,086	19.9
ARIZONA				
Mesa				
2000 (42)	397,215	352,669	44,546	11.2
1990 (53)	288,091	274,077	14,014	4.9
1980 (-)	152,453	145,873	6,580	4.3
1970 (-)	62,990	61,023	1,967	3.1
1960 (-)	33,772	32,600	1,172	3.5
Phoenix				
2000* (6)	1,320,994	1,063,669	257,325	19.5
1990* (9)	983,403	898,731	84,672	8.6
1980* (9)	789,704	745,042	44,662	5.7
1970* (20)	581,466	559,810	21,656	3.7

Table 26. (Continued)

State, urban place and year (rank in total population)	Total	Native	Foreign born	
			Number	Percent
1960* (29)	439,170	419,732	19,438	4.4
1950* (99)	106,310	98,895	7,415	7.0
1940 (-)	65,414	61,092	4,322	6.6
1930 (-)	48,118	(NA)	(NA)	(NA)
1920 (-)	29,053	24,907	4,146	14.3
1910 (-)	11,134	(NA)	(NA)	(NA)
1900 (-)	5,544	4,609	935	16.9
1890 (-)	3,152	2,079	1,073	34.0
Tucson				
2000* (30)	486,591	417,115	69,476	14.3
1990* (33)	405,390	361,993	43,397	10.7
1980* (45)	330,537	304,331	26,206	7.9
1970* (53)	262,933	246,662	16,271	6.2
1960* (54)	212,892	199,200	13,692	6.4
1950 (-)	45,454	(NA)	(NA)	(NA)
1940 (-)	36,818	32,365	4,453	12.1
1930 (-)	32,506	(NA)	(NA)	(NA)
1920 (-)	20,292	(NA)	(NA)	(NA)
1910 (-)	13,193	(NA)	(NA)	(NA)
1900 (-)	7,531	5,179	2,352	31.2
1890 (-)	5,150	2,685	2,465	47.9
1880 (-)	7,007	3,065	3,942	56.3
1870 (-)	3,224	1,026	2,198	68.2
CALIFORNIA				
Fresno				
2000* (37)	427,224	340,287	86,937	20.3
1990* (47)	354,202	293,467	60,735	17.1
1980* (65)	218,202	200,147	18,055	8.3
1970* (83)	165,972	155,912	10,060	6.1
1960* (91)	133,929	123,216	10,713	8.0
1950 (-)	91,669	(NA)	(NA)	(NA)
1940 (-)	60,685	51,768	8,917	14.7
1930 (-)	52,513	42,245	10,268	19.6
1920 (-)	45,086	35,371	9,715	21.5
1910 (-)	24,892	(NA)	(NA)	(NA)
1900 (-)	12,470	9,171	3,299	26.5
1890 (-)	10,818	7,678	3,140	29.0
Long Beach				
2000* (34)	461,381	329,213	132,168	28.6
1990* (32)	429,433	325,283	104,150	24.3
1980* (37)	361,334	309,923	51,411	14.2
1970* (40)	358,622	334,370	24,252	6.8
1960* (35)	344,153	322,700	21,453	6.2
1950* (40)	250,135	233,875	16,260	6.5
1940 (53)	164,271	151,542	12,729	7.7
1930 (57)	142,032	127,640	14,392	10.1

Table 26. (Continued)

State, urban place and year (rank in total population)	Total	Native	Foreign born	
			Number	Percent
1920 (-)	55,593	48,493	7,100	12.8
Los Angeles				
2000* (2)	3,694,834	2,182,114	1,512,720	40.9
1990* (2)	3,485,398	2,148,733	1,336,665	38.4
1980* (3)	2,966,850	2,162,032	804,818	27.1
1970* (3)	2,815,998	2,405,128	410,870	14.6
1960* (3)	2,481,456	2,169,779	311,677	12.6
1950* (4)	1,965,150	1,702,210	262,940	13.4
1940 (5)	1,504,277	1,277,240	227,037	15.1
1930 (5)	1,238,048	990,913	247,135	20.0
1920 (10)	576,673	454,542	122,131	21.2
1910 (17)	319,198	253,065	66,133	20.7
1900 (36)	102,479	82,515	19,964	19.5
1890 (57)	50,395	37,643	12,752	25.3
1880 (-)	11,183	7,979	3,204	28.7
1870 (-)	5,728	3,724	2,004	35.0
Oakland				
2000* (41)	399,477	293,361	106,116	26.6
1990* (39)	372,242	298,718	73,524	19.8
1980* (43)	339,337	296,758	42,579	12.5
1970* (38)	361,607	329,368	32,239	8.9
1960* (33)	367,548	332,369	35,179	9.6
1950* (27)	383,200	342,455	40,745	10.6
1940 (29)	302,163	257,622	44,541	14.7
1930 (30)	284,063	230,032	54,031	19.0
1920 (31)	216,261	166,366	49,895	23.1
1910 (32)	150,174	109,328	40,846	27.2
1900 (56)	66,960	49,704	17,256	25.8
1890 (60)	48,682	34,145	14,537	29.9
1880 (51)	34,555	23,534	11,021	31.9
1870 (-) [1]	10,500	(NA)	(NA)	(NA)
Sacramento				
2000* (40)	407,075	324,459	82,616	20.3
1990* (41)	369,365	318,796	50,569	13.7
1980* (52)	275,741	248,033	27,708	10.0
1970* (55)	254,417	236,928	17,489	6.9
1960* (63)	191,667	175,016	16,651	8.7
1950* (67)	137,675	123,465	14,210	10.3
1940 (85)	105,958	92,238	13,720	12.9
1930 (96)	93,750	76,482	17,268	18.4
1920 (-)	65,908	52,920	12,988	19.7
1910 (-)	44,696	33,651	11,045	24.7
1900 (-)	29,282	22,559	6,723	23.0
1890 (-)	26,386	18,712	7,674	29.1
1880 (90)	21,420	14,372	7,048	32.9
1870 (89)	16,283	10,081	6,202	38.1

Table 26. (Continued)

State, urban place and year (rank in total population)	Total	Native	Foreign born	
			Number	Percent
San Diego				
2000* (7)	1,223,341	909,114	314,227	25.7
1990* (6)	1,110,549	878,411	232,138	20.9
1980* (8)	875,538	744,632	130,906	15.0
1970* (14)	696,474	643,497	52,977	7.6
1960* (18)	573,224	532,797	40,427	7.1
1950* (31)	333,865	308,605	25,260	7.6
1940 (43)	203,341	183,228	20,113	9.9
1930 (53)	147,995	126,409	21,586	14.6
1920 (93)	74,361	60,327	14,034	18.9
1910 (-)	39,578	31,749	7,829	19.8
1900 (-)	17,700	13,932	3,768	21.3
1890 (-)	16,159	12,060	4,099	25.4
San Francisco [2]				
2000* (13)	776,733	491,192	285,541	36.8
1990* (14)	723,959	477,925	246,034	34.0
1980* (13)	678,974	486,770	192,204	28.3
1970* (13)	715,673	561,166	154,507	21.6
1960* (12)	740,316	597,785	142,531	19.3
1950* (11)	775,075	638,065	137,010	17.7
1940 (12)	634,536	494,513	140,023	22.1
1930 (11)	634,394	462,753	171,641	27.1
1920 (12)	506,676	357,481	149,195	29.4
1910 (11)	416,912	274,614	142,298	34.1
1900 (9)	342,782	225,897	116,885	34.1
1890 (8)	298,997	172,186	126,811	42.4
1880 (9)	233,959	129,715	104,244	44.6
1870 (10)	149,473	75,754	73,719	49.3
1860 (15)	56,802	28,348	28,454	50.1
San Jose				
2000* (11)	893,889	564,132	329,757	36.9
1990* (11)	782,225	575,184	207,041	26.5
1980* (17)	629,442	538,528	90,914	14.4
1970* (31)	447,025	413,063	33,962	7.6
1960* (57)	204,196	186,766	17,430	8.5
1950 (-)	95,280	(NA)	(NA)	(NA)
1940 (-)	68,457	59,182	9,275	13.5
1930 (-)	57,651	47,266	10,385	18.0
1920 (-)	39,642	31,368	8,274	20.9
1910 (-)	28,946	22,524	6,422	22.2
1900 (-)	21,500	16,923	4,577	21.3
1890 (-)	18,060	13,308	4,752	26.3
1880 (-)	12,567	8,733	3,834	30.5
1870 (-)	9,089	5,334	3,755	41.3

Table 26. (Continued)

State, urban place and year (rank in total population)	Total	Native	Foreign born	
			Number	Percent
COLORADO				
Colorado Springs				
2000 (48)	360,798	335,534	25,264	7.0
1990 (54)	281,140	267,891	13,249	4.7
1980 (66)	215,150	204,403	10,747	5.0
1970 (-)	135,059	131,447	3,612	2.7
1960 (-)	70,194	67,612	2,582	3.7
1950 (-)	45,472	(NA)	(NA)	(NA)
1940 (-)	36,789	35,109	1,680	4.6
1930 (-)	33,237	(NA)	(NA)	(NA)
1920 (-)	30,105	27,466	2,639	8.8
1910 (-)	29,078	26,059	3,019	10.4
1900 (-)	21,085	18,785	2,300	10.9
1890 (-)	11,140	9,673	1,467	13.2
1880 (-)	4,226	3,711	515	12.2
Denver				
2000* (24)	554,636	458,035	96,601	17.4
1990* (26)	467,610	432,895	34,715	7.4
1980* (24)	492,365	461,653	30,712	6.2
1970* (25)	514,678	493,752	20,926	4.1
1960* (23)	493,887	470,134	23,753	4.8
1950* (24)	415,760	392,650	23,110	5.6
1940 (24)	322,412	297,430	24,982	7.7
1930 (29)	287,861	255,004	32,857	11.4
1920 (25)	256,491	218,261	38,230	14.9
1910 (27)	213,381	173,632	39,749	18.6
1900 (25)	133,859	108,558	25,301	18.9
1890 (26)	106,713	81,249	25,464	23.9
1880 (50)	35,629	26,924	8,705	24.4
1870 (-)	4,759	3,621	1,138	23.9
CONNECTICUT				
Bridgeport				
2000* (-)	139,529	110,891	28,638	20.5
1990* (-)	141,686	120,955	20,731	14.6
1980* (-)	142,546	123,408	19,138	13.4
1970* (88)	156,542	136,542	20,000	12.8
1960* (80)	156,748	133,941	22,807	14.6
1950* (63)	157,710	128,460	29,250	18.5
1940 (59)	147,121	113,453	33,668	22.9
1930 (54)	146,716	105,654	41,062	28.0
1920 (44)	143,555	96,773	46,782	32.6
1910 (49)	102,054	65,790	36,264	35.5
1900 (54)	70,996	48,715	22,281	31.4
1890 (59)	48,866	34,677	14,189	29.0
1880 (71)	27,643	20,204	7,439	26.9
1870 (76)	18,969	13,585	5,384	28.4

Table 26. (Continued)

State, urban place and year (rank in total population)	Total	Native	Foreign born	
			Number	Percent
Hartford				
2000* (-)	121,578	98,907	22,671	18.6
1990* (-)	139,739	118,297	21,442	15.3
1980* (-)	136,392	112,496	23,896	17.5
1970* (86)	158,017	133,347	24,670	15.6
1960* (78)	162,178	133,540	28,638	17.7
1950* (54)	177,050	144,275	32,775	18.5
1940 (51)	166,267	129,572	36,695	22.1
1930 (47)	164,072	119,416	44,656	27.2
1920 (46)	138,036	97,124	40,912	29.6
1910 (51)	98,915	67,561	31,354	31.7
1900 (49)	79,850	56,092	23,758	29.8
1890 (54)	53,230	38,774	14,456	27.2
1880 (43)	42,015	31,420	10,595	25.2
1870 (34)	37,180	26,363	10,817	29.1
1860 (31)	26,917	(NA)	(NA)	(NA)
1850 (53)	13,555	10,640	2,915	21.5
New Haven				
2000* (-)	123,626	109,276	14,350	11.6
1990* (-)	130,474	119,841	10,633	8.1
1980* (-)	126,109	115,179	10,930	8.7
1970* (-)	137,721	123,937	13,784	10.0
1960* (82)	152,048	132,002	20,046	13.2
1950* (59)	164,225	138,900	25,325	15.4
1940 (54)	160,605	127,882	32,723	20.4
1930 (49)	162,655	122,111	40,544	24.9
1920 (39)	162,537	116,413	46,124	28.4
1910 (35)	133,605	90,616	42,989	32.2
1900 (31)	108,027	77,225	30,802	28.5
1890 (32)	81,298	58,304	22,994	28.3
1880 (26)	62,882	47,214	15,668	24.9
1870 (25)	50,840	36,484	14,356	28.2
1860 (23)	39,267	(NA)	(NA)	(NA)
1850 (33)	20,345	16,648	3,697	18.2
DELAWARE				
Wilmington				
2000* (-)	72,664	69,016	3,648	5.0
1990* (-)	71,529	69,054	2,475	3.5
1980* (-)	70,195	67,511	2,684	3.8
1970* (-)	80,381	76,422	3,959	4.9
1960* (-)	95,827	89,920	5,907	6.2
1950* (95)	109,755	101,860	7,895	7.2
1940 (75)	112,504	101,969	10,535	9.4
1930 (80)	106,597	93,911	12,686	11.9
1920 (62)	110,168	93,831	16,337	14.8
1910 (61)	87,411	73,698	13,713	15.7

Table 26. (Continued)

State, urban place and year (rank in total population)	Total	Native	Foreign born	
			Number	Percent
1900 (51)	76,508	66,030	10,478	13.7
1890 (44)	61,431	52,332	9,099	14.8
1880 (42)	42,478	36,804	5,674	13.4
1870 (43)	30,841	25,689	5,152	16.7
1860 (43)	21,258	(NA)	(NA)	(NA)
1850 (51)	13,979	12,216	1,763	12.6
DISTRICT OF COLUMBIA				
Washington				
2000* (21)	572,059	498,498	73,561	12.9
1990* (19)	606,900	548,013	58,887	9.7
1980* (15)	638,333	597,774	40,559	6.4
1970* (9)	756,492	722,930	33,562	4.4
1960* (9)	763,956	724,985	38,971	5.1
1950* (9)	800,830	758,090	42,740	5.3
1940 (11)	663,091	628,175	34,916	5.3
1930 (14)	486,869	456,136	30,733	6.3
1920 (14)	437,571	408,206	29,365	6.7
1910 (16)	331,069	306,167	24,902	7.5
1900 (15)	278,718	258,599	20,119	7.2
1890 (14)	230,392	211,622	18,770	8.1
1880 (14)	147,293	133,051	14,242	9.7
1870 (12)	109,199	95,442	13,757	12.6
1860 (14)	61,122	(NA)	(NA)	(NA)
1850 (18)	40,001	35,719	4,282	10.7
FLORIDA				
Jacksonville [3]				
2000* (14)	735,503	691,842	43,661	5.9
1990* (15)	635,230	613,467	21,763	3.4
1980* (22)	540,920	525,436	15,484	2.9
1970* (23)	528,865	519,169	9,696	1.8
1960* (61)	201,030	197,594	3,436	1.7
1950* (49)	204,275	199,995	4,280	2.1
1940 (47)	173,065	168,970	4,095	2.4
1930 (63)	129,549	124,987	4,562	3.5
1920 (79)	91,558	87,414	4,144	4.5
1910 (95)	57,699	55,011	2,688	4.7
1900 (-)	28,429	27,263	1,166	4.1
1890 (-)	17,201	16,137	1,064	6.2
1880 (-)	7,650	6,920	730	9.5
1870 (-)	6,912	6,485	427	6.2
Miami				
2000* (47)	362,563	146,824	215,739	59.5
1990* (46)	358,548	144,420	214,128	59.7
1980* (41)	346,865	160,585	186,280	53.7
1970* (42)	335,062	194,855	140,207	41.8
1960* (44)	291,688	242,442	49,246	16.9

Table 26. (Continued)

State, urban place and year (rank in total population)	Total	Native	Foreign born	
			Number	Percent
1950* (42)	248,970	218,850	30,120	12.1
1940 (48)	172,172	155,547	16,625	9.7
1930 (78)	110,637	96,866	13,771	12.4
1920 (-)	29,571	22,173	7,398	25.0
Tampa				
2000* (57)	303,512	266,485	37,027	12.2
1990* (55)	280,015	257,724	22,291	8.0
1980* (53)	271,523	252,863	18,660	6.9
1970* (50)	277,748	261,381	16,367	5.9
1960* (48)	274,970	258,986	15,984	5.8
1950* (85)	124,645	113,745	10,900	8.7
1940 (84)	108,391	96,990	11,401	10.5
1930 (91)	101,161	85,994	15,167	15.0
1920 (-)	51,608	40,256	11,352	22.0
1910 (-)	37,782	26,979	10,803	28.6
1900 (-)	15,839	10,754	5,085	32.1
1890 (-)	5,532	3,748	1,784	32.2
GEORGIA				
Atlanta				
2000* (39)	416,629	389,277	27,352	6.6
1990* (36)	394,017	380,663	13,354	3.4
1980* (29)	425,022	415,245	9,777	2.3
1970* (27)	497,046	491,194	5,852	1.2
1960* (24)	487,275	482,680	4,595	0.9
1950* (32)	331,210	327,015	4,195	1.3
1940 (28)	302,288	297,934	4,354	1.4
1930 (32)	270,366	265,574	4,792	1.8
1920 (33)	200,616	195,827	4,789	2.4
1910 (31)	154,839	150,338	4,501	2.9
1900 (43)	89,872	87,341	2,531	2.8
1890 (42)	65,533	63,662	1,871	2.9
1880 (49)	37,409	35,993	1,416	3.8
1870 (61)	21,789	20,699	1,090	5.0
Savannah				
2000* (-)	131,603	126,538	5,065	3.8
1990* (-)	137,557	134,881	2,676	1.9
1980* (-)	141,378	138,329	3,049	2.2
1970* (-)	118,344	116,996	1,348	1.1
1960* (83)	149,245	147,112	2,133	1.4
1950* (88)	119,365	117,640	1,725	1.4
1940 (99)	95,996	94,095	1,901	2.0
1930 (-)	85,024	82,493	2,531	3.0
1920 (85)	83,252	79,916	3,336	4.0
1910 (86)	65,064	61,616	3,448	5.3
1900 (69)	54,244	50,810	3,434	6.3
1890 (69)	43,189	39,781	3,408	7.9

Table 26. (Continued)

State, urban place and year (rank in total population)	Total	Native	Foreign born	
			Number	Percent
1880 (62)	30,709	27,715	2,994	9.7
1870 (48)	28,235	24,564	3,671	13.0
1860 (41)	22,292	(NA)	(NA)	(NA)
1850 (44)	15,312	12,878	2,434	15.9
HAWAII				
Honolulu [4]				
2000* (46)	371,619	277,724	93,895	25.3
1990* (44)	365,272	286,957	78,315	21.4
1980* (36)	365,048	297,010	68,038	18.6
1970* (44)	324,869	289,644	35,225	10.8
1960* (43)	294,194	263,216	30,978	10.5
ILLINOIS				
Chicago				
2000* (3)	2,895,964	2,267,061	628,903	21.7
1990* (3)	2,783,726	2,314,539	469,187	16.9
1980* (2)	3,005,078	2,569,846	435,232	14.5
1970* (2)	3,362,947	2,989,028	373,919	11.1
1960* (2)	3,550,404	3,112,012	438,392	12.3
1950* (2)	3,611,580	3,078,610	532,970	14.8
1940 (2)	3,396,808	2,721,661	675,147	19.9
1930 (2)	3,376,438	2,517,029	859,409	25.5
1920 (2)	2,701,705	1,893,147	808,558	29.9
1910 (2)	2,185,283	1,401,855	783,428	35.9
1900 (2)	1,698,575	1,111,463	587,112	34.6
1890 (2)	1,099,850	649,184	450,666	41.0
1880 (4)	503,185	298,326	204,859	40.7
1870 (5)	298,977	154,420	144,557	48.4
1860 (9)	109,260	54,636	54,624	50.0
1850 (24)	29,963	14,281	15,682	52.3
INDIANA				
Indianapolis [3]				
2000* (12)	782,414	746,347	36,067	4.6
1990* (13)	731,321	717,358	13,963	1.9
1980* (12)	700,719	687,294	13,425	1.9
1970* (11)	744,768	733,895	10,873	1.5
1960* (26)	476,258	467,642	8,616	1.8
1950* (23)	426,945	418,015	8,930	2.1
1940 (20)	386,972	376,344	10,628	2.7
1930 (21)	364,161	350,307	13,854	3.8
1920 (21)	314,194	297,098	17,096	5.4
1910 (22)	233,650	213,808	19,842	8.5
1900 (21)	169,164	152,042	17,122	10.1
1890 (27)	105,436	90,949	14,487	13.7
1880 (24)	75,056	62,446	12,610	16.8
1870 (27)	48,244	37,587	10,657	22.1
KANSAS				

Table 26. (Continued)

State, urban place and year (rank in total population)	Total	Native	Foreign born	
			Number	Percent
Wichita				
2000 (50)	343,997	316,059	27,938	8.1
1990 (51)	304,011	291,752	12,259	4.0
1980 (51)	279,272	270,275	8,997	3.2
1970 (51)	276,718	273,496	3,222	1.2
1960 (51)	254,698	251,897	2,801	1.1
1950 (58)	166,980	164,545	2,435	1.5
1940 (74)	114,966	112,774	2,192	1.9
1930 (77)	111,110	108,305	2,805	2.5
1920 (96)	72,217	69,173	3,044	4.2
1910 (-)	52,450	49,570	2,880	5.5
1900 (-)	24,671	23,224	1,447	5.9
1890 (-)	23,853	21,945	1,908	8.0
1880 (-)	4,911	4,501	410	8.3
KENTUCKY				
Louisville				
2000* (66)	256,420	246,770	9,650	3.8
1990* (58)	269,157	265,110	4,047	1.5
1980* (49)	298,455	294,293	4,162	1.4
1970* (39)	361,496	358,058	3,438	1.0
1960* (31)	390,639	386,683	3,956	1.0
1950* (29)	367,375	362,485	4,890	1.3
1940 (25)	319,077	312,832	6,245	2.0
1930 (24)	307,745	298,714	9,031	2.9
1920 (29)	234,891	223,224	11,667	5.0
1910 (24)	223,928	206,455	17,473	7.8
1900 (18)	204,731	183,304	21,427	10.5
1890 (20)	161,129	137,619	23,510	14.6
1880 (16)	123,758	100,602	23,156	18.7
1870 (14)	100,753	75,085	25,668	25.5
1860 (12)	68,033	(NA)	(NA)	(NA)
1850 (14)	43,194	30,733	12,461	28.8
LOUISIANA				
New Orleans				
2000* (31)	484,674	464,093	20,581	4.2
1990* (24)	496,938	476,154	20,784	4.2
1980* (21)	557,515	535,806	21,709	3.9
1970* (19)	593,467	575,358	18,109	3.1
1960* (15)	627,525	612,945	14,580	2.3
1950* (16)	568,680	553,335	15,345	2.7
1940 (15)	494,537	479,334	15,203	3.1
1930 (16)	458,762	437,716	21,046	4.6
1920 (17)	387,219	359,854	27,365	7.1
1910 (15)	339,075	310,742	28,333	8.4
1900 (12)	287,104	256,779	30,325	10.6
1890 (12)	242,039	207,670	34,369	14.2

Table 26. (Continued)

State, urban place and year (rank in total population)	Total	Native	Foreign born	
			Number	Percent
1880 (10)	216,090	174,933	41,157	19.0
1870 (9)	191,418	142,943	48,475	25.3
1860 (6)	168,675	104,054	64,621	38.3
1850 (5)	116,375	67,774	48,601	41.8
MAINE				
Portland				
2000* (-)	64,257	59,362	4,895	7.6
1990* (-)	64,358	61,065	3,293	5.1
1980* (-)	61,572	58,794	2,778	4.5
1970* (-)	65,116	61,877	3,239	5.0
1960* (-)	72,566	67,023	5,543	7.6
1950 (-)	77,634	(NA)	(NA)	(NA)
1940 (-)	73,643	63,732	9,911	13.5
1930 (-)	70,810	59,064	11,746	16.6
1920 (-)	69,272	55,926	13,346	19.3
1910 (91)	58,571	46,420	12,151	20.7
1900 (78)	50,145	39,710	10,435	20.8
1890 (83)	36,425	28,600	7,825	21.5
1880 (53)	33,810	26,908	6,902	20.4
1870 (41)	31,413	24,401	7,012	22.3
1860 (32)	26,341	(NA)	(NA)	(NA)
1850 (31)	20,815	17,303	3,512	16.9
MARYLAND				
Baltimore				
2000* (17)	651,154	621,516	29,638	4.6
1990* (12)	736,014	712,547	23,467	3.2
1980* (10)	786,775	762,108	24,667	3.1
1970* (7)	905,757	877,047	28,710	3.2
1960* (6)	939,024	899,337	39,687	4.2
1950* (6)	945,940	893,295	52,645	5.6
1940 (7)	859,100	797,402	61,698	7.2
1930 (8)	804,874	729,426	75,448	9.4
1920 (8)	733,826	649,017	84,809	11.6
1910 (7)	558,485	480,823	77,662	13.9
1900 (6)	508,957	440,357	68,600	13.5
1890 (7)	434,439	365,436	69,003	15.9
1880 (7)	332,313	276,177	56,136	16.9
1870 (6)	267,354	210,870	56,484	21.1
1860 (4)	212,418	159,921	52,497	24.7
1850 (2)	169,054	133,562	35,492	21.0
MASSACHUSETTS				
Boston				
2000* (20)	589,141	437,305	151,836	25.8
1990* (20)	574,283	459,686	114,597	20.0
1980* (20)	562,994	475,938	87,056	15.5
1970* (16)	641,056	557,068	83,988	13.1

Table 26. (Continued)

State, urban place and year (rank in total population)	Total	Native	Foreign born	
			Number	Percent
1960* (13)	697,938	587,974	109,964	15.8
1950* (10)	800,590	651,590	149,000	18.6
1940 (9)	770,816	586,736	184,080	23.9
1930 (9)	781,188	547,501	233,687	29.9
1920 (7)	748,060	505,441	242,619	32.4
1910 (5)	670,585	427,220	243,365	36.3
1900 (5)	560,892	363,763	197,129	35.1
1890 (6)	448,477	290,305	158,172	35.3
1880 (5)	362,839	248,043	114,796	31.6
1870 (7)	250,526	162,540	87,986	35.1
1860 (5)	177,841	114,050	63,791	35.9
1850 (3)	136,881	90,204	46,677	34.1
Cambridge				
2000* (-)	101,355	75,137	26,218	25.9
1990* (-)	95,802	74,452	21,350	22.3
1980* (-)	95,322	77,759	17,563	18.4
1970* (-)	100,417	84,943	15,474	15.4
1960* (-)	107,716	91,305	16,411	15.2
1950* (87)	120,320	98,950	21,370	17.8
1940 (78)	110,879	85,313	25,566	23.1
1930 (74)	113,643	80,050	33,593	29.6
1920 (63)	109,694	76,398	33,296	30.4
1910 (47)	104,839	69,511	35,328	33.7
1900 (41)	91,886	61,420	30,466	33.2
1890 (41)	70,028	46,177	23,851	34.1
1880 (31)	52,669	37,001	15,668	29.7
1870 (33)	39,634	27,579	12,055	30.4
Charlestown [5]				
1870 (47)	28,323	21,399	6,924	24.4
Fall River				
2000* (-)	91,938	73,722	18,216	19.8
1990* (-)	92,703	73,496	19,207	20.7
1980* (-)	92,574	72,199	20,375	22.0
1970* (-)	96,976	81,417	15,559	16.0
1960* (-)	99,942	86,398	13,544	13.6
1950* (93)	111,765	93,495	18,270	16.3
1940 (73)	115,428	90,725	24,703	21.4
1930 (71)	115,274	83,056	32,218	27.9
1920 (54)	120,485	78,064	42,421	35.2
1910 (42)	119,295	68,337	50,958	42.7
1900 (33)	104,863	54,821	50,042	47.7
1890 (40)	74,398	36,664	37,734	50.7
1880 (37)	48,961	25,386	23,575	48.2
1870 (50)	26,766	15,288	11,478	42.9
Lawrence				
2000* (-)	72,043	50,032	22,011	30.6

Table 26. (Continued)

State, urban place and year (rank in total population)	Total	Native	Foreign born	
			Number	Percent
1990* (-)	70,207	55,534	14,673	20.9
1980* (-)	63,175	53,823	9,352	14.8
1970* (-)	66,915	57,218	9,697	14.5
1960* (-)	70,933	59,548	11,385	16.1
1950 (-)	80,536	(NA)	(NA)	(NA)
1940 (-)	84,323	61,342	22,981	27.3
1930 (-)	85,068	56,382	28,686	33.7
1920 (73)	94,270	55,069	39,201	41.6
1910 (63)	85,892	44,421	41,471	48.3
1900 (57)	62,559	33,982	28,577	45.7
1890 (64)	44,654	24,136	20,518	45.9
1880 (46)	39,151	21,885	17,266	44.1
1870 (45)	28,921	16,204	12,717	44.0
Lowell				
2000* (-)	105,167	81,900	23,267	22.1
1990* (-)	103,439	86,441	16,998	16.4
1980* (-)	92,418	83,946	8,472	9.2
1970* (-)	94,280	86,053	8,227	8.7
1960* (-)	92,107	82,904	9,203	10.0
1950 (-)	97,249	(NA)	(NA)	(NA)
1940 (88)	101,389	81,937	19,452	19.2
1930 (93)	100,234	74,059	26,175	26.1
1920 (61)	112,759	74,643	38,116	33.8
1910 (46)	106,294	62,800	43,494	40.9
1900 (39)	94,969	53,995	40,974	43.1
1890 (37)	77,696	43,095	34,601	44.5
1880 (27)	59,475	36,421	23,054	38.8
1870 (31)	40,928	26,493	14,435	35.3
Lynn				
2000* (-)	89,122	68,774	20,348	22.8
1990* (-)	81,245	70,008	11,237	13.8
1980* (-)	78,471	71,257	7,214	9.2
1970* (-)	90,289	81,081	9,208	10.2
1960* (-)	94,478	82,382	12,096	12.8
1950 (-)	99,738	(NA)	(NA)	(NA)
1940 (95)	98,123	76,967	21,156	21.6
1930 (87)	102,320	75,039	27,281	26.7
1920 (69)	99,148	71,010	28,138	28.4
1910 (59)	89,336	61,731	27,605	30.9
1900 (55)	68,513	50,771	17,742	25.9
1890 (51)	55,727	41,762	13,965	25.1
1880 (48)	38,274	31,234	7,040	18.4
1870 (49)	28,233	23,298	4,935	17.5
Worcester				
2000* (-)	172,648	147,551	25,097	14.5
1990* (-)	169,759	154,687	15,072	8.9

Table 26. (Continued)

State, urban place and year (rank in total population)	Total	Native	Foreign born	
			Number	Percent
1980* (92)	161,799	148,040	13,759	8.5
1970* (73)	176,617	159,359	17,258	9.8
1960* (66)	186,587	161,911	24,676	13.2
1950* (50)	202,940	168,925	34,015	16.8
1940 (44)	193,694	153,634	40,060	20.7
1930 (42)	195,311	144,150	51,161	26.2
1920 (35)	179,754	126,227	53,527	29.8
1910 (33)	145,986	97,389	48,597	33.3
1900 (29)	118,421	80,769	37,652	31.8
1890 (33)	84,655	57,952	26,703	31.5
1880 (28)	58,291	42,667	15,624	26.8
1870 (30)	41,105	29,159	11,946	29.1
MICHIGAN				
Detroit				
2000* (10)	951,270	905,729	45,541	4.8
1990* (7)	1,027,974	993,484	34,490	3.4
1980* (6)	1,203,339	1,135,036	68,303	5.7
1970* (5)	1,511,322	1,391,975	119,347	7.9
1960* (5)	1,670,144	1,468,431	201,713	12.1
1950* (5)	1,846,660	1,568,400	278,260	15.1
1940 (4)	1,623,452	1,300,764	322,688	19.9
1930 (4)	1,568,662	1,162,780	405,882	25.9
1920 (4)	993,678	702,794	290,884	29.3
1910 (9)	465,766	308,232	157,534	33.8
1900 (13)	285,704	189,201	96,503	33.8
1890 (15)	205,876	124,167	81,709	39.7
1880 (18)	116,340	70,695	45,645	39.2
1870 (18)	79,577	44,196	35,381	44.5
1860 (19)	45,619	(NA)	(NA)	(NA)
1850 (30)	21,019	11,092	9,927	47.2
Flint				
2000* (-)	124,939	123,107	1,832	1.5
1990* (-)	140,761	138,475	2,286	1.6
1980* (96)	159,611	155,343	4,268	2.7
1970* (67)	193,379	186,254	7,125	3.7
1960* (62)	196,940	186,302	10,638	5.4
1950* (60)	162,350	150,125	12,225	7.5
1940 (56)	151,543	135,627	15,916	10.5
1930 (50)	156,492	135,028	21,464	13.7
1920 (78)	91,599	76,386	15,213	16.6
1910 (-)	38,550	31,820	6,730	17.5
1900 (-)	13,103	10,938	2,165	16.5
1890 (-)	9,803	7,916	1,887	19.2
1880 (-)	8,409	6,654	1,755	20.9
1870 (-)	5,386	4,194	1,192	22.1

Table 26. (Continued)

State, urban place and year (rank in total population)	Total	Native	Foreign born	
			Number	Percent
Grand Rapids				
2000* (93)	197,846	177,032	20,814	10.5
1990* (83)	189,126	181,670	7,456	3.9
1980* (75)	181,843	173,103	8,740	4.8
1970* (65)	197,461	187,605	9,856	5.0
1960* (71)	177,313	163,094	14,219	8.0
1950* (55)	175,980	159,520	16,460	9.4
1940 (52)	164,292	143,918	20,374	12.4
1930 (46)	168,592	141,243	27,349	16.2
1920 (48)	137,634	109,207	28,427	20.7
1910 (44)	112,571	84,184	28,387	25.2
1900 (44)	87,565	63,669	23,896	27.3
1890 (47)	60,278	40,874	19,404	32.2
1880 (58)	32,016	22,016	10,000	31.2
1870 (88)	16,507	10,782	5,725	34.7
MINNESOTA				
Minneapolis				
2000* (45)	382,452	326,977	55,475	14.5
1990* (42)	368,383	345,759	22,624	6.1
1980* (34)	370,951	352,691	18,260	4.9
1970* (32)	434,408	413,533	20,875	4.8
1960* (25)	482,872	448,424	34,448	7.1
1950* (17)	519,245	470,455	48,790	9.4
1940 (16)	492,370	428,006	64,364	13.1
1930 (15)	464,356	383,233	81,123	17.5
1920 (18)	380,582	292,334	88,248	23.2
1910 (18)	301,408	215,309	86,099	28.6
1900 (19)	202,718	141,697	61,021	30.1
1890 (18)	164,738	104,180	60,558	36.8
1880 (38)	46,887	31,874	15,013	32.0
1870 (-)	13,066	8,613	4,453	34.1
St Paul				
2000* (59)	287,151	246,013	41,138	14.3
1990* (57)	272,235	252,342	19,893	7.3
1980* (54)	270,230	257,095	13,135	4.9
1970* (46)	310,004	297,966	12,038	3.9
1960* (40)	313,411	295,997	17,414	5.6
1950* (35)	310,220	285,755	24,465	7.9
1940 (33)	287,736	254,020	33,716	11.7
1930 (31)	271,606	226,954	44,652	16.4
1920 (30)	234,698	182,976	51,722	22.0
1910 (26)	214,744	158,087	56,657	26.4
1900 (23)	163,065	116,246	46,819	28.7
1890 (23)	133,156	79,979	53,177	39.9
1880 (45)	41,473	26,398	15,075	36.3
1870 (71)	20,030	11,343	8,687	43.4

Table 26. (Continued)

State, urban place and year (rank in total population)	Total	Native	Foreign born	
			Number	Percent
MISSOURI				
Kansas City				
2000* (36)	441,269	415,637	25,632	5.8
1990* (31)	435,141	422,754	12,387	2.8
1980* (27)	448,154	435,415	12,739	2.8
1970* (26)	507,247	496,995	10,252	2.0
1960* (27)	476,500	463,329	13,171	2.8
1950* (20)	456,710	440,660	16,050	3.5
1940 (19)	399,178	379,758	19,420	4.9
1930 (19)	399,746	373,548	26,198	6.6
1920 (19)	324,410	296,827	27,583	8.5
1910 (20)	248,381	222,915	25,466	10.3
1900 (22)	163,752	145,342	18,410	11.2
1890 (24)	132,716	111,858	20,858	15.7
1880 (30)	55,785	46,484	9,301	16.7
1870 (38)	32,260	24,581	7,679	23.8
St Joseph				
2000* (-)	73,829	73,059	770	1.0
1990* (-)	71,852	71,291	561	0.8
1980* (-)	76,691	75,699	992	1.3
1970* (-)	72,932	71,848	1,084	1.5
1960* (-)	79,673	78,227	1,446	1.8
1950 (-)	78,588	(NA)	(NA)	(NA)
1940 (-)	75,711	72,951	2,760	3.6
1930 (-)	80,935	76,827	4,108	5.1
1920 (87)	77,939	71,501	6,438	8.3
1910 (70)	77,403	69,272	8,131	10.5
1900 (34)	102,979	94,555	8,424	8.2
1890 (55)	52,324	45,251	7,073	13.5
1880 (57)	32,431	26,775	5,656	17.4
1870 (73)	19,565	14,339	5,226	26.7
St Louis				
2000* (49)	348,189	328,647	19,542	5.6
1990* (34)	396,685	386,651	10,034	2.5
1980* (26)	453,085	441,207	11,878	2.6
1970* (18)	622,234	605,974	16,260	2.6
1960* (10)	750,026	723,547	26,479	3.5
1950* (8)	853,490	811,435	42,055	4.9
1940 (8)	816,048	756,401	59,647	7.3
1930 (7)	821,960	740,614	81,346	9.9
1920 (6)	772,897	669,271	103,626	13.4
1910 (4)	687,029	560,806	126,223	18.4
1900 (4)	575,238	463,882	111,356	19.4
1890 (5)	451,770	336,894	114,876	25.4
1880 (6)	350,518	245,505	105,013	30.0
1870 (4)	310,864	198,615	112,249	36.1

Table 26. (Continued)

State, urban place and year (rank in total population)	Total	Native	Foreign born	
			Number	Percent
1860 (8)	160,773	(NA)	(NA)	(NA)
1850 (8)	77,860	39,463	38,397	49.3
NEBRASKA				
Omaha				
2000* (44)	390,112	364,425	25,687	6.6
1990* (48)	335,795	326,393	9,402	2.8
1980* (48)	314,267	304,103	10,164	3.2
1970* (41)	347,790	337,053	10,737	3.1
1960* (42)	301,598	287,215	14,383	4.8
1950* (41)	249,740	232,210	17,530	7.0
1940 (39)	223,844	201,455	22,389	10.0
1930 (39)	214,006	184,480	29,526	13.8
1920 (34)	191,601	155,956	35,645	18.6
1910 (41)	124,096	96,917	27,179	21.9
1900 (35)	102,555	79,003	23,552	23.0
1890 (21)	140,452	105,413	35,039	24.9
1880 (63)	30,518	20,588	9,930	32.5
1870 (91)	16,083	9,763	6,320	39.3
NEVADA				
Las Vegas				
2000 (32)	478,868	388,212	90,656	18.9
1990 (63)	258,295	231,801	26,494	10.3
1980 (89)	164,674	151,557	13,117	8.0
1970 (-)	125,606	120,391	5,215	4.2
1960 (-)	64,405	61,361	3,044	4.7
NEW JERSEY				
Camden				
2000* (-)	79,904	72,804	7,100	8.9
1990* (-)	87,492	84,056	3,436	3.9
1980* (-)	84,910	82,267	2,643	3.1
1970* (-)	102,551	98,201	4,350	4.2
1960* (-)	117,159	108,817	8,342	7.1
1950* (86)	123,955	111,595	12,360	10.0
1940 (71)	117,536	102,471	15,065	12.8
1930 (68)	118,700	99,984	18,716	15.8
1920 (58)	116,309	95,955	20,354	17.5
1910 (56)	94,538	78,765	15,773	16.7
1900 (52)	75,935	65,838	10,097	13.3
1890 (49)	58,313	50,580	7,733	13.3
1880 (44)	41,659	37,164	4,495	10.8
1870 (69)	20,045	17,462	2,583	12.9
Jersey City				
2000* (72)	240,055	158,501	81,554	34.0
1990* (67)	228,537	172,211	56,326	24.6
1980* (61)	223,532	187,180	36,352	16.3
1970* (54)	260,549	233,914	26,635	10.2

Table 26. (Continued)

State, urban place and year (rank in total population)	Total	Native	Foreign born	
			Number	Percent
1960* (47)	276,101	245,128	30,973	11.2
1950* (37)	299,130	257,740	41,390	13.8
1940 (30)	301,173	247,797	53,376	17.7
1930 (23)	316,715	246,027	70,688	22.3
1920 (22)	298,103	221,809	76,294	25.6
1910 (19)	267,779	189,792	77,987	29.1
1900 (17)	206,433	148,009	58,424	28.3
1890 (19)	163,003	109,645	53,358	32.7
1880 (17)	120,722	81,464	39,258	32.5
1870 (17)	82,546	50,711	31,835	38.6
Newark				
2000* (63)	273,546	207,489	66,057	24.1
1990* (56)	275,221	223,798	51,423	18.7
1980* (46)	329,248	281,509	47,739	14.5
1970* (35)	382,374	342,270	40,104	10.5
1960* (30)	405,220	355,261	49,959	12.3
1950* (21)	437,540	365,730	71,810	16.4
1940 (18)	429,760	338,889	90,871	21.1
1930 (18)	442,337	326,202	116,135	26.3
1920 (15)	414,524	296,975	117,549	28.4
1910 (14)	347,469	236,462	111,007	31.9
1900 (16)	246,070	174,707	71,363	29.0
1890 (17)	181,830	126,259	55,571	30.6
1880 (15)	136,508	96,178	40,330	29.5
1870 (13)	105,059	69,175	35,884	34.2
1860 (11)	71,941	(NA)	(NA)	(NA)
1850 (19)	38,894	26,572	12,322	31.7
Paterson				
2000* (-)	149,222	100,298	48,924	32.8
1990* (-)	140,891	105,536	35,355	25.1
1980* (-)	137,970	112,433	25,537	18.5
1970* (95)	144,835	123,834	21,001	14.5
1960* (86)	143,663	120,188	23,475	16.3
1950* (66)	139,135	111,025	28,110	20.2
1940 (64)	139,656	105,463	34,193	24.5
1930 (60)	138,513	95,748	42,765	30.9
1920 (49)	135,875	90,633	45,242	33.3
1910 (40)	125,600	80,115	45,485	36.2
1900 (32)	105,171	66,380	38,791	36.9
1890 (36)	78,347	47,185	31,162	39.8
1880 (34)	51,031	32,329	18,702	36.6
1870 (37)	33,579	20,711	12,868	38.3
Trenton				
2000* (-)	85,258	73,234	12,024	14.1
1990* (-)	88,675	81,980	6,695	7.6
1980* (-)	92,124	85,981	6,143	6.7

Table 26. (Continued)

State, urban place and year (rank in total population)	Total	Native	Foreign born	
			Number	Percent
1970* (-)	104,521	96,498	8,023	7.7
1960* (-)	114,167	101,040	13,127	11.5
1950* (80)	127,875	109,835	18,040	14.1
1940 (67)	124,697	102,790	21,907	17.6
1930 (65)	123,356	96,479	26,877	21.8
1920 (55)	119,289	89,121	30,168	25.3
1910 (52)	96,815	70,439	26,376	27.2
1900 (53)	73,307	56,514	16,793	22.9
1890 (50)	57,458	43,410	14,048	24.4
1880 (64)	29,910	24,191	5,719	19.1
1870 (58)	22,874	17,855	5,019	21.9
NEW MEXICO				
Albuquerque				
2000* (35)	448,627	408,865	39,762	8.9
1990* (38)	384,736	363,426	21,310	5.5
1980* (44)	331,767	316,711	15,056	4.5
1970* (58)	243,751	238,734	5,017	2.1
1960* (60)	201,189	196,686	4,503	2.2
1950 (-)	96,815	(NA)	(NA)	(NA)
1940 (-)	35,449	33,909	1,540	4.3
1930 (-)	26,570	(NA)	(NA)	(NA)
1920 (-)	15,157	(NA)	(NA)	(NA)
1910 (-)	11,020	(NA)	(NA)	(NA)
1900 (-)	6,238	5,282	956	15.3
1890 (-)	3,785	3,084	701	18.5
NEW YORK				
Albany				
2000* (-)	95,658	87,436	8,222	8.6
1990* (-)	101,082	93,297	7,785	7.7
1980* (-)	101,727	94,625	7,102	7.0
1970* (-)	115,875	108,067	7,808	6.7
1960* (94)	129,726	119,548	10,178	7.8
1950* (69)	134,325	122,120	12,205	9.1
1940 (65)	130,577	115,334	15,243	11.7
1930 (64)	127,412	109,388	18,024	14.1
1920 (60)	113,344	95,649	17,695	15.6
1910 (50)	100,253	82,035	18,218	18.2
1900 (40)	94,151	76,433	17,718	18.8
1890 (29)	94,923	72,630	22,293	23.5
1880 (21)	90,758	66,993	23,765	26.2
1870 (20)	69,422	47,215	22,207	32.0
1860 (13)	62,367	(NA)	(NA)	(NA)
1850 (10)	50,763	34,172	16,591	32.7
Brooklyn [6]				
1890 (4)	806,343	544,643	261,700	32.5
1880 (3)	566,663	388,969	177,694	31.4

Table 26. (Continued)

State, urban place and year (rank in total population)	Total	Native	Foreign born	
			Number	Percent
1870 (3)	396,099	251,381	144,718	36.5
Buffalo				
2000* (58)	292,648	279,792	12,856	4.4
1990* (50)	328,123	313,382	14,741	4.5
1980* (39)	357,870	335,845	22,025	6.2
1970* (28)	462,781	427,529	35,252	7.6
1960* (20)	532,759	477,739	55,020	10.3
1950* (15)	577,825	507,320	70,505	12.2
1940 (14)	575,901	483,500	92,401	16.0
1930 (13)	573,076	454,135	118,941	20.8
1920 (11)	506,775	384,951	121,824	24.0
1910 (10)	423,715	305,026	118,689	28.0
1900 (8)	352,387	248,135	104,252	29.6
1890 (11)	255,664	166,179	89,485	35.0
1880 (13)	155,134	103,866	51,268	33.0
1870 (11)	117,714	71,477	46,237	39.3
New York [7]				
2000* (1)	8,008,278	5,137,246	2,871,032	35.9
1990* (1)	7,322,564	5,239,633	2,082,931	28.4
1980* (1)	7,071,639	5,401,440	1,670,199	23.6
1970* (1)	7,894,798	6,457,740	1,437,058	18.2
1960* (1)	7,783,314	6,224,624	1,558,690	20.0
1950* (1)	7,887,380	6,026,450	1,860,930	23.6
1940 (1)	7,454,995	5,316,338	2,138,657	28.7
1930 (1)	6,930,446	4,571,760	2,358,686	34.0
1920 (1)	5,620,048	3,591,888	2,028,160	36.1
1910 (1)	4,766,883	2,822,526	1,944,357	40.8
1900 (1)	3,437,202	2,167,122	1,270,080	37.0
1890 (1)	1,515,301	875,358	639,943	42.2
1880 (1)	1,206,299	727,629	478,670	39.7
1870 (1)	942,292	523,198	419,094	44.5
1860 (1)	813,669	429,952	383,717	47.2
1850 (1)	515,547	279,814	235,733	45.7
Bronx borough [7]				
2000* (X)	1,332,650	946,823	385,827	29.0
1990* (X)	1,203,789	928,996	274,793	22.8
1980* (X)	1,168,972	953,659	215,313	18.4
1970* (X)	1,471,686	1,242,476	229,210	15.6
1960* (X)	1,424,814	1,118,222	306,592	21.5
1950 (X)	1,451,277	(NA)	(NA)	(NA)
1940 (X)	1,394,711	931,258	463,453	33.2
1930 (X)	1,265,258	785,807	479,451	37.9
1920 (X)	732,016	464,274	267,742	36.6
1910 (X)	430,980	281,553	149,427	34.7
1900 (X)	200,507	138,965	61,542	30.7

Table 26. (Continued)

State, urban place and year (rank in total population)	Total	Native	Foreign born	
			Number	Percent
Brooklyn borough [7]				
2000* (X)	2,465,326	1,533,557	931,769	37.8
1990* (X)	2,300,664	1,628,095	672,569	29.2
1980* (X)	2,230,936	1,699,963	530,973	23.8
1970* (X)	2,601,974	2,145,338	456,636	17.5
1960* (X)	2,628,230	2,111,881	516,349	19.6
1950 (X)	2,738,175	(NA)	(NA)	(NA)
1940 (X)	2,698,285	1,920,231	778,054	28.8
1930 (X)	2,560,401	1,678,830	881,571	34.4
1920 (X)	2,018,356	1,352,168	666,188	33.0
1910 (X)	1,634,351	1,059,621	574,730	35.2
1900 (X)	1,166,582	810,885	355,697	30.5
Manhattan borough [7]				
2000* (X)	1,537,195	1,084,755	452,440	29.4
1990* (X)	1,487,536	1,103,670	383,866	25.8
1980* (X)	1,428,285	1,079,704	348,581	24.4
1970* (X)	1,539,225	1,231,595	307,630	20.0
1960* (X)	1,698,285	1,323,587	374,698	22.1
1950 (X)	1,960,101	(NA)	(NA)	(NA)
1940 (X)	1,889,924	1,307,029	582,895	30.8
1930 (X)	1,867,312	1,177,806	689,506	36.9
1920 (X)	2,284,103	1,333,839	950,264	41.6
1910 (X)	2,331,542	1,215,065	1,116,477	47.9
1900 (X)	1,850,093	1,060,751	789,342	42.7
Queens borough [7]				
2000* (X)	2,229,379	1,201,040	1,028,339	46.1
1990* (X)	1,951,598	1,244,445	707,153	36.2
1980* (X)	1,891,325	1,350,507	540,818	28.6
1970* (X)	1,986,470	1,569,583	416,887	21.0
1960* (X)	1,809,994	1,474,371	335,623	18.5
1950 (X)	1,550,849	(NA)	(NA)	(NA)
1940 (X)	1,297,634	1,018,697	278,937	21.5
1930 (X)	1,079,129	810,770	268,359	24.9
1920 (X)	469,042	356,871	112,171	23.9
1910 (X)	284,041	204,712	79,329	27.9
1900 (X)	152,999	108,187	44,812	29.3
Staten Island borough [7]				
2000* (X)	443,728	371,071	72,657	16.4
1990* (X)	378,977	334,427	44,550	11.8
1980* (X)	352,121	317,607	34,514	9.8
1970* (X)	295,443	268,748	26,695	9.0
1960* (X)	221,991	196,563	25,428	11.5
1950 (X)	191,555	(NA)	(NA)	(NA)
1940 (X)	174,441	139,123	35,318	20.2
1930 (X)	158,346	118,547	39,799	25.1
1920 (X)	116,531	84,736	31,795	27.3

Table 26. (Continued)

State, urban place and year (rank in total population)	Total	Native	Foreign born	
			Number	Percent
1910 (X)	85,969	61,575	24,394	28.4
1900 (X)	67,021	48,334	18,687	27.9
Rochester				
2000* (79)	219,766	203,689	16,077	7.3
1990* (66)	231,636	217,213	14,423	6.2
1980* (57)	241,741	221,466	20,275	8.4
1970* (49)	296,233	265,003	31,230	10.5
1960* (38)	318,611	276,567	42,044	13.2
1950* (33)	330,990	281,945	49,045	14.8
1940 (23)	324,975	264,737	60,238	18.5
1930 (22)	328,132	253,293	74,839	22.8
1920 (23)	295,750	224,339	71,411	24.1
1910 (25)	218,149	159,073	59,076	27.1
1900 (24)	162,608	121,860	40,748	25.1
1890 (22)	133,896	94,121	39,775	29.7
1880 (22)	89,366	62,744	26,622	29.8
1870 (22)	62,386	41,202	21,184	34.0
Syracuse				
2000* (-)	147,326	136,112	11,214	7.6
1990* (-)	163,860	153,284	10,576	6.5
1980* (86)	170,105	157,079	13,026	7.7
1970* (66)	197,332	181,625	15,707	8.0
1960* (53)	216,038	194,842	21,196	9.8
1950* (47)	218,830	195,335	23,495	10.7
1940 (41)	205,967	178,335	27,632	13.4
1930 (40)	209,326	174,176	35,150	16.8
1920 (37)	171,717	139,334	32,383	18.9
1910 (34)	137,249	106,401	30,848	22.5
1900 (30)	108,374	84,617	23,757	21.9
1890 (31)	88,143	65,801	22,342	25.3
1880 (32)	51,792	38,774	13,018	25.1
1870 (29)	43,051	29,061	13,990	32.5
Troy				
2000* (-)	49,170	46,298	2,872	5.8
1990* (-)	54,269	50,897	3,372	6.2
1980* (-)	56,638	53,314	3,324	5.9
1970* (-)	62,907	59,397	3,510	5.6
1960* (-)	67,492	63,189	4,303	6.4
1950 (-)	72,311	(NA)	(NA)	(NA)
1940 (-)	70,304	62,739	7,565	10.8
1930 (-)	72,763	62,516	10,247	14.1
1920 (98)	72,013	60,488	11,525	16.0
1910 (72)	76,813	61,365	15,448	20.1
1900 (62)	60,651	46,267	14,384	23.7
1890 (46)	60,956	43,691	17,265	28.3
1880 (29)	56,747	39,809	16,938	29.8

Table 26. (Continued)

State, urban place and year (rank in total population)	Total	Native	Foreign born	
			Number	Percent
1870 (28)	46,465	30,246	16,219	34.9
Utica				
2000* (-)	60,679	53,448	7,231	11.9
1990* (-)	68,637	64,919	3,718	5.4
1980* (-)	75,632	70,744	4,888	6.5
1970* (-)	91,727	84,245	7,482	8.2
1960* (-)	100,410	89,006	11,404	11.4
1950* (-)	101,040	86,570	14,470	14.3
1940 (92)	100,518	83,166	17,352	17.3
1930 (89)	101,740	80,413	21,327	21.0
1920 (74)	94,156	70,865	23,291	24.7
1910 (73)	74,419	53,103	21,316	28.6
1900 (66)	56,383	42,913	13,470	23.9
1890 (67)	44,007	32,238	11,769	26.7
1880 (52)	33,914	24,581	9,333	27.5
1870 (46)	28,804	18,955	9,849	34.2
NORTH CAROLINA				
Charlotte				
2000* (26)	542,131	482,282	59,849	11.0
1990* (35)	396,003	380,884	15,119	3.8
1980* (47)	314,447	305,705	8,742	2.8
1970* (60)	241,130	238,093	3,037	1.3
1960* (59)	201,564	199,767	1,797	0.9
1950* (70)	133,800	132,555	1,245	0.9
1940 (91)	100,899	99,991	908	0.9
1930 (-)	82,675	81,759	916	1.1
1920 (-)	46,338	45,816	522	1.1
1910 (-)	34,014	33,534	480	1.4
1900 (-)	18,091	17,804	287	1.6
1890 (-)	11,557	11,371	186	1.6
1880 (-)	7,094	6,901	193	2.7
1870 (-)	4,473	4,305	168	3.8
OHIO				
Akron				
2000* (81)	217,088	210,177	6,911	3.2
1990* (71)	223,019	216,208	6,811	3.1
1980* (59)	237,177	228,476	8,701	3.7
1970* (52)	275,420	263,173	12,247	4.4
1960* (45)	290,351	272,988	17,363	6.0
1950* (39)	273,710	252,855	20,855	7.6
1940 (38)	244,791	219,313	25,478	10.4
1930 (35)	255,040	223,346	31,694	12.4
1920 (32)	208,435	170,414	38,021	18.2
1910 (81)	69,067	55,818	13,249	19.2
1900 (87)	42,728	35,601	7,127	16.7
1890 (-)	27,601	21,608	5,993	21.7

Table 26. (Continued)

State, urban place and year (rank in total population)	Total	Native	Foreign born	
			Number	Percent
1880 (-)	16,512	12,901	3,611	21.9
1870 (-)	10,006	7,402	2,604	26.0
Cincinnati				
2000* (54)	330,662	318,201	12,461	3.8
1990* (45)	364,040	353,995	10,045	2.8
1980* (32)	385,457	374,833	10,624	2.8
1970* (29)	452,376	440,039	12,337	2.7
1960* (21)	502,550	485,950	16,600	3.3
1950* (18)	502,010	481,485	20,525	4.1
1940 (17)	455,610	429,712	25,898	5.7
1930 (17)	451,160	416,174	34,986	7.8
1920 (16)	401,247	358,326	42,921	10.7
1910 (13)	363,591	306,732	56,859	15.6
1900 (10)	325,902	267,941	57,961	17.8
1890 (9)	296,908	225,500	71,408	24.1
1880 (8)	255,139	183,480	71,659	28.1
1870 (8)	216,239	136,627	79,612	36.8
1860 (7)	161,044	87,430	73,614	45.7
1850 (6)	115,435	60,894	54,541	47.2
Cleveland				
2000* (33)	478,393	457,021	21,372	4.5
1990* (23)	505,616	484,641	20,975	4.1
1980* (18)	573,822	540,475	33,347	5.8
1970* (10)	750,932	694,532	56,400	7.5
1960* (8)	876,050	779,466	96,584	11.0
1950* (7)	912,840	779,960	132,880	14.6
1940 (6)	878,336	698,552	179,784	20.5
1930 (6)	900,429	669,483	230,946	25.6
1920 (5)	796,841	556,668	240,173	30.1
1910 (6)	560,663	364,493	196,170	35.0
1900 (7)	381,768	257,137	124,631	32.6
1890 (10)	261,353	164,258	97,095	37.2
1880 (11)	160,146	100,737	59,409	37.1
1870 (15)	92,829	54,014	38,815	41.8
Columbus				
2000* (15)	711,644	663,931	47,713	6.7
1990* (16)	632,958	609,487	23,471	3.7
1980* (19)	564,866	548,411	16,455	2.9
1970* (21)	539,469	528,275	11,194	2.1
1960* (28)	471,316	460,264	11,052	2.3
1950* (30)	362,205	351,740	10,465	2.9
1940 (26)	306,087	294,035	12,052	3.9
1930 (28)	290,564	275,122	15,442	5.3
1920 (28)	237,031	220,844	16,187	6.8
1910 (29)	181,511	165,148	16,363	9.0
1900 (28)	125,560	113,232	12,328	9.8

Table 26. (Continued)

State, urban place and year (rank in total population)	Total	Native	Foreign born	
			Number	Percent
1890 (30)	88,150	75,662	12,488	14.2
1880 (33)	51,647	42,576	9,071	17.6
1870 (42)	31,274	23,663	7,611	24.3
Dayton				
2000* (-)	166,193	162,948	3,245	2.0
1990* (89)	182,044	179,438	2,606	1.4
1980* (70)	203,371	199,230	4,141	2.0
1970* (59)	243,405	239,206	4,199	1.7
1960* (49)	262,332	256,234	6,098	2.3
1950* (44)	243,050	234,985	8,065	3.3
1940 (40)	210,718	201,357	9,361	4.4
1930 (41)	200,982	188,888	12,094	6.0
1920 (43)	152,559	139,394	13,165	8.6
1910 (43)	116,577	102,685	13,892	11.9
1900 (45)	85,333	75,280	10,053	11.8
1890 (45)	61,220	51,633	9,587	15.7
1880 (47)	38,678	31,432	7,246	18.7
1870 (44)	30,473	23,050	7,423	24.4
Toledo				
2000* (56)	313,587	304,112	9,475	3.0
1990* (49)	332,943	323,680	9,263	2.8
1980* (40)	354,635	343,625	11,010	3.1
1970* (34)	384,067	371,601	12,466	3.2
1960* (39)	318,003	302,620	15,383	4.8
1950* (36)	303,725	283,650	20,075	6.6
1940 (34)	282,349	257,493	24,856	8.8
1930 (27)	290,718	256,717	34,001	11.7
1920 (26)	243,164	204,868	38,296	15.7
1910 (30)	168,497	136,353	32,144	19.1
1900 (26)	131,822	104,000	27,822	21.1
1890 (34)	81,434	59,245	22,189	27.2
1880 (35)	50,137	35,788	14,349	28.6
1870 (40)	31,584	20,485	11,099	35.1
Youngstown				
2000* (-)	82,026	80,421	1,605	2.0
1990* (-)	95,732	92,853	2,879	3.0
1980* (-)	115,435	109,878	5,557	4.8
1970* (98)	139,720	130,680	9,040	6.5
1960* (75)	166,689	149,838	16,851	10.1
1950* (57)	168,065	146,530	21,535	12.8
1940 (49)	167,720	141,002	26,718	15.9
1930 (45)	170,002	136,771	33,231	19.5
1920 (50)	132,358	98,413	33,945	25.6
1910 (67)	79,066	54,170	24,896	31.5
1900 (84)	44,885	32,678	12,207	27.2
1890 (91)	33,220	22,684	10,536	31.7

Table 26. (Continued)

State, urban place and year (rank in total population)	Total	Native	Foreign born	
			Number	Percent
1880 (-)	15,435	10,678	4,757	30.8
1870 (-)	8,075	5,258	2,817	34.9
OKLAHOMA				
Oklahoma City				
2000* (29)	505,963	463,078	42,885	8.5
1990* (29)	444,730	425,998	18,732	4.2
1980* (31)	403,243	391,791	11,452	2.8
1970* (37)	366,756	362,877	3,879	1.1
1960* (37)	324,253	320,757	3,496	1.1
1950* (45)	242,085	239,380	2,705	1.1
1940 (42)	204,424	201,573	2,851	1.4
1930 (43)	185,389	181,667	3,722	2.0
1920 (80)	91,295	87,730	3,565	3.9
1910 (87)	64,205	60,868	3,337	5.2
1900 (-)	10,037	9,466	571	5.7
1890 (-)	4,151	3,808	343	8.3
Tulsa				
2000* (43)	393,051	367,386	25,665	6.5
1990* (43)	367,193	356,183	11,010	3.0
1980* (38)	360,919	351,570	9,349	2.6
1970* (43)	331,768	328,269	3,499	1.1
1960* (50)	261,685	258,738	2,947	1.1
1950* (51)	182,705	180,485	2,220	1.2
1940 (62)	142,157	139,963	2,194	1.5
1930 (58)	141,258	138,420	2,838	2.0
1920 (97)	72,075	70,009	2,066	2.9
OREGON				
Portland				
2000* (28)	529,025	460,049	68,976	13.0
1990* (30)	437,398	403,797	33,601	7.7
1980* (35)	366,423	340,440	25,983	7.1
1970* (36)	381,927	360,847	21,080	5.5
1960* (32)	372,664	345,238	27,426	7.4
1950* (28)	373,105	338,185	34,920	9.4
1940 (27)	305,394	265,389	40,005	13.1
1930 (25)	301,815	251,587	50,228	16.6
1920 (24)	258,288	208,510	49,778	19.3
1910 (28)	207,214	156,902	50,312	24.3
1900 (42)	90,426	64,550	25,876	28.6
1890 (61)	46,385	29,062	17,323	37.3
1880 (-)	17,577	11,265	6,312	35.9
1870 (-)	8,293	5,715	2,578	31.1
PENNSYLVANIA				
Allegheny [8]				
1900 (27)	129,896	99,680	30,216	23.3
1890 (28)	105,287	79,152	26,135	24.8

Table 26. (Continued)

State, urban place and year (rank in total population)	Total	Native	Foreign born	
			Number	Percent
1880 (23)	78,682	59,245	19,437	24.7
1870 (23)	53,180	37,872	15,308	28.8
Philadelphia				
2000* (5)	1,517,550	1,380,345	137,205	9.0
1990* (5)	1,585,577	1,480,763	104,814	6.6
1980* (4)	1,688,210	1,580,259	107,951	6.4
1970* (4)	1,948,608	1,821,712	126,896	6.5
1960* (4)	2,002,509	1,824,082	178,427	8.9
1950* (3)	2,068,095	1,830,300	237,795	11.5
1940 (3)	1,931,334	1,638,788	292,546	15.1
1930 (3)	1,950,961	1,578,883	372,078	19.1
1920 (3)	1,823,779	1,423,035	400,744	22.0
1910 (3)	1,549,008	1,164,301	384,707	24.8
1900 (3)	1,293,697	998,357	295,340	22.8
1890 (3)	1,046,964	777,484	269,480	25.7
1880 (2)	847,170	642,835	204,335	24.1
1870 (2)	674,022	490,398	183,624	27.2
1860 (2)	565,529	396,099	169,430	30.0
Pittsburgh				
2000* (-)	334,563	315,689	18,874	5.6
1990* (40)	369,879	352,933	16,946	4.6
1980* (30)	423,938	401,743	22,195	5.2
1970* (24)	520,146	488,871	31,275	6.0
1960* (16)	604,332	559,079	45,253	7.5
1950* (12)	675,465	609,895	65,570	9.7
1940 (10)	671,659	586,756	84,903	12.6
1930 (10)	669,817	560,132	109,685	16.4
1920 (9)	588,343	467,551	120,792	20.5
1910 (8)	533,905	392,981	140,924	26.4
1900 (11)	321,616	236,738	84,878	26.4
1890 (13)	238,617	165,328	73,289	30.7
1880 (12)	156,389	111,784	44,605	28.5
1870 (16)	86,076	58,254	27,822	32.3
Reading				
2000* (-)	81,201	72,685	8,516	10.5
1990* (-)	78,380	75,018	3,362	4.3
1980* (-)	78,686	75,802	2,884	3.7
1970* (-)	87,647	84,013	3,634	4.1
1960* (-)	98,177	93,068	5,109	5.2
1950* (96)	109,245	102,695	6,550	6.0
1940 (79)	110,568	102,688	7,880	7.1
1930 (76)	111,171	101,584	9,587	8.6
1920 (64)	107,784	98,211	9,573	8.9
1910 (55)	96,071	87,248	8,823	9.2
1900 (50)	78,961	73,021	5,940	7.5
1890 (48)	58,661	53,929	4,732	8.1

Table 26. (Continued)

State, urban place and year (rank in total population)	Total	Native	Foreign born	
			Number	Percent
1880 (41)	43,278	39,654	3,624	8.4
1870 (36)	33,930	30,059	3,871	11.4
Scranton				
2000* (-)	76,415	74,040	2,375	3.1
1990* (-)	81,805	79,715	2,090	2.6
1980* (-)	88,117	84,950	3,167	3.6
1970* (-)	103,446	98,904	4,542	4.4
1960* (-)	111,443	104,230	7,213	6.5
1950* (83)	125,300	112,645	12,655	10.1
1940 (63)	140,404	122,015	18,389	13.1
1930 (55)	143,433	117,976	25,457	17.7
1920 (47)	137,783	109,196	28,587	20.7
1910 (38)	129,867	94,745	35,122	27.0
1900 (38)	102,026	73,053	28,973	28.4
1890 (39)	75,215	49,642	25,573	34.0
1880 (39)	45,850	29,993	15,857	34.6
1870 (35)	35,092	19,205	15,887	45.3
RHODE ISLAND				
Providence				
2000* (-)	173,618	129,671	43,947	25.3
1990* (-)	160,728	129,196	31,532	19.6
1980* (100)	156,804	135,643	21,161	13.5
1970* (71)	179,231	161,000	18,231	10.2
1960* (56)	207,498	181,480	26,018	12.5
1950* (43)	248,520	209,085	39,435	15.9
1940 (37)	253,504	201,655	51,849	20.5
1930 (37)	252,981	187,626	65,355	25.8
1920 (27)	237,595	167,700	69,895	29.4
1910 (23)	224,326	147,327	76,999	34.3
1900 (20)	175,597	119,742	55,855	31.8
1890 (25)	132,146	91,782	40,364	30.5
1880 (20)	104,857	76,782	28,075	26.8
1870 (21)	68,904	51,727	17,177	24.9
1860 (16)	50,666	(NA)	(NA)	(NA)
1850 (17)	41,513	31,834	9,679	23.3
SOUTH CAROLINA				
Charleston				
2000* (-)	96,086	92,676	3,410	3.5
1990* (-)	80,414	78,508	1,906	2.4
1980* (-)	69,510	67,872	1,638	2.4
1970* (-)	66,934	66,079	855	1.3
1960* (-)	65,925	65,014	911	1.4
1950 (-)	70,174	(NA)	(NA)	(NA)
1940 (-)	71,275	69,956	1,319	1.9
1930 (-)	62,265	60,626	1,639	2.6
1920 (-)	67,957	65,723	2,234	3.3

Table 26. (Continued)

State, urban place and year (rank in total population)	Total	Native	Foreign born	
			Number	Percent
1910 (90)	58,833	56,385	2,448	4.2
1900 (68)	55,807	53,215	2,592	4.6
1890 (53)	54,955	51,822	3,133	5.7
1880 (36)	49,984	46,034	3,950	7.9
1870 (26)	48,956	44,064	4,892	10.0
1860 (22)	40,522	(NA)	(NA)	(NA)
1850 (15)	42,985	38,342	4,643	10.8
TENNESSEE				
Memphis				
2000* (18)	649,845	623,770	26,075	4.0
1990* (18)	610,337	602,039	8,298	1.4
1980* (14)	646,356	637,969	8,387	1.3
1970* (17)	623,753	618,652	5,101	0.8
1960* (22)	497,524	493,112	4,412	0.9
1950* (26)	394,985	390,650	4,335	1.1
1940 (32)	292,942	288,431	4,511	1.5
1930 (36)	253,143	247,816	5,327	2.1
1920 (40)	162,351	156,507	5,844	3.6
1910 (37)	131,105	124,585	6,520	5.0
1900 (37)	102,320	97,210	5,110	5.0
1890 (43)	64,495	59,095	5,400	8.4
1880 (54)	33,592	29,621	3,971	11.8
1870 (32)	40,226	33,446	6,780	16.9
1860 (38)	22,623	(NA)	(NA)	(NA)
1850 (73)	8,841	7,440	1,401	15.8
Nashville [3]				
2000* (25)	545,549	506,613	38,936	7.1
1990* (25)	488,518	476,347	12,171	2.5
1980* (25)	455,663	448,000	7,663	1.7
1970* (30)	448,003	444,315	3,688	0.8
1960* (73)	170,874	169,497	1,377	0.8
1950* (56)	173,580	172,205	1,375	0.8
1940 (50)	167,402	165,846	1,556	0.9
1930 (51)	153,866	152,055	1,811	1.2
1920 (56)	118,342	115,930	2,412	2.0
1910 (45)	110,364	107,347	3,017	2.7
1900 (47)	80,865	77,828	3,037	3.8
1890 (38)	76,168	72,374	3,794	5.0
1880 (40)	43,350	40,325	3,025	7.0
1870 (52)	25,865	23,056	2,809	10.9
1860 (54)	16,988	(NA)	(NA)	(NA)
1850 (63)	10,165	9,217	948	9.3
TEXAS				
Austin				
2000* (16)	656,302	547,296	109,006	16.6
1990* (27)	465,577	425,951	39,626	8.5

Table 26. (Continued)

State, urban place and year (rank in total population)	Total	Native	Foreign born	
			Number	Percent
1980* (42)	345,544	328,840	16,704	4.8
1970* (56)	251,791	246,294	5,497	2.2
1960* (67)	186,545	182,209	4,336	2.3
1950* (73)	131,645	127,930	3,715	2.8
1940 (-)	87,930	84,910	3,020	3.4
1930 (-)	53,120	50,078	3,042	5.7
1920 (-)	34,876	32,314	2,562	7.3
1910 (-)	29,860	27,405	2,455	8.2
1900 (-)	22,258	20,146	2,112	9.5
1890 (-)	14,575	12,737	1,838	12.6
1880 (-)	11,013	9,628	1,385	12.6
1870 (-)	4,428	3,812	616	13.9
Dallas				
2000* (8)	1,188,204	897,768	290,436	24.4
1990* (8)	1,006,831	880,969	125,862	12.5
1980* (7)	904,074	849,162	54,912	6.1
1970* (8)	844,280	826,854	17,426	2.1
1960* (14)	679,684	666,964	12,720	1.9
1950* (22)	432,970	424,620	8,350	1.9
1940 (31)	294,734	287,339	7,395	2.5
1930 (33)	260,475	251,014	9,461	3.6
1920 (42)	158,976	150,175	8,801	5.5
1910 (58)	92,104	86,840	5,264	5.7
1900 (88)	42,638	39,257	3,381	7.9
1890 (77)	38,067	34,089	3,978	10.4
1880 (-)	10,358	9,035	1,323	12.8
El Paso				
2000* (22)	564,280	416,775	147,505	26.1
1990* (22)	515,342	394,910	120,432	23.4
1980* (28)	425,259	334,352	90,907	21.4
1970* (45)	322,261	277,919	44,342	13.8
1960* (46)	276,687	233,673	43,014	15.5
1950* (76)	130,505	108,655	21,850	16.7
1940 (98)	96,810	74,688	22,122	22.9
1930 (86)	102,421	66,118	36,303	35.4
1920 (89)	77,560	43,905	33,655	43.4
1910 (-)	39,279	24,775	14,504	36.9
1900 (-)	15,906	9,597	6,309	39.7
1890 (-)	10,338	6,519	3,819	36.9
Fort Worth				
2000* (27)	535,420	448,300	87,120	16.3
1990* (28)	447,619	407,319	40,300	9.0
1980* (33)	385,166	366,854	18,312	4.8
1970* (33)	393,516	387,577	5,939	1.5
1960* (34)	356,729	351,913	4,816	1.4
1950* (38)	277,585	273,465	4,120	1.5

Table 26. (Continued)

State, urban place and year (rank in total population)	Total	Native	Foreign born	
			Number	Percent
1940 (46)	177,662	174,098	3,564	2.0
1930 (48)	163,447	158,514	4,933	3.0
1920 (65)	106,482	98,980	7,502	7.0
1910 (75)	73,312	69,032	4,280	5.8
1900 (-)	26,688	24,895	1,793	6.7
1890 (-)	23,076	21,053	2,023	8.8
1880 (-)	6,663	6,137	526	7.9
Houston				
2000* (4)	1,954,848	1,438,743	516,105	26.4
1990* (4)	1,630,672	1,340,298	290,374	17.8
1980* (5)	1,595,167	1,439,590	155,577	9.8
1970* (6)	1,231,572	1,194,071	37,501	3.0
1960* (7)	938,219	913,920	24,299	2.6
1950* (14)	594,585	577,030	17,555	3.0
1940 (21)	384,514	369,050	15,464	4.0
1930 (26)	292,352	274,415	17,937	6.1
1920 (45)	138,276	126,188	12,088	8.7
1910 (68)	78,800	72,392	6,408	8.1
1900 (85)	44,633	40,228	4,405	9.9
1890 (-)	27,557	24,442	3,115	11.3
1880 (-)	16,513	14,240	2,273	13.8
1870 (-)	9,382	7,811	1,571	16.7
San Antonio				
2000* (9)	1,144,554	1,010,879	133,675	11.7
1990* (10)	935,927	848,378	87,549	9.4
1980* (11)	785,809	720,933	64,876	8.3
1970* (15)	654,468	615,779	38,689	5.9
1960* (17)	588,042	548,258	39,784	6.8
1950* (25)	407,335	374,340	32,995	8.1
1940 (36)	253,854	225,558	28,296	11.1
1930 (38)	231,542	190,830	40,712	17.6
1920 (41)	161,379	124,555	36,824	22.8
1910 (54)	96,614	79,119	17,495	18.1
1900 (71)	53,321	43,973	9,348	17.5
1890 (81)	37,673	28,670	9,003	23.9
1880 (96)	20,550	14,952	5,598	27.2
1870 (-)	12,256	8,136	4,120	33.6
VIRGINIA				
Norfolk				
2000* (73)	234,403	222,769	11,634	5.0
1990* (62)	261,229	251,463	9,766	3.7
1980* (55)	266,979	256,327	10,652	4.0
1970* (47)	307,951	300,477	7,474	2.4
1960* (41)	305,872	300,091	5,781	1.9
1950* (48)	214,360	209,290	5,070	2.4
1940 (60)	144,332	140,562	3,770	2.6

Table 26. (Continued)

State, urban place and year (rank in total population)	Total	Native	Foreign born	
			Number	Percent
1930 (62)	129,710	125,167	4,543	3.5
1920 (59)	115,777	108,779	6,998	6.0
1910 (82)	67,452	63,776	3,676	5.4
1900 (80)	46,624	44,919	1,705	3.7
1890 (88)	34,871	33,744	1,127	3.2
1880 (83)	21,966	21,131	835	3.8
1870 (75)	19,229	18,490	739	3.8
Richmond				
2000* (94)	197,790	190,147	7,643	3.9
1990* (76)	203,056	199,336	3,720	1.8
1980* (64)	219,214	215,165	4,049	1.8
1970* (57)	249,621	246,422	3,199	1.3
1960* (52)	219,958	216,970	2,988	1.4
1950* (46)	229,655	225,800	3,855	1.7
1940 (45)	193,042	189,555	3,487	1.8
1930 (44)	182,929	178,810	4,119	2.3
1920 (38)	171,667	166,954	4,713	2.7
1910 (39)	127,628	123,492	4,136	3.2
1900 (46)	85,050	82,185	2,865	3.4
1890 (35)	81,388	77,915	3,473	4.3
1880 (25)	63,600	60,260	3,340	5.3
1870 (24)	51,038	47,260	3,778	7.4
1860 (25)	37,910	(NA)	(NA)	(NA)
1850 (26)	27,570	25,468	2,102	7.6
Virginia Beach				
2000* (38)	425,257	396,981	28,276	6.6
1990* (37)	393,069	372,552	20,517	5.2
1980* (56)	262,199	251,229	10,970	4.2
1970* (79)	172,106	168,977	3,129	1.8
1960* (-)	8,091	7,911	180	2.2
WASHINGTON				
Seattle				
2000* (23)	563,375	468,423	94,952	16.9
1990* (21)	516,259	448,523	67,736	13.1
1980* (23)	493,846	438,230	55,616	11.3
1970* (22)	530,860	482,437	48,423	9.1
1960* (19)	557,087	497,367	59,720	10.7
1950* (19)	466,110	406,845	59,265	12.7
1940 (22)	368,302	304,832	63,470	17.2
1930 (20)	365,583	287,241	78,342	21.4
1920 (20)	315,312	234,336	80,976	25.7
1910 (21)	237,194	169,738	67,456	28.4
1900 (48)	80,671	58,668	22,003	27.3
1890 (70)	42,837	29,181	13,656	31.9
1880 (-)	3,533	(NA)	(NA)	(NA)
1870 (-)	1,107	828	279	25.2

Table 26. (Continued)

State, urban place and year (rank in total population)	Total	Native	Foreign born	
			Number	Percent
Spokane				
2000* (96)	196,143	185,047	11,096	5.7
1990* (94)	177,196	170,199	6,997	3.9
1980* (82)	171,300	163,679	7,621	4.4
1970* (80)	170,516	164,008	6,508	3.8
1960* (68)	181,608	171,550	10,058	5.5
1950* (62)	161,160	148,785	12,375	7.7
1940 (68)	122,001	109,046	12,955	10.6
1930 (70)	115,514	99,021	16,493	14.3
1920 (66)	104,437	87,341	17,096	16.4
1910 (48)	104,402	82,582	21,820	20.9
1900 (-)	36,848	29,015	7,833	21.3
1890 (-)	19,922	14,299	5,623	28.2
WISCONSIN				
Milwaukee				
2000* (19)	596,956	550,834	46,122	7.7
1990* (17)	628,088	598,421	29,667	4.7
1980* (16)	636,212	604,494	31,718	5.0
1970* (12)	717,110	677,534	39,576	5.5
1960* (11)	741,324	684,310	57,014	7.7
1950* (13)	636,005	572,815	63,190	9.9
1940 (13)	587,472	503,531	83,941	14.3
1930 (12)	578,249	467,638	110,611	19.1
1920 (13)	457,147	346,987	110,160	24.1
1910 (12)	373,857	262,328	111,529	29.8
1900 (14)	285,315	196,324	88,991	31.2
1890 (16)	204,468	124,892	79,576	38.9
1880 (19)	115,587	69,514	46,073	39.9
1870 (19)	71,440	37,667	33,773	47.3
1860 (20)	45,246	(NA)	(NA)	(NA)
1850 (35)	20,061	7,279	12,782	63.7

Footnotes:

* Indicates sample data.

(X) Not applicable. The boroughs are part of New York City. (NA) Not available.

(-) Not among the 100 largest urban places in this year.

[1]Population of Oakland township in 1870: total, 11,104; native, 6,940; foreign-born, 4,164; percent foreign-born, 37.5.

[2]1850 census results for San Francisco were destroyed by fire. The population of San Francisco according to the 1852 state census was 34,776. Population of San Francisco county in 1852: total, 36,154; native, 16,851; foreign-born, 19,303; percent foreign-born, 53.4 percent.

[3]See text for Table 23 regarding consolidated cities from 1970 to 2000.

[4]Data for Honolulu not shown prior to statehood for Hawaii. See general text.

[5]Charlestown annexed by Boston in 1874.

[6]Brooklyn annexed by New York in 1898. For 1900-1990, see Brooklyn borough.

[7]Data are shown separately for each of the five boroughs of New York City from 1900 to 1990. The five boroughs were formed in 1898.

[8]Allegheny annexed by Pittsburgh in 1907.

Internet Release Date: February 2, 2006

REFERENCES

Anderson, Margo J. 1988. The American Census: a Social History. New Haven, CT: Yale University Press.

Bohme, Frederick G. et al. 1973. Population and Housing Inquiries in U.S. Decennial Censuses, 1790-1970. U.S. Bureau of the Census, Working Paper No. 39. Washington DC: U.S. Government Printing Office.

Dahmann, Donald C. 1992. "Accounting for the Geography of Population: 200 Years of Census Bureau Practice with Macro-Scale Sub-National Regions." Paper presented at the Annual Meeting of the Association of American Geographers, San Diego, CA, 18-22 April 1992.

Dubester, Henry J. 1950. Catalog of United States Census Publications: 1790-1945. Washington, DC: U.S. Government Printing Office. (Reprinted in U.S. Bureau of the Census, 1974.)

Eckler, Ross A. 1972. The Bureau of the Census. New York, NY: Praeger Publishers.

Fay, Robert E. et al. 1988. "The Coverage of Population in the 1980 Census." Bureau of the Census, Evaluation and Research Reports, PHC80-E4. Washington, DC: U.S. Government Printing Office.

Forstall, Richard L. 1996. Population of States and Counties of the United States: 1790 to 1990. U.S. Bureau of the Census. Washington, DC: U.S. Government Printing Office.

Gibson, Campbell. 1998. Population of the 100 Largest Cities and Other Urban Places in the United States: 1790 to 1990. Population Division Working Paper No. 27. Washington, DC: U.S. Bureau of the Census.

Gibson, Campbell and Emily Lennon, 1999. Historical Census Statistics on the Foreign-Born Population of the United States: 1850 to 1990. Population Division Working Paper No. 29. Washington, DC: U.S. Bureau of the Census.

Robinson, J. Gregory. 2001. ESCAP II: Demographic Analysis Results. U.S. Census Bureau, <http://www.census.gov/dmd/www/pdf/Report1.PDF>.

Robinson, J. Gregory et al. 1993. "Estimation of Population Coverage in the 1990 United States Census Based on Demographic Analysis," Journal of the American Statistical Association, Vol. 88, No. 423 (September 1993), pp. 1061-1079.

Truesdell, Leon E. 1949. "The Development of the Urban-Rural Classification in the United States: 1874 to 1949." Bureau of the Census, Current Population Reports, Series P-23, No. 1. Washington, DC: U.S. Government Printing Office.

United Nations. No date. 2002 Demographic Yearbook. Department for Economic and Social Information and Policy Analysis, Statistics Division. New York: United Nations, <http://unstats.un.org/unsd/demographic/products/dyb/dyb2.htm>.

U.S. Bureau of the Census. 1949. Historical Statistics of the United States, 1789-1945. Washington, DC: U.S. Government Printing Office.

1960. Historical Statistics of the United States, Colonial Times to 1957. Washington, DC: U.S. Government Printing Office.

1974. Catalog of Publications: 1790-1972. Washington, D.C.: U.S. Government Printing Office.

1975. Historical Statistics of the United States, Colonial Times to 1970. Washington, DC: U.S. Government Printing Office.

1984. Bureau of the Census Catalog: 1984. Washington, DC: U.S. Government Printing Office.

1994. Census Catalog and Guide: 1994. Washington, DC: U.S. Government Printing Office.

U.S. Census Bureau. 2001a. Report of the Executive Steering Committee for Accuracy and Coverage Evaluation Policy on Adjustment for Non-Redistricting Uses, <http://www.census.gov/dmd/www/pdf/Recommend2.pdf>.

2001b. Overview of Race and Hispanic Origin:2000. Census 2000 Brief. C2KBR/01-1. Washington, DC: U.S. Government Printing Office, <http://www.census.gov/prod/2001pubs/c2kbr01-1.pdf>.

U.S. Immigration and Naturalization Service. 1997. Statistical Yearbook of the Immigration and Naturalization Service, 1996. Washington, DC: U.S. Government Printing Office.

U.S. Office of Management and Budget. 1977. Race and Ethnic Standards for Federal Statistics and Administrative Reporting. Statistical Policy Directive No. 15. Washington, DC: U.S. Office of Management and Budget.

1997. Revisions to the Standards for the Classification of Federal Data on Race and Ethnicity. Federal Register, Vol. 62, No. 210 (October 30), pp. 58782-58790.

2000. Standards for Defining Metropolitan and Micropolitan Statistical Areas. Federal Register, Vol. 65, No. 249 (December 27), pp. 82228-82238.

Voegelin, C.F. and F.M. 1977. Classification and Index of the World's Languages. New York, NY: Elsevier North Holland, Inc.

Wright, Carroll D. and William C. Hunt. 1900. The History and Growth of the United States Census. Washington, DC: U.S. Government Printing Office.

DECENNIAL CENSUS DATA PUBLICATIONS

(References are listed chronologically, starting with publications from the U.S. Census Office followed by publications from the U.S. Bureau of the Census and the U.S. Census Bureau. Dubester numbers are from Henry J. Dubester, Catalog of United States Census Publications: 1790-1945. See General References. Lengthy titles are shortened for references cited in Dubester, which includes full titles and annotations.)

U.S. Census Office. 1853. Census of Population: 1850. The Seventh Census of the United States (Dubester #30). Washington, DC: Robert Armstrong, public printer.

1854. Census of Population: 1850, Statistical View of the United States (Dubester #33). Washington, DC: Beverley Tucker, Senate Printer.

1864. Census of Population: 1860. Population of the United States (Dubester #37). Washington, DC. U.S. Government Printing Office.

1872a. Census of Population: 1870, Vol. I, The Statistics of the Population of the United States (Dubester #45). Washington, DC: U.S. Government Printing Office.

1872b. Census of Population: 1870, Vol. II, The Vital Statistics of the United States (Dubester #49). Washington, DC: U.S. Government Printing Office.

1883. Census of Population: 1880, Vol. I. Statistics of the Population of the United States (Dubester #61). Washington, DC: U.S. Government Printing Office.

1895. Census of Population: 1890, Vol. I, Report on Population of the United States, Part 1 (Dubester #177). Washington, DC: U.S. Government Printing Office.

1897. Census of Population: 1890, Vol. I, Report on Population of the United States, Part 2 (Dubester # 178). Washington, DC: U.S. Government Printing Office.

1901. Census of Population: 1900, Vol. I, Population, Part 1 (Dubester #252). Washington, DC: U.S. Government Printing Office.

1902. Census of Population: 1900, Vol. II, Population, Part 2 (Dubester #254). Washington, DC: U.S. Government Printing Office.

U.S. Bureau of the Census. 1906. Census of Population: 1900, Supplementary Analysis and Derivative Tables (Dubester #273). Washington, DC: U.S. Government Printing Office.

1909. A Century of Population Growth from the First Census of the United States to the Twelfth: 1790 to 1900 (Dubester #2785). Washington, DC: Government Printing Office.

1913a. Census of Population: 1910, Vol. I, General Report and Analysis (Dubester #296). Washington, DC: U.S. Government Printing Office.

1913b. Census of Population: 1910, Vol. II, Reports by States – Alabama-Montana (Dubester #313). Washington, DC: U.S. Government Printing Office.

1913c. Census of Population: 1910, Vol. III, Reports by States – Nebraska-Wyoming, Alaska, Hawaii, and Porto Rico (Dubester #314). Washington, DC: U.S. Government Printing Office.

1922a. Census of Population: 1920, Vol. II, General Report and Analytical Tables (Dubester #453). Washington, DC: U.S. Government Printing Office.

1922b. Census of Population: 1920, Vol. III, Composition and Characteristics of the Population by States (Dubester #470). Washington, DC: U.S. Government Printing Office.

1933a. Census of Population: 1930, Vol. II, General Report (Dubester #653). Washington, DC: U.S. Government Printing Office

1933b. Census of Population: 1930, Vol. III, Reports by States (Dubester #668). Washington, DC: U.S. Government Printing Office.

1943a. Census of Population: 1940, Vol. II, Characteristics of the Population, Parts 1 to 7, (Dubester #956). Washington, DC: U.S. Government Printing Office.

1943b. Census of Population: 1940, Vol. IV, Characteristics by Age, Part 1 (Dubester #971). Washington, DC: U.S. Government Printing Office.

1943c. Census of Population: 1940, Characteristics of the Nonwhite Population by Race (Dubester #976). Washington, DC: U.S. Government Printing Office.

1943d. Census of Population: 1940, Mother Tongue (Dubester #1004). Washington, DC: U.S. Government Printing Office.

1953a. Census of Population: 1950, Vol. II, Characteristics of the Population, Part 1, United States Summary. Washington, DC: U.S. Government Printing Office. 1953b. Census of

Population: 1950, Vol. II, Characteristics of the Population, Parts 2-52, Alabama to Wyoming, Alaska, and Hawaii. Washington, DC: U.S. Government Printing Office.

1953c. Census of Population: 1950, Vol. IV, Special Reports, Part 3, No. 3B, Nonwhite Population by Race. Washington, DC: U.S. Government Printing Office.

1953d. Census of Population: 1950, Vol. IV, Special Reports, Part 3, No. 3D, Puerto Ricans in Continental United States. Washington, DC: U.S. Government Printing Office.

1963a. Census of Population: 1960, Vol. II, Subject Reports, 1C, Nonwhite Population by Race. Washington, DC: U.S. Government Printing Office.

1963b. Census of Population: 1960, Vol. II, Subject Reports, 1D, Puerto Ricans in the United States. Washington, DC: U.S. Government Printing Office.

1963c. Census of Population: 1960, Vol. II, Subject Reports, 2A, State of Birth. Washington, DC: U.S. Government Printing Office.

1964a. Census of Population: 1960, Vol. I, Characteristics of the Population, Part 1, United States Summary. Washington, DC: U.S. Government Printing Office.

1964b. Census of Population: 1960, Vol. I, Characteristics of the Population, Parts 2-52, Alabama to Wyoming. Washington, DC: U.S. Government Printing Office.

1965. Census of Population: 1960, Vol. II, Subject Reports, 1A, Nativity and Parentage. Washington, DC: U.S. Government Printing Office.

1966. Census of Population: 1960, Vol. II, Subject Reports, 1E, Mother Tongue of the Foreign Born. Washington, DC: U.S. Government Printing Office.

1973a. Census of Population: 1970, Vol. 1, Characteristics of the Population, Part 1, United States Summary. Washington, DC: U.S. Government Printing Office.

1973b. Census of Population: 1970, Vol. 1, Characteristics of the Population, Parts 2-52, Alabama to Wyoming. Washington, DC: U.S. Government Printing Office.

1973c. Census of Population: 1970, Vol. II, Subject Reports, 1A, National Origin and Language. Washington, DC: U.S. Government Printing Office.

1973d. Census of Population: 1970, Vol. II, Subject Reports, 1B, Negro Population. Washington, DC: U.S. Government Printing Office.

1973e. Census of Population: 1970, Vol. II, Subject Reports, 1C, Persons of Spanish Origin. Washington, DC: U.S. Government Printing Office.

1973f. Census of Population: 1970, Vol. II, Subject Reports, 1D, Persons of Spanish Surname. Washington, DC: U.S. Government Printing Office.

1973g. Census of Population: 1970, Vol. II, Subject Reports, 1E, Puerto Ricans in the United States. Washington, DC: U.S. Government Printing Office.

1973h. Census of Population: 1970, Vol. II, Subject Reports, 1F, American Indians. Washington, DC: U.S. Government Printing Office.

1973i. Census of Population: 1970, Vol. II, Subject Reports, 1G, Japanese, Chinese, and Filipinos in the United States. Washington, DC: U.S. Government Printing Office.

1973j. Census of Population: 1970, Supplementary Report, PC(S1)-30, Persons of Spanish Ancestry. Washington, DC: U.S. Government Printing Office.

1982. Census of Population: 1980, General Population Characteristics, Alabama to Wyoming, PC80-1-B2 - B52 (Vol.1,Ch. B, Parts 2-52). Washington, DC: U.S. Government Printing Office.

1983a. Census of Population: 1980, General Population Characteristics, United States Summary, PC80-1-B1 (Vol. 1, Ch. B, Part 1). Washington, DC: U.S. Government Printing Office.

1983b. Census of Population: 1980, General Social and Economic Characteristics, United States Summary, PC80-1-C1 (Vol. 1, Ch. C, Part 1). Washington, DC: U.S. Government Printing Office.

1992a. Census of Population: 1990, General Population Characteristics, United States, 1990 CP-1-1. Washington, DC: U.S. Government Printing Office.

1992b. Census of Population: 1990, General Population Characteristics, Alabama to Wyoming, 1990 CP-1-2 to 1-52. Washington, DC: U.S. Government Printing Office.

1993a. Census of Population: 1990, Social and Economic Characteristics, United States. 1990 CP-2-1, Washington, DC: U.S. Government Printing Office.

1993b. Census of Population: 1990, The Foreign-Born Population in the United States, 1990 CP-3-1. Washington, DC: U.S. Government Printing Office.

1993c. Census of Population: 1990, Supplementary Reports, Metropolitan Areas as Defined by the Office of Management and Budget, June 30, 1993. Washington, DC: U.S. Government Printing Office.

U.S. Census Bureau. 2000. Census of Population: 2000, Summary Social, Economic, and Housing Characteristics, United States Summary, PHC-2-1. Washington, DC: U.S. Government Printing Office.

POPULATION DIVISION WORKING PAPER SERIES

For copies of these working papers, please contact the Statistical Information Staff, Population Division, Bureau of the Census, Washington, DC 20233-8800 (301)763-2422/pop@census.gov

No. 1 - The Census Bureau Approach for Allocating International Migration to States, Counties, and Places: 1981-1991. David L. Word. Issued October 1992.

No. 2 - Geographic Coding of Administrative Records--Past Experience and Current Research. Douglas K.Sater. Issued April 1993.

No. 3 - Postcensal Population Estimates: States, Counties, and Places. John F. Long. Issued August 1993.

No. 4 - Evaluating the Passel-Word Spanish Surname List: 1990 Decennial Census Post Enumeration Survey Results. R. Colby Perkins. Issued August 1993.

No. 5 - Evaluation of Postcensal County Estimates for the 1980s. Sam T. Davis. Issued March 1994.

No. 6 - Metropolitan Growth and Expansion in the 1980s. Richard L. Forstall and James D. Fitzsimmons. Issued April 1993.

No. 7 - Geographic Coding of Administrative Records -- Current Research in ZIP/Sector-to-County Coding Process. Douglas K. Sater. Issued June 1994.

No. 8 - Illustrative Ranges of the Distribution of Undocumented Immigrants by State. Edward W. Fernandez and J. Gregory Robinson. Issued October 1994.

No. 9 - Estimates of Emigration of the Foreign-Born Population: 1980-1990. Bashir Ahmed and J. Gregory Robinson. Issued December 1994.

No. 10 - Estimation of the Annual Emigration of U.S. Born Persons by Using Foreign Censuses and Selected Administrative Data: Circa 1980. Edward W. Fernandez. Issued January 1995.

No. ll -Using Analytic Techniques to Evaluate the 1990 Census Coverage of Young Hispanics. Edward Fernandez. Issued May 1995.

No. 12 - Metropolitan and Nonmetropolitan Areas: New Approaches to Geographical Definition. Donald C. Dahmann and James D. Fitzsimmons. Issued October 1995.

No. 13 - Building a Spanish Surname List for the 1990's--New Approach to An Old Problem. David L. Word and R. Colby Perkins, Jr. Issued February 1996.

No. 14 - Fertility of American Men. Amara Bachu. Issued March 1996.

No. 15 - Comparisons of Selected Social and Economic Characteristics Between Asians, Hawaiians, Pacific Islanders, and American Indians (Including Alaskan Natives). Edward W. Fernandez. Issued June 1996.

No. 16 - Findings on Questions on Race and Hispanic Origin Tested in the 1996 National Content Survey. Prepared in the Population Division by the Racial Statistics Branch and the Ethnic and Hispanic Statistics Branch. Issued December 1996.

No. 17 - Race and Ethnicity Classification Consistency Between the Census Bureau and the National Center for Health Statistics. Larry Sink. Issued February 1997.

No. 18 - Results of the 1996 Race and Ethnic Targeted Test. Issued May 1997.

No. 19 - Who Responds/Who Doesn't? Analyzing Variation in Mail Response Rates During the 1990 Census. David L. Word. Issued July 1997.

No. 20 - Trends in Marital Status of U.S. Women at First Birth: 1930 to 1994. Amara Bachu. Issued March 1998.

No. 21 - State Estimates of Organized Child Care Facilities. Lynne Casper and Martin Issued March 1998.

No. 22 - How Well Does the Current Population Survey Measure the Foreign-Born Population in the United States Dianne Schmidley and J. Gregory Robinson. Issued April 1998

No. 23 - Poverty, Family Structure, and Child Well-Being: Indicators from the SIPP. Jason Fields and Kristin Smith. Issued April 1998

No. 24 - Child Well-Being Indicators from the SIPP. Kristin Smith, Loretta Bass, and Jason Fields. Issued April 1998

No. 25 - Timing of First Births: 1930-34, 1990-94. Amara Bachu. Issued May 1998

No. 26 - Co-Resident Grandparents and Grandchildren: Grandparent Maintained Families. Lynne Casper and Ken Bryson. Issued March 1998.

No. 27 - Population of the 100 Largest Cities and Other Urban Places in the United States: 1790 to 1990. Campbell Gibson. Issued June 1998

No. 28 - Are There Differences in Voting Behavior Between Naturalized and Native-born Americans? Loretta E. Bass and Lynne M. Casper. Issued March 1999.

No. 29 - Historical Census Statistics on the Foreign-born Population of the United States: 1850-1990. Campbell J. Gibson. Issued February 1999

No. 30 - Direct Measures of Poverty as Indicators of Economic Need: Evidence from the Survey of Income and Program Participation. Kurt J. Bauman. November 1998

No. 31 - American Community Survey and Intercensal Population Estimates: Where Are the Crossroads? Amy Symens. Issued December 1998

No. 32 - Women's abor Force Attachment Patterns and Maternity Leave: A Review of the Literature. Kristen Smith and Amara Bachu. Issued January 1999

No. 33 - Evaluation of Relationship, Marital Status, and Grandparents Items on the Census 2000 Dress Rehearsal Charles Clark and Jason Fields. Issued April 1999.

No. 34 - Unbinding the Ties: Edit Effects of Marital Status on Same Gender Couples. Charles Clark and Jason Fields. Issued April 1999.

No. 35 - Racial-Ethnic and Gender Differences in Returns to Cohabitation and Marriage: Evidence from the Current Population Survey. Philip N. Cohen. Issued May 1999.

No. 36 - How Does POSSLQ Measure Up? Historical Estimates of Cohabitation. Lynne Casper, Philip N. Cohen, and Tavia Simmons. Issued May 1999.

No. 37 - Childlessness Among American Women On the Rise? Amara Bachu. Issued May 1999.

No. 38 - Methodology and Assumptions for the Population Projections of the United States: 1999 to 2100. Frederick Hollman, Tammany Mulder, and Jeffrey Kallan. Issued January 1999.

No. 39 - What Do We Know About the Undercount of Children? Kirsten K. West and J. Gregory Robinson. Issued August 1999.

No. 40 - Canceled

No. 41 - Canceled

No. 42 - Measures of Help Available to Households in Need: Their Relationship to Well-Being, Welfare, and Work. Kurt Bauman and Barbara Downs. Issued May 2000

No. 43 - Have We Reached the Top? Educational Attainment Projections of the U.S. Population. Jennifer Cheeseman Day and Kurt Bauman. Issued May 2000.

No. 44 - The Emerging American Voter: An Examination of the Increase in the Black Vote in November 1998. Avalaura L. Gaither and Eric C. Newburger. Issued June 2000

No. 45 - An Analysis of State and County Population Changes by Characteristics: 1990-1999. Amy Symens Smith, Bashir Ahmed, and Larry Sink. Issued November 2000.

No. 46 - The Effect of Work and Welfare on Living Conditions in Single Parent Households. Kurt Bauman. Issued August 2000.

No. 47 - Canceled

No. 48 - Canceled

No. 49 - Variations in State Mortality From 1960 to 1990. Monique Oosse. Issued September 2003.

No. 50 - Accuracy of the U.S. Census Bureau National Population Projections and Their Respective Components of Change. Tammany Mulder. Issued November 2002.

No. 51 - U.S. Census Bureau Measurement of Net International Migration to the United States: 1990 to 2000. Tammany Mulder, Frederick Hollmann, Lisa Lollock, Rachel Cassidy, Joseph Costanzo, and Josephine Baker. Issued February 2002.

No. 52 - At-Risk Conditions of U.S. School-Age Children. Robert Kominski, Amie Jamieson, and Gladys Martinez. Issued June 2001.

No. 53 - Home Schooling in the United States: Trends and Characteristics. K. J. Bauman. Issued August 2001.

No. 54 - Evaluation of the 1990 School District Level Population Estimates Based on the Synthetic Ratio Approach. E. R. Miller. Issued September 2001.

No. 55 - State Estimates of Child Care Establishments 1977-1997. Grace O'Neil and Martin O'ConnellIssued August 2001.

No. 56 - Historical Census Statistics on Population Totals by Race, 1790 to 1990, and by Hispanic Origin, 1970 to 1990, for the United States, Regions, Divisions, and States. Campbell Gibson and Kay Jung. Issued September 2002.

No. 57 - Evaluating Forecast Error in State Population Projections Using Census 2000 Counts. Paul Campbell. Issued July 2002.

No. 58 - Evaluating Components of International Migration: Estimates of the Foreign-Born Population by Migrant Status: 2000. Kevin Deardorff and Lisa Blumerman. Issued November 2002.

No. 59 - Evaluating Components of International Migration: Legal Migrants. Marc Perry, Barbara Van der Vate, Lea Auman, and Kathy Morris. Issued November 2001.

No. 60 - Evaluating Components of International Migration: Temporary (Legal) Migrants. Rachel Cassidy and Lucinda Pearson. Issued November 2001

No. 61 - Evaluating Components of International Migration: The Residual Foreign Born.

Joe Costanzo, Cynthia Davis, Caribert Irazi, Daniel Goodkind, Roberto Ramirez. Issued January 2002.

No. 62 - Evaluating Components of International Migration: Foreign-Born Emigrants. Tammany Mulder, Betsy ela Brittingham. Issued June 2002.

No. 63 - Evaluating Components of Internation Migration: Native-Born Emigrants. Jim C. Gibbs, Gregory S. Harper, Marc J. Rubin, and Hyon B. Shin. Issued January 2003.

No. 64 - Evaluating Components of International Migration: Migration Between Puerto Rico and the United States. Matt Christenson. Issued January 2002.

No. 65 - Evaluating Components of International Migration: Quality of Foreign-Born and Hispanic Population Data. Art Cresce, Roberto Ramirez, and Gregory Spencer. Issued July 2002.

No. 66 - Evaluating Components of International Migration: Consistency of 2000 Nativity Data. Nolan Malone. Issued January 2002.

No. 67 - Evaluation of Census Bureau's1995-2025 State Population Projections. Ching Li Wang. Issued October 2002.

No. 68 - Guide To International Migration Statistics: The Sources, Collection, and Processing of Foreign-Born Population Data at the U.S. Census Bureau. Joseph M. Costanzo, Cynthia J. Davis, and Nolan Malone. Issued October 2002.

No. 69 - Seasonality of Moves and Duration and Tenure of Residence: 1996. Jason Schachter and Jeffrey Kuenzi. Issued December 2002.

No. 70 - Evaluation of 2000 Subcounty Population Estimates. Greg Harper, Chuck Coleman, and Jason Devine. Issued May 2003.

No. 71 - People Might Move Out but Housing Units Do t: An Evaluation of the State and County Housing Unit Estimates. Jason Devine and Charles Coleman. Issued April 2003.

No. 72 - Analysis of General Hispanic Responses in Census 2000. Arthur R. Cresce and Roberto R. Ramirez. Issued September 2003.

No. 73 - Measuring the Foreign-Born Population in the United States With the Current Population Survey: 1994-2002. A. Dianne Schmidley and J. Gregory Robinson. Issued October 2003.

No. 74 - Evaluation of April 1, 2000 School District Population Estimates Based on the Synthetic Ratio Method. Monique Oosse. Issued June 2004.

No. 75 - Identification of Hispanic Ethnicity in Census 2000: Analysis of Data Quality for the Question on Hispanic Origin. Arthur R. Cresce, Audrey Dianne Schmidley and Robert R. Ramirez Issued July 2004.

No. 76 - Historical Census Statistics On Population Totals By Race, 1790 To 1990, And By Hispanic Origin, 1970 To 1990, For Large Cities And Other Urban Places In The United States. Campbell Gibson and Kay Jung. Issued July 2005.

No. 77 - Analysis of Multiple Origin Reporting to the Hispanic Origin Question in Census 2000. Roberto Ramirez. Issued November 2005.

No. 78 - Changes in the Lives of U.S. Children: 1990-2000. Julia Overturf Johnson. Issued July 2005.

No. 79 - Matched Race and Hispanic Origin Responses from Census 2000 and Current Population Survey February to May 2000. Jorge del Pinal and A. Dianne Schmidley. Issued January 2006.

No. 80 - Thirty-Five Years of Tracking Hispanic Ethnicity: Evaluation of Current Population Survey Data Quality for the Question of Hispanic Origin, 1969 to 2004. A. Dianne Schmidley and Arthur R. Cresce. Release Pending.

No. 81 - Historical Census Statistics on the Foreign-Born Population of the United States: 1850 to 2000 Campbell Gibson and Kay Jung. Issued February 2006.

INDEX

A

B

C

D

E

F

G

H

I

J

K

L

M

U

V

W

Y

Z